REMOTE VIRTUE

Recent Titles in Psychology, Religion, and Spirituality
J. Harold Ellens, Series Editor

The Invisible Church: Finding Spirituality Where You Are
J. Pittman McGehee and Damon Thomas

The Spirituality of Sex
J. Harold Ellens

The Healing Power of Spirituality: How Faith Helps Humans Thrive,
3 volumes
J. Harold Ellens, editor

Families of the Bible: A New Perspective
Kamila Blessing

Explaining Evil, 3 volumes
J. Harold Ellens, editor

Cruel God, Kind God: How Images of God Shape Belief, Attitude,
and Outlook
Zenon Lotufo, Jr.

100 Years of Happiness: Insights and Findings from the Experts
Nathan Carlin and Donald Capps

Heaven, Hell, and the Afterlife: Eternity in Judaism, Christianity, and Islam
J. Harold Ellens, editor

Winning Revolutions: The Psychosocial Dynamics of Revolts for Freedom,
Fairness, and Rights, 3 volumes
J. Harold Ellens, editor

Seeking the Sacred with Psychoactive Substances: Chemical Paths to
Spirituality and to God
J. Harold Ellens, editor

The Psychedelic Policy Quagmire: Health, Law, Freedom, and Society
J. Harold Ellens and Thomas B. Roberts, editors

Being Called: Scientific, Secular, and Sacred Perspectives
David Bryce Yaden, Theo D. McCall, and J. Harold Ellens, editors

REMOTE VIRTUE

A Christian Guide to
Intentional Media Viewing

Jen Letherer

Psychology, Religion, and Spirituality
J. Harold Ellens, Series Editor

 PRAEGER™

An Imprint of ABC-CLIO, LLC
Santa Barbara, California • Denver, Colorado

Library of Congress Cataloging-in-Publication Data

Letherer, Jen.
    Remote virtue : a Christian guide to intentional media viewing / Jen Letherer.
        pages cm. — (Psychology, religion, and spirituality)
    Includes bibliographical references and index.
        ISBN 978-1-4408-3708-1 (alk. paper) — ISBN 978-1-4408-3709-8 (ebook)
    1. Motion pictures—Religious aspects—Christianity. 2. Motion pictures—Moral and ethical aspects.   3. Television broadcasting—Religious aspects.   I. Title.
    PN1995.5.L48 2015
    261.5'7—dc23   2015021803

ISBN: 978-1-4408-3708-1
EISBN: 978-1-4408-3709-8

19 18 17 16 15   1 2 3 4 5

This book is also available on the World Wide Web as an eBook.
Visit www.abc-clio.com for details.

Praeger
An Imprint of ABC-CLIO, LLC

ABC-CLIO, LLC
130 Cremona Drive, P.O. Box 1911
Santa Barbara, California 93116–1911

This book is printed on acid-free paper ∞
Manufactured in the United States of America

Contents

Series Editor's Foreword   vii

Acknowledgments   ix

Introduction   xi

Chapter 1   An Imperative to Understand the Moving Image   1

Chapter 2   What Happened to Movies and Television?   11

Chapter 3   A Brief Guide to Film Criticism   23

Chapter 4   A Brief Guide to Christian Film Criticism   35

Chapter 5   The Moving Image as Modern Literature   49

Chapter 6   Visual Literacy: A Viewing Primer   61

Chapter 7   Redemptive Narratives   81

Chapter 8   Truth and the Moving Image   101

Chapter 9   Putting It into Practice   119

Chapter 10   *Top Chef*: A Study in Gastronomic Criticism and
             Human Behavior   131

Chapter 11   *Modern Family*: Not Normal Is the New Normal   145

Chapter 12   *The Walking Dead*: Perspectives on Undeath   159

Contents

Chapter 13   *Downton Abbey*: Social Progressivism Meets Period
              (Mellow) Drama   173

Conclusion   187

Index   191

Series Editor's Foreword

J. Harold Ellens

This foreword is brief. There is a good reason. You bought this book to get right to the heart of the issue. You are mostly like me, impatient with long forewords that try to tell you the book's message in a single essay. That is neither necessary nor possible—especially for this stunning volume. This is a book of substantive content, written engagingly, on an important and entertaining topic. Jen Letherer has given us a cultural gift that raises all the right questions, and answers them in delightfully good humor. She knows everything about everything related to television, film, theater, and human communication. Her book is a great pleasure to discover.

This book is mainly about moving pictures. It asks important questions. Are movies and television supposed to entertain, teach, provoke us to think about life's rights and wrongs, entice us to philosophical discussion about goals, or keep our cultural values in line? Almost every person has an opinion on that question. Some of us feel very strongly about one or other of those possibilities. Some of us do not care to think about such questions and just like to "go along for the ride," so to speak. Jen Letherer is a deeply thoughtful person with a vast understanding of the history and content of TV programming and film development. She addresses all of those questions about film, TV shows, videos, and nearly every type of moving image that you and I see. She has a comprehensive understanding of the latest applications that are possible in moving-image communication. And she tells the story with a delightful entertaining style and a vigorous and humorful prose. Every page of her work is studded with a lively panoply of illustrations taken from the history of films and programs that have made TV the dominant presence in our lives from its beginnings in the 1950s to the shows aired today.

Letherer asks whether moving images enhance our culture or affect it negatively. In the end, it is not her goal to judge but to raise all the questions for us to consider deeply. She is generally delighted with the entertainment value of movies and television. She realizes that one can love a film, TV program, or series just for the surface story, while that same story may have an underlying meaning that requires much deeper thought. It may show us a side of our culture that we do not think about. It may point out the flaws in it, spotlight for us great wonders that we had not noticed, and highlight heroic achievements of humans in ordinary life that we might otherwise have missed altogether. Letherer's analysis is penetrating, illuminating, and comprehensive in "covering the waterfront" of human life portrayed by the characters and situations depicted on the screen.

As I close this piece I want to give you a little taste of this marvelously definitive, blithely entertaining, and very readable book. Letherer declares that movies and TV shape the beliefs and values in our culture. Our popular culture is a bit like a funhouse mirror. As we view ourselves in the mirror of a film or TV show, it shoots our image back to us in a twisted and distorted way that makes us think about the exaggerated aspects of it humorously, and in ways that we had not realized before. It is a kind of revelation that gives us a chance to see ourselves, and laugh or cry about what we see. Movies and television show us and our society in ways that tell a certain truth, but are always distorted in some revealing way. "They are funhouse mirrors" for our entertainment, instruction, and education. Not a bad arrangement for an instrument that dominates the attention of the citizens of our culture.

Now you want nothing further from me. You want to get right to the heart of the matter that Jen Letherer has prepared for you with delightful imagination.

ACKNOWLEDGMENTS

Having spent my adult life in the collaborative worlds of theater and moving-image production, I found it no surprise that even writing a book was indeed a group effort. I am indebted to many for their help and support, the first and most notable of which must be Dr. J. Harold Ellens, who contacted me several years ago about authoring a book about television from a Christian perspective. His patience, insight, persistence, and encouragement have been instrumental. I am honored to know him, and quite humbled to have been guided and encouraged by him. I am also grateful for the mentorship and support of Robert H. Woods Jr., Paul Patton, Wally Metts, and Quentin Schultze, who have shepherded my writing and teaching with a graciousness I am far below deserving. My respect and gratitude for these gentlemen is without bounds.

I have also found it providential to work with the much admired and sought after Marsha Daigle-Williamson, whose editing prowess exceeded even her high reputation. She was always thorough, articulate, and kind to a young author. I know my personal style is quirky to say the least, and she required me to explain and re-reason the things that needed it, as well as dotting all the necessary i's and crossing all the t's (a skill I wish I had the patience for). Debbie Carvalko at Praeger also proved to be a skilled guide and the kind of editor every author wants to work with, and I appreciate so much all of her replies, information, advice, and knowledge.

I think I am safe in assuming that I have been blessed with the kind of support system that should make anyone jealous, and it includes colleagues and friends alike who do not mind my constantly talking shop and potentially ruining every movie we watch. Two of the first who need mentioning are Melissa Yekulis and Maggie Tibus, both of whom have looked over manuscript sections, who told me when I was not making sense (in writing and in general conversation), and with whom I would watch movies and television programs any day of the week. I also owe great thanks to my mother, Jean Letherer, who loves movies and televisions so much that she remains the only person who will play classic movie trivia with me. And to my father, Donald Letherer, who, when I was in tenth grade, took away the family television (only to return it months later) because my brother Ted and I stayed up too late laughing at David Letterman. The brother also deserves a note here, since that episode of *Late Night*, with Richard Simmons as guest, was one of the funniest things I have ever seen. My eldest brother Joe and his family (actually all of my nieces and nephews) can also recite the plot to every episode of *Little House on the Prairie*, chapter and verse, and my Aunt Judy can do the same with *Sex and the City*. My media-loving family taught and encouraged me to cherish and understand what I love, and to watch with prudence and integrity.

Lastly, I wish to thank my film and video students, whose insight and growth have challenged and encouraged me, my church family at Hudson Wesleyan Church (including Pastor Wesley Rowan and his wife, my dear friend Carrie, who understand me well enough to know I will get a reference that Pastor Wes makes to *The Princess Bride* from the pulpit), and mostly, my grandmother Genevieve Siegel. It is to her legacy and memory I dedicate *Remote Virtue*, because, I think, she would have liked it very much.

INTRODUCTION

I think anybody who takes the trouble to write what we refer to as a serious play is holding a mirror up to people, saying: Look, this is how you behave, this is who you are. If you don't like it, why don't you change?

—*Edward Albee*[1]

The medium is the message.

—*Marshall McLuhan*[2]

We are in a race between education and disaster.

—*Neil Postman*[3]

The above quotes have indelibly shaped my approach to understanding and teaching moving-image media. As a storyteller, Albee's sentiment about the power of story has helped me appreciate the vitality of dramatic narrative and its redemptive potential. McLuhan's sentiment is often cited by media critics, and I am no exception, because understanding the very nature of moving-image stories is a vital part of understanding what they say. The tools of storytelling are a part of the story itself. Those trying to understand moving-image stories must on some level understand the art of the moving image if they are to grasp the story's power and significance. Postman's recitation of Aldous Huxley's sentiment reminds me of the imperative. Our entertainment-driven and sodden culture is losing something vital: it is losing perspective and thereby losing control over the effect moving-image media has upon us.

Therefore, the intention of this text is educate in order to avoid the "disaster" Postman is referring to. Stories have power. They have the power to make us question our own beliefs and the nature of the world around us. For Christians, or for anyone seeking insight, that quality is necessary if we are to grow. Moving-image stories have their own kind of power, and their physical production, construction, exhibition technologies, and audience-viewing habits are a part of that power. With training in the areas of moving-image stories and the moving-image medium, viewers may be educated in order to avoid "disaster."

But what really is this disaster? Postman discusses how the forms of moving-image entertainment change viewer perception and expectation for reality. The disaster is that viewers are profoundly affected by the moving images they see. What we watch affects us. By gaining insight, viewers can take back control of the effects moving-image stories have on them. Therefore, this text is intended to put forth a methodology for understanding, demystifying, and ultimately finding more perspective and control over moving-image narratives and the effects they have on viewers.

To that end, the opening chapter outlines the need to understand moving-image media's capacity to instill ideologies into viewer's minds. The worldviews and ways of thinking that moving-image stories show as "normal" or "good" are worth questioning. Chapter 1 intends to help viewers understand how and why moving images tell viewers what is "good" or "normal." Chapter 2 helps viewers understand more about what moving-image media means by outlining the convergence of the discrete mediums of film and television into a shared identity as "moving-image content;" stories that are shown as moving images and can be viewed over a variety of devices and exhibition platforms.

The next two chapters discuss a foundation of critical insight into moving-image stories laid down by both the traditions of academic film criticism and by Christian critics. This knowledge brings helpful insights that those studying moving images have already gained and gives viewers perspective in the development of Christian media criticism.

Chapter 5 intends to lay the groundwork for developing moving image "visual" literacy by comparing moving-image criticism to literary criticism, discussing what "literacy" really means, and why it is both attainable and necessary. To further quote Postman, "The solution must be found in *how* we watch" [italics original].[4] Chapter 6 then outlines the tools that can be used in order to practice visual literacy by explaining what aspects of story and form (the construction of the moving image and all of its elements) can be examined and how.

In order to truly understand moving images, however, it is important to put their ideology in perspective, so Chapter 7 is devoted to discussing the idea of a redemptive narrative. This area is a subject of much discussion in

Christian media circles, and in this chapter different kinds of potentially redemptive elements and approaches are examined. Chapter 8 is intended to highlight one other important aspect of visual literacy, that is, discussing the inherent pitfalls of photographed stories and their potential to become an alternate, false reality for viewers.

Chapter 9 then distills the concepts of visual literacy laid down in Chapter 6, giving viewers a "primer" set of questions that can be used when watching moving-image narratives. The last four chapters of the text put that primer into practice by utilizing the tools outlined in the previous chapters to examine four popular contemporary television programs: *Top Chef, Modern Family, The Walking Dead,* and *Downton Abbey.*

In our media-saturated world, moving-image stories are a part of our daily experience. Movies and television have become pastimes, diversions, shared realities, and, at their worst, preferred dream states in which viewers may lose some touch with reality and are influenced by program ideologies. If so many of us spend so much time watching movies and television, why do we not understand the effects those narratives have on us? What can we do to regain control over the effects of moving-image narratives?

The first step is to want to. By opening this text, we may assume the reader has at least some desire to have a deeper understanding of moving images and their influence. Being aware is a good place to start. Before we do, however, one note: while this book may increase your understanding of movies and television, I believe it will not lessen your enjoyment of them in any way. Instead, it will instill a sense of empowerment in understanding and appreciation of content and form. It is my sincere belief that those who study moving images only love them more as the study continues. The magic is not really gone; it is simply explained.

Consider how often we avoid food labels, not wanting to know how many calories or what potentially unwanted ingredients lurk in our snacks and suppers. However, when we face our fears we become empowered, knowing that our mac and cheese, for instance, contains both protein and carbs. Some things we may enjoy less, realizing that the ingredients contain unhealthy products. Other things we will enjoy with more certainty, knowing we are ingesting quality ingredients.

Likewise, some programs will remain guilty pleasures, but we will know why. Others we will watch with more confidence, knowing why we are drawn to them and how they can be beneficial to us. In all cases, we will be more empowered to bring balance to our media diet. In the end, understanding moving-image media by being visually literate will aid both our understanding and enjoyment of moving-image stories.

We begin by considering why this understanding is necessary. Moving images have power. By the conclusion of this text, it is the sincere hope and confidence of this author that the reader will be able to "read the label" for moving-image stories and by knowing more will have more control. That control will lead to a more virtuous practice of viewing. Visual literacy, the skill this book intends to teach, is what is necessary for practicing "remote" virtue.

NOTES

1. Edward Albee, in Buzz McLaughlin, *The Playwright's Process: Learning the Craft from Today's Leading Dramatists* (New York: Backstage Books, 1997) 31.

2. Marshall McLuhan, *Understanding Media: The Extensions of Man,* repr., ed. (Boston: MIT Press, 1994), 7.

3. Neil Postman, *Amusing Ourselves to Death: Public Discourse in the Age of Show Business* (New York: Penguin Books, 1985), 163.

4. Ibid., 160.

CHAPTER 1

AN IMPERATIVE TO UNDERSTAND THE MOVING IMAGE

Therefore, analysis can be seen to have several clear benefits. It allows us to reach more valid and definite conclusions on the film's meanings and value, it helps us "lock" the experience of a film into our minds, and it sharpens our critical judgments.

—*Joseph M. Boggs*[1]

Movies and television are an alternate reality into which viewers can escape every time they go to a theater, turn on a television, or queue up a video online. What viewers see in moving-image narratives cannot help but affect them. Moving-image stories, like all stories, come from the perspective of those telling the story and are designed to be sold to those who would enjoy them. All moving-image stories, whether they intend to or not, contain an agenda for what they purport is good, right, or worthwhile; they all contain ideology.

"I'm giving you a choice," Nada (played by Roddy Piper in John Carpenter's 1988 film *They Live*) says to his friend Frank (Keith David); "Either put on the glasses [to see the aliens taking over earth] or start eating that trash can." In the 2012 Sophie Fiennes's film *The Pervert's Guide to Ideology*, writer and on-screen narrator Slavoj Zizek interrupts the clip from *They Live* to tell viewers, "I already am eating from the trash can all the time. The name of this trash can is ideology. The material force of ideology makes me not see what I'm effectively eating. It's not only our reality which enslaves us. The tragedy of our predicament when we are within ideology is that when we think that we escape it into our dreams, at that point we are within ideology."[2] Films, as Zizek explains, are always feeding us a message. Films may be our dreams, our escape from harsh or even simply mundane realities, but we are not safe there. Even in these seemingly innocent diversions there are messages constantly shaping our mind. We are what we eat, and we conform to what we continually put before our eyes.

This idea is not new and does not only apply to the cinema. Contemporary scholars like Hyeseung Yang and Mary Beth Oliver may debate what influence television programming has on the perceived quality of life of different classes (as they do in a 2010 essay for *Mass Communication and Society*[3]), but even the Motion Picture Production Code of 1930, the document intended to self-regulate Hollywood product and fend off boycotts by religious and educational groups and the censorship of state legislatures, warned, ". . . . the *moral importance* of entertainment is something which has been universally recognized. It enters intimately into the lives of men and women and affects them closely; it occupies their minds and affections during leisure hours, and ultimately touches the whole of their lives [italics original]."[4] Moving images carry powerful messages that deeply affect our lives. They craft our perceptions. They become both our realities and our dreams. As such their importance must not be overlooked. The activity may seem frivolous; the effects are not.

Some films and television programs telegraph their explicit message. There's no mistaking that *The Passion of the Christ* is a pro-Jesus film. The 2014 film *Noah*, directed by Darren Aronofsky, is easily perceived as pro-environment and as pro-theistic evolution. (The Big Bang sequence is pretty self-evident.) Some messages are easy to see. A moving-image story may be overt, explicit, in what it values. But as writers Jean-Louis Comolli and Jean Narboni once famously wrote in the first serious film journal, *Cahiers du Cinéma*, "Every film is political, inasmuch as it is determined by the ideology which produces it."[5] Every film comes from a point of view. Every narrative television program is part of a larger social ethos. And while some messages are easy to see and intentionally foregrounded, many impact audiences in more subtle and more lasting ways.

Whether they intend to or not, moving images convey value judgments. They constantly tell us what is worthwhile, what is admirable, and what is that most pejorative of twenty-first-century words: boring. These value judgments become our personal and social culture: our beliefs and values. Moving images have indelibly shaped our cultural consciousness and our individual psyches, and they continue to shape them. Those implied messages, those implicit points of view, are both the hardest to read and the most important.

Teaching audiences to understand both the implicit and explicit messages of moving images is a modern educational mandate. Educator Harold

Foster published *The New Literacy: The Language of Film and Television* in 1979 to educate English teachers and encourage them to make this type of media literacy a more viable part of secondary curriculum. Although media literacy has grown and is growing, films like Zizek and Fiennes's *Pervert's Guide* demonstrate that insight into the messages of films is still largely an academic exercise, and not an understood social imperative. "In addition to the outward manifestations of the media's power," Foster writes, "there are more pervasive forms of manipulation that are harder to measure and define. Many of these nuances of attitudes, values, beliefs, habits, and lifestyles that are influenced by television or film are too nebulous to be adequately measured."[6] Studies of the effects of violent content on viewers can be conducted, but implicit messages are hard to measure. Yet they are affecting attitudes, values, beliefs, habits, and lifestyles, and understanding those effects is left to academics.

In an age of self-help, social awareness, and self-actualization, why are we not taking responsibility for the messages that some of our most pervasive forms of media put forth? Why are we not fully aware of the ideas and ideologies that come into common acceptance because television or movies make them normal or popular? We are generally capable, but we are also generally untrained, or trained to ignore the potential for influence and just accept the fantasies. Still, it is human nature to resist being trained, and this points to a problem larger than a lack of education. Why do we hesitate to want to truly understand ideologies and implicit messages in moving images?

The answer is simple: we do not want to know.

Whatever else they sell, television and movies have always been crafted to sell themselves. They sell ideas, and the biggest idea is their own importance. In the golden age of Hollywood, the studios promoted the nickname "dream factories." If the movies did not tell us what we wanted to hear, we would not watch them, and if television did not placate us by affirming our own habits, we would find something else to stimulate us in our downtime. We do not want to understand them because while they have the potential to carry complex messages in complicated and interesting ways, the path of least resistance is the one that gains the most profit, and the production companies that fund production, compensate artists, and distribute the moving-picture products are commercial industries first and foremost.

Take, for instance, two movies about state-champion football teams: Disney's 2000 *Remember the Titans* and Destination Films' 2006 *Facing the Giants*. Both revolve around underdog teams training for their seasons. Both deal with social and personal issues on and off the field and with coaches who must lead under trying circumstances, and in both films the "home" team ultimately wins their state championship. One is based on a true account; the other carries a gospel imperative and call for revival. Both are loaded with explicit and implicit messages. Both are also intended to appeal to audiences who want to see underdogs succeed against long odds. These are "feel good" movies. And while they both affirm points of view many would consider positive (racial reconciliation and gospel revival), they do not do much more than that on the surface: they do not challenge social assumptions or leave the viewer sorting out the complex realities of race in America and spirit-led revival. They get to the happy ending and leave it there. They are intended for audiences who already agree with their explicit messages and serve only to affirm their "feel good-ness." But underneath the explicit messages are all kinds of value judgments about body image, social type, masculinity, and "winning." The positive attributes are used to "sell" the rest of their explicit and implicit messages, which may or may not be pernicious or beneficial. The point here is that the "feel good" story is easy to sell and becomes an excuse for viewers to overlook—or not even consider—the other messages the film is selling.

My conservative Christian mom loves the 1995 Rob Reiner film *The American President*. She does not approve of President Andrew Shepherd (Michael Douglas) and his love interest, lobbyist Sydney Ellen Wade (Annette Bening) "jumping into bed together," but she thinks it is a cute movie, and that he seems to be a good father and a responsible guy. These elements are the explicit message the movie sends viewers, but their implications include implicit ideologies: romance is fun (even if there are some conservative objections to pleasure over prudence) and the president can be a likable, conscientious guy like Michael Douglas (which does not excuse his bedroom behavior but does make it more acceptable). Furthermore, the film ties these ideas together: good guy/love interest and conscientious leader of the free world. *The American President* may play like an innocent romantic comedy with charismatic stars and emotional sympathy, but it is loaded with moral and political judgments.

Reiner's film is inherently political, and Shepherd is obviously a Democrat with a strong agenda for gun control and the environment. Whether or not that platform is good or bad is beside the point: the film associates it with a "responsible guy." The protagonist is a political figure, and the narrative asks us to feel empathy with him. If that guy were real, we would vote for him, regardless of party politics. Why? We trust him. He is nice. He is Michael Douglas, and not the same Michael Douglas as the *Wall Street* Michael Douglas, but more like an extension of the *Romancing the Stone* Michael Douglas. *The American President* was written by Aaron Sorkin, who would go on to write *The West Wing* for NBC. Neither the television show nor the film is a true model of the American political system. Each is instead a dream of what we would like it to be, with charismatic actors helping us invest in their points of view. If this were not true, they would not be popular. Later shows like *House of Cards* paint a less idealistic version of Washington, but even they are still responses to what viewers would like to see (aha! we knew it was corrupt!) set in a dramatic arc, mixing political rhetoric with dramatic plot and character sympathy. Politics is mixed with narrative crafting of "good guys" and "bad guys" and the actions they do that determine how we should feel about them in a plot intended to grab our interest.

Not only do both *The American President* and *The West Wing* show overt political points of view and associate them with likable characters whom we will intrinsically "root for," they also portray our governmental system in an exaggerated, dramatized way that gives a false impression. "Watching any one episode is enough to make that clear," Graeme McMillan writes for *Time.* "*The West Wing* worked so well because it was based on a particular fantasy: not that there are some good people in Washington, but that it is *filled* with them. That fantasy is as much part of the charm of *The West Wing* as the fast-paced dialogue and Martin Sheen's wondrous ability to glower or charm."[7] McMillan's article calls *The West Wing* a "stirring, comforting fantasy." That is television and film in a nutshell. Certainly, not all moving pictures are chock full of nothing less than comforting lies, but so many of the most popular shows fit the profile of an exaggerated circumstance intended to excite and engage us, full of characters with less impulse control than polite society recommends. More often than not, these characters and plots are crafted into stories that fulfill a deep desire that is not as easy to fill in reality. They are our fantasies; with problems neatly wrapped up or actions without real consequence.

Do these false impressions of reality stop audiences from enjoying the programs? Should they? A stirring, comforting fantasy is a diversion, not a source of reality and truth. Are moving-image makers even aware of their own biases?

The short answer is "yes." Movies and television have always been made to have broad appeal. They are commercial ventures. Producers, directors, and writers know how to craft narratives to give us enjoyment while shaping perceptions. In her 2013 book *I Do and I Don't: A History of Marriage and the Movies*, film historian Jeanine Basinger details how Hollywood learned to sell pictures with a marriage plot. She first differentiates romantic comedies (how couples get together and eventually get married) from films that depict a married couple and their married life. The latter type, movies that depict a married couple, needed a plot (since marriage is really about loving sacrificially, forgiving, finding harmony, and being a helpmeet through everyday life, none of which is any good as plot), and Hollywood found a standard: find an obstacle that derails the marriage (she calls this the "what happened to us?" moment) and then find a way to get the two protagonists back together again.

The working out of that plot was the kind of romantic intrigue and character work that was Hollywood storytelling's bread and butter. "This ultimate strategy of the marriage film followed the sly-boots tricks of all Hollywood movies with their crime-doesn't-pay (but isn't it fun?) and sin-isn't-good (but let's have a look at some) approach."[8] Hollywood knew how to give audiences an escape from reality and from both moral and social obligations without undermining the social status quo. Cheating is bad. But I don't blame him for wanting more excitement. Life is more than riches. But look at that fantastic fur coat.

In fact, getting around the Production Code was an art form for writers and directors. Movies were and are big bold pictures. But there was always more to the picture than what met the eye. Basinger continues:

> There is no comprehension of Hollywood and its product without the realization that planned subtext is not a modern, after-the-fact discovery or interpretation. Hollywood was run by canny men who came out of salesmanship and poverty. . . . Dissembling was something they understood. . . . Moviemakers shrewdly hinted, covered up, misdirected, double-talked, and became vague. . . . Underneath every movie story runs another story, and it often contradicts or questions the one on the surface.[9]

Movies not only talked (and still talk) in subtext, but the subtext was also used to subvert the explicit message. Basinger uses the 1947 Universal Pictures' *The Egg and I* with Claudette Colbert and Fred MacMurray as an example. When MacMurray's Bob MacDonald comes home and tells Colbert's Betty MacDonald he has quit his office job and bought a chicken farm in the country, she says that whatever her husband does is fine with her. "What she says is one thing," Basinger tells us, but "how she looks when she says it is quite another."[10] Colbert, a master at sarcasm, says one thing and means something much more complex that is never so clear as to be offensive or blatant. It was subtle, but it was a value judgment. Leaving his stable office job to start a chicken farm was going to be bad news for his long-suffering wife, and she knew it. So she let the audience know it too, but in an indirect way. That was the language Hollywood perfected and still uses.

When Hollywood was at its most successful, when it became the purveyor of cultural dreams for the nation (and in many ways the world), filmmakers were working on the proven assumption that they could gain audience sympathy and engage audience emotion by reacting to a story at the same time they told it. The story is never just the story; the pictures are never just the pictures. They always come from a point of view. The frame always isolates and excludes, and the message is always given within a context of acceptance. This is why movies and television shows both appeal to us and change our perceptions. That is ideology at work.

Film ideology has been under discussion academically for years, and academic television discussions are changing. The editors of a collection of essays on television texts titled *How to Watch Television* note, "TV content is overwhelmingly regarded as self-explanatory, as most people assume that we all just know how to watch television." They then add, "We disagree. . . . The goal of such textual analysis [as contained in the essays] is to connect the program to its broader contexts, and make an argument about the text's cultural significance, thus providing a model for how you can watch television with a critical eye."[11] The critical essays in works like *How to Watch Television* provide models, because as the editors and other scholars keep noting, there is an imperative to truly understand the moving image. We think we "get" television and movies. But do we really? How much are we missing?

What *How to Watch Television* does not do is lay out guidelines for viewers to make their own close watching and critical examination of television and movie texts. How much better if audiences not only read what critics were saying about the messages purveyed by movies and television but were also able to discern them themselves?

In order to begin to do this, two obstacles must be considered. The first is the understanding that what is "good" or "evil" depends on one's own set of beliefs and values. What should audiences watch? What is good or bad about what they watch? This is entirely dependent upon what will be either edifying or degrading to them. As St. Paul told the church at Corinth, "'I have the right to do anything,' you say—but not everything is beneficial. 'I have the right to do anything'—but not everything is constructive" (1 Cor. 10:23, NIV). All moving images are available for consumption, but not all of them—or not all aspects of them—may be constructive. Audiences will have to lay out what a movie or television program is saying first, and then use whatever trustworthy moral guideposts they find to decide whether the explicit, implicit, and contextual messages are beneficial or pernicious.

Christian writers trying to help audiences discern aspects of popular culture also often cite St. Paul's letter to the Philippians: "whatever is true, whatever is noble, whatever is right, whatever is pure, whatever is lovely, whatever is admirable—if anything is excellent or praiseworthy—think about such things" (Phil. 4:8, NIV). What is noble and lovely? There are cultural standards of art. Some art is "better" (of higher artistic merit, etc.) than others. There are models of virtue. Some things have more virtue than others. It is the intention of this text to enable television and movie viewers to bring to their experience of those mediums their own moral judgments, instead of unknowingly or blindly accepting those the media put forth. Those moral judgments should be dependent on sources outside of not only the movies and television themselves, but also outside of critics and cultural perceptions. Viewers must attune their own moral compass to discern what is worthy of praise. What this text hopes to offer are tools to help know what the programs are saying. With those tools viewers can discern the messages and bring their own value judgments to them.

Audience awareness that they must know their own moral compasses is the first obstacle. The second is the reminder that must continually be kept in front of all audiences if they are to understand the effects of moving-image ideologies: we just do not want to have to work that hard. There are times when the content may offend us (rattling us to consciousness), or we may truly care and not be sure how to go about gaining understanding, but we must remember that most popular movies and television programs do not ask us to think much about what we are watching, and we will by and large respond by accepting them as harmless, mindless entertainment if there is no overt objectionable content. Movies and television shows, especially the ones most celebrated by popular culture, will not ask us to consider them as other than pure enjoyment, and our human nature will be tempted to play along.

Movies and television are important players in a larger system of beliefs and values: our popular culture. "Popular culture," critics Jack Nachbar and Kevin Lause tell us, "is a 'Funhouse Mirror' because it both reflects our 'image' back to us but also *alters* our image in the process of doing so." Understanding this dual function "makes the study of it a valuable 'survival manual.' . . . We may *choose* to believe something rather than merely being *led* to do so [italics original]."[12] The pictures movies and television use to reflect our society show images that may have some veracity but are always skewed in some way. They are funhouse mirrors.

They are also mirrors like the one that the ubiquitous twenty-first-century popular culture hero Harry Potter looks into in *Harry Potter and the Philosopher's Stone*, the Mirror of Erised, which shows us pictures of what we would wish to see. In the story, Harry looks into the enchanted mirror and sees himself with his parents; his friend Ron looks in and sees himself as Head Boy and Quidditch Captain. Erised is "desire" spelled backward (reflected in the mirror). An inscription on the outside of the mirror reads "erised stra ehru oyt ube cafru oyt on wohs I," which, when reflected says, "I show not your face but your heart's desire." That is an apt metaphor for the moving image too. Movies and television comfort us with comforting pictures we would like to be true. They show our desires for adventure, for drama, for romance, for riches, for satisfaction, but they cannot truly satisfy them. Like Harry, if we stand and stare at our own mirror, the moving image, we will be given "neither knowledge or truth" as Harry's headmaster Dumbledore warns him.[13] We may very well waste away, watching and wishing.

While we look in these mirrors—these moving-picture stories that distort and alter reality at the same time they create it—we need to learn to discern. And discerning values from movies and television will take thought work. While as a whole the mediums tend to serve us most easily by not requiring us to do much thinking, some formal aspects of production will encourage us to be discerning. For instance, watching a movie with subtitles makes the viewer's brain a more active participant in creating meaning. But as Philip Kerr says in his article "How to Become an Armchair Polyglot," subtitles can be a turn-off. "American audiences generally don't want to go to the movies to read. They'd rather the experience flow over them, be spoon-fed rather than interactive. Reading dialog takes them out of the movie, they say, shattering the illusion."[14] We may have to gain an appreciation for the work that encourages us to think as we watch, knowing that those elements keep us from taking in messages without thinking. We may also need to develop our own tools, our own reality totems (tools to help us separate the moving image world from the real world), that remind us we are standing at the mirror, and that the images are nothing but images.

The price we pay for not growing in discernment and healthy viewing habits is a loss in our perception of reality, in our gratitude for the three-dimensional existence in front of us, and in a healthy perspective on what life ought to be. But with a critical eye, we will be able to separate the benefit from the danger. Moving images have a lot to offer, and while there are ideological pitfalls at every turn, there are also deep beauties and powerful truths. We will find the pitfalls and the truth when we can truly separate message from medium, narrative from agenda, and reality from fiction.

Movies and television grew up as industries next door to each other. As such they have always been closely related. But current technology and trends mean that although film has been discreetly studied for decades, and television has recently seen great growth in content analysis, these two mediums can no longer be studied without consideration of each other. Both work to create meaning in the same general ways. Both heavily impact popular thought. Understanding and empowering potential impact first means understanding how these two mediums have really become one, and how they work in tandem.

NOTES

1. Joseph M. Boggs, *The Art of Watching Films* (Menlo Park, CA: The Benjamin/Cummings Publishing Company, 1978), 10.

2. Sophie Fiennes, dir., *The Pervert's Guide to Ideology*, written and performed by Slavoj Zizek (Los Angeles: I Wonder Pictures, Officine UBU and Zeitgeist Films, 2013).

3. Hyeseung Yang, "Exploring the Effects of Television Viewing on Perceived Life Quality: A Combined Perspective of Material Value and Upward Social Comparison," *Mass Communication and Society* 13, no. 2 (2010): 118–138.

4. Motion Picture Producers and Distributors of America, "The Motion Picture Production Code," 1930, in *Hollywood's America: United States History through Its Films*, 3rd ed., eds. Steven Mintz and Randy Roberts (New York: Brandywine Press, 2001), 143.

5. Jean-Louis Comolli and Jean Narboni, "Cinema/Ideology/Criticism," in *Movies and Methods*, ed. Bill Nichols, vol. 1 (Berkeley: University of California Press, 1976), 22.

6. Harold Foster, *The New Literacy: The Language of Film and Television* (Urbana, IL: The National Council of Teachers of English, 1979), 4.

7. Graeme McMillan, "Revisiting *The West Wing*: A Stirring, Comforting Fantasy," *Time*, April 19, 2013, accessed September 23, 2014, http://entertainment.time.com/2013/04/19/revisiting-the-west-wing-a-stirring-comforting-fantasy/.

8. Jeanine Basinger, *I Do and I Don't: A History of Marriage and the Movies* (New York: Knopf, 2013), 123.

9. Ibid., 31.

10. Ibid., 124.

11. Ethan Thompson and Jason Mittell, eds., *How to Watch Television* (New York: New York University Press, 2013), 1, 4.

12. Jack Nachbar and Kevin Lause, eds., *Popular Culture: An Introductory Text.* (Bowling Green, OH: Bowling Green State University Popular Press, 1992), 7.

13. J. K. Rowling, *Harry Potter and the Philosopher's Stone* (London: Bloomsbury Children's Press, 1997), 213.

14. Philip Kerr, "How to Become an Armchair Polyglot," *New Statesman*, September 23, 2002, accessed September 23, 2014, http://www.newstatesman.com/node/143860.

Chapter 2

What Happened to Movies and Television?

I think old media, new media, those walls are coming down. It's all storytelling. There are principles around storytelling. There are different use cases around storytelling, and there are different experiences around the way you consume news and information. And in a digital world you consume it differently than we did. My parents consumed it differently than I do. This is part of the natural evolution of the great use cases of technologies of our time.

—Journalist Andrew Lack[1]

Everyone seems to believe in the imminent arrival of convergence but may still disagree about what the principle will mean in practical terms.

—John Caldwell[2]

Who knows how much will change between this book passing from my hand to yours? You should be ready for the loss of theaters and video stores. Be open to something like Apple TV, activated by voice controls. . . . Be prepared for the word "movie" being replaced by "hit" or "bite"—or "viddies." (a term Anthony Burgess used in *A Clockwork Orange* in 1962)

—David Thomson[3]

Both cinema and television are media with great capacity for storytelling by means of the moving image. But the moving image has always been inherently dependent upon technology. Without the development of silver nitrate film and the intermittent motion of both film cameras and projectors, there would have been no movies. Without radio transmission, receivers, or cathode ray tubes, there would have been no television. And yet, because of the development of both of these mediums, all of this technology is now outdated.

It is the nature of technology to change over time, and the twentieth and twenty-first centuries have been times of intense technological progress. As these technologies have developed, the nature of the storytelling, methods of production, and methods of delivery have changed. In recent years, the lines between these two discrete but related forms of entertainment have blurred to the point that they are now so overlapped it almost becomes pointless to try to separate them. What were once the television and film mediums are now moving-image media.

They began, however, as quite separate entities, albeit with shared personalities and production aspects. Both film and television production companies started in New York and eventually moved west to Los Angeles. The film industry moved to southern California to make use of cheaper labor, a myriad of shooting locations, and year-round warm weather. The television industry would find a place in Hollywood easily, since they needed on-air talent, sets, locations, lights, sound stages, and costumes, and Hollywood already had them. Movies and television have shared the same production space and have been intertwined, with movie stars popping up in television programs, and television-sized budgets being used for some productions (like the 1956 low-budget MGM feature *The Catered Affair*). Television also became the second-run theater for many Hollywood films, and it is there that the divested vaults of the studios, which lost their star contracts in the 1950s and 1960s and began to break apart, found new audiences. Films like *It's a Wonderful Life* and *Citizen Kane* owe television much of their notoriety. The mediums have always been related. But they utilized different technologies, and they found their audiences in different places. These differences are significant.

BROADCAST VERSUS THE BIG SCREEN

The differences between television and film start with their intentions and origins. Film began as a purely visual form, the revolving peep show flip-books of the kinetoscope parlors, the nickelodeons, and eventually the epics of D. W. Griffith and Cecil B. DeMille. In the United States, movies were mostly silent until the late 1920s, when Warner Brothers' *The Jazz Singer* created a market for the sync sound film. Movies stumbled over sound equipment for a while but regained their footing early in the Depression, and going to the movies became the thing to do on any given night of the week. But it still meant going out: leaving the house and entering into the corner

Bijou or Rex or Palladium movie house to sit in the dark and escape into the shadows of the silver screen.

Television came to life after World War II. The technology had been around, but the war effort and other factors hampered its growth until the machines of war were turned into the industries of peacetime. Television was in essence a broadcasted picture: it was radio with faces. Radio had been the household entertainment of the 1930s. While one went "out" to the movies, one stayed "in" and listened to the radio. The radio ran all day and sometimes all night. Radio was in the home, right there in the living room or kitchen, bringing the outside world in.

Television would do the same thing. It would need to fill its hours with something to broadcast. In fact, it was the radio networks that first made the shift: NBC, CBS, and other radio affiliates were already in the broadcast business when television became a viable broadcast market. The film remained an event, while television, like radio, was the creation of programming: something to fill broadcast hours. Different times of day drew different audiences. Radio producers had learned this. The farm report needed to be broadcast in the morning, before farmers went out into the field for the day. Saturday was a good day for programming for kids. Afternoons were a good time to run melodramas and romances for women listening in at home. All of these practices transferred over to television.

The mediums were funded differently too. People bought a ticket to the movies, but they needed only a receiver to get television, so block sponsors initially funded the programming. Cigarette manufacturer Phillip Morris funded *I Love Lucy*; Pet Milk funded *The Red Skelton Show*. Eventually, producers would move to magazine-style, short "commercial" ads, which did not require one sponsor to carry a whole show and worked much better when shows went into syndication. So while films used (and still use) product placement and merchandise sales (not a significant profit line until the 1970s and 1980s), their major funding was the backing of the studios, which knew they would get a return on ticket sales (and eventually, VHS and DVD sales). Television, however, depended largely on commercial ads.

GLAMOUR VERSUS FAMILIARITY

The differences gave contrasting connotations to the mediums, so they affected audiences in different ways. The size of the screen, the environment in which to watch, and the focus of attention changed the experience for viewers. "Movies were an escape," Jeanine Basinger tells us; "television was a distraction. When people entered a darkened motion-picture theater, often into icy-cold air conditioning (or cozy warmth, depending on the season), they left behind the outer world and sank into a plush seat, ready to soar away from everything known. When they watched television, they were in their own homes, possibly doing another task, subject to interruptions from the telephone, the doorbell, family members, etc. Television even interrupted itself—with commercials."[4]

Movies retained the air of an experience. They were an event; they were an excuse for a date or an evening out; they were special. What happened in the theater had a different effect than just listening to or watching a broadcast. Television was an everyday medium. Its explosion as a mass medium coincided with America's exodus from metropolitan downtowns to the suburbs. Television was the medium of the new American home: a modern ranch on a quiet suburban street, with a television aerial on the roof. The television, like radio, was company during the day and distraction for busy children. It did not command a person's attention the same way the movies did. Viewers might set out TV trays for frozen TV dinners to watch a favorite program, but they made that, not the medium itself, an event.

> The screen was smaller than you were, and you looked down toward it, not upward as you did for the gigantic movie shows. What you saw on TV could be anything—local and international news, weather, game shows, variety shows, westerns, sitcoms—but they were all there in front of you at the same time. You could control them, moving up and down on the dial; no longer did the image take over and dominate you. The reverse happened: you dominated it, easily eliminating anything you didn't like and changing to something else.[5]

Audiences did not get to pick what came to the local theater, but with television they had options. They could turn it off and turn it on again to find something different to watch.

The film industry generally looked down on television. It was not the shimmering silver screen, with its lavish sets, high production values, and shining stars. It was a glowing box that talked incessantly with second-rate stars and third-rate photography. There were no "long sequences without dialogue in which the camera lingered over a star's face, allowing a viewer to feel, think, and empathize with the character, imposing his or her own feelings onto the actor. Audiences just sat and listened, because everything was dialogue-driven: an actor talking was what the little set could provide."[6] To combat the financial threat television provided, movies began using color photography more often. The innovation of anamorphic lenses meant the picture had more scope with a wider screen, so the camera could still linger over stars' faces and over vast landscapes. There were gimmicks and promotions and biblical epics intended to do what television could not and could continue to give audiences a special experience.

The difference in production value, event versus every day, and placement in a special darkened room versus at home in the living room, meant audiences saw film and television stars differently. The movie stars had big, glamorous faces. Movie stars like Clark Gable or Rita Hayworth were distant, elusive, glamorized. Comedienne Carol Burnett, who grew up going to the movies with her grandmother living just north of Hollywood, went on to famously spoof movies on her hit variety series *The Carol Burnett Show*: "People watched me between their toes in bed, whereas you look at Cary Grant up there, you know, he's 80 feet tall on the silver screen. They were much more removed."[7] Movie stars were glamorous, while television stars were familiar.

Television became a part of the family. Photographs from the 1950s reveal that television sets sometimes had family pictures placed on top or around them. Television historian John Carey notes, "This probably reflects the increasing time people were spending with TV and the acceptance of television as 'part of the family.'"[8] Television personalities were people we knew, and television was at home with us. Allison Arngrim, known to *Little House on the Prairie* fans as the villainous and nettling Nellie Oleson, parlayed her time on the long-running hit series into an adult career in comedy (mostly mining her snobby childhood character for humor in a one-woman show called *Confessions of a Prairie Bitch*). In an interview about the show's popularity and impact, her childhood marred by abuse, and her close relationship to cast members as well as the show's production community, Arngrim said that viewers found watching the program about wholesome, traditional American values and more innocent times to be cathartic. *Little House on the Prairie* was a television program that was an escape, a substitute family for viewers. And Arngrim comments, "Well, it was the same for me."[9] Television was a different kind of escape. It was not one experience; it was weekly or daily time spent with people. It was an ongoing relationship, even more intimate than the ones audience developed with individual movie stars. Television personalities became family.

PRODUCTION VALUES AND REMOTE CONTROLS

Television never developed the strong ties to the art community that film had. There was no French Surrealist or German Expressionist television phase. Likewise, television never got the same critical attention. Movies were promoted, reviewed, and then digested by critics. Film theorists had been critically discussing the medium nearly since its invention, and many notable filmmakers like Sergei Eisenstein, François Truffaut, and Peter Bogdanovich were writing about cinema as much as they were producing it. Although television had critics of the medium too, they centered on television's effect on audiences (notably, studies on violence, like the infamous experiments with the Bobo doll, conducted by Albert Bandura in the early 1960s[10]) and not on the art of the medium itself. Films got reviewed. Television programs got promoted. They were by and large overlooked as fodder for academic pursuit.

But all that has changed. As television technology improved and budgets got bigger, production values went up, and with them cinematic quality went up. Nearly coinciding was the introduction of new technologies like the VCR and consumer video equipment. With them came more "home movies," now without the difficulty of developing an 8 mm film and projecting it, and the sales and rental of Hollywood films both old and new for home consumption. The advent of cable and satellite "pay" television, starting with HBO in 1972[11], also led to more home consumption of films.

Another significant technology from this time period is noted by Carey: the remote control. The evolution and popularization of this device is indicative of our interaction with all moving-image media. It signifies the way all viewing technology has gone and indicates something important about viewing tendencies. "With multiple sets, remote controls and a larger number of channels available, TV viewing became more personalized and channel changing became more common."[12] What to watch, when, and where became viewer choice. With more options available all the time, viewers are still being given more options. Consumption of the moving image was popularized as a group activity, first at the theater, then as the family gathered around the television. But over time, in both mediums, especially in the 1970s and 1980s when they really began to overlap, the significant factor was the ability of the viewers to more closely control their individual viewing habits.

COMPETITION, CONTENT, AND CONTROL

In a sense, viewers have always had control. Ratings determined what survived on television, and ticket sales determined what kinds of films would be made and what stars would be in them. But more direct control meant subtle and significant changes to the production of both mediums, and, more importantly, more competition. Films changed a great deal when television viewing was a threat to ticket sales. VCRs gave Hollywood a new market and a new major income stream, as home VHS and DVD sales were now a part of measuring how well each film would do. Take, for instance, the popularization of the Disney sequels released straight to video. Titles like *Beauty and the Beast: The Enchanted Christmas* and *Cinderella II: Dreams Come True* would be costly to bring to the big screen, with limited profit. But straight release of a video to VHS could be marketed to families that could not as easily get out to the theater and that were looking for a distraction for their children, who already had developed a relationship with the original film, thereby utilizing a brand loyalty to Belle or Cinderella (or Disney, or Disney princesses in general).[13]

The VCR thus made films a viable competitor with television programming. Cable television, like HBO, Cinemax, and Showtime, were competitors too, gaining subscriptions and running full-length films in people's homes with no commercial interruptions. Soon, HBO would start producing content: first, feature films, then series programs like the critically acclaimed *The Garry Shandling Show* and *The Sopranos*. HBO's highly praised and highly sought original productions on cable were so successful they spawned a new market, and AMC, Showtime, and others started creating their own high-production-value programs.[14] To compete with that, other television content began to change. The growing list of cable channels added to this market, and network programming answered by co-opting the most popular practices of cable networks (like reality shows, which started with MTV's *The Real World*).

Movies responded by once again utilizing new technology to make movie-going a special experience. The past 20 years have seen the evolution and resurgence of IMAX films and 3D films. Innovative Steadicam uses, like those used to make the camera "weightless" in Alfonso Cuarón's 2013 *Gravity*, pull audiences to the theater. Likewise, just as they did in the 1950s and 1960s, big screen epics lure viewers with an experience that is not the same on a small screen. *Ben-Hur* in 1959 was comparable in its successful attempt to draw audiences with its scope and heavy production value to the *Lord of the Rings* trilogy in the late 1990s/early 2000s.

Then in the early 2000s, HBO once again found a key way to reach ancillary markets by releasing *The Sopranos* and *Sex and the City* in boxed sets. A *Los Angeles Daily News* article from 2003 points to the trend that took off during that time, stating, "Now new and old television shows are being released at such a blistering pace that the genre is becoming the fastest-growing segment of the booming home video industry."[15] The advent of television programming suddenly available beyond "Nick at Night" meant television programs, like Hollywood movies with the advent of VHS, now had a new life. With that came more critical attention and in-depth academic discussion of individual television programs. Once they could be reviewed more closely, paused, rewound, restarted, and watched multiple times, critics could analyze the programs more closely.

Television on DVD also meant sales beyond syndication, so old shows were now a commodity. Since conglomerates now owned television networks, studios, and distribution arms, content was shared between mediums more eagerly, since a profit was a profit wherever they could get it. The

Internet, along with DVD sales and conglomerate hierarchy, meant both television and movies could be turned into "content" instead of existing only as new releases. This "rhetorical shift from talking about productions as 'programs' to talking about them as 'content' underscores the centrality of repurposing in industrial practice."[16] Television stations still broadcast, but what they create is now called "content" instead of programming. Unlike programming, which is accessed primary by "tuning in" at the right time and to the right channel, content is something viewers can seek and find at their own volition. Content can cross mediums. Content can be rerun, redelivered, re-packaged, and re-marketed. Content has a shelf life that neither television nor film in their early days could maintain.

More recently, streaming video and other Internet providers have once again changed the nature of how moving-image media have evolved, and they are indicative of why the intertwined mediums are now so blurred they can barely be discerned from each other. While movies have always been shown on television, and television has always produced its own lower-budget feature-length productions, the trends in both of those mediums have changed. More and more films are divided along production value lines, and independent or low-budget cinema competes with high-budget films in different ways. The success of some Miramax imports in the 1980s began to challenge Hollywood's blockbusters, but the commercial viability of independently produced films, like the Sundance Film Festival darlings *Little Miss Sunshine* and *Napoleon Dynamite*, meant the Hollywood blockbuster was not the only kind of movie making a profit.

Furthermore, television production values have continued to rise. AMC's *Breaking Bad* cost around $3 million per episode, what a *Variety* editor called "on the high end of most basic cable dramas."[17] HBO and AMC started producing higher-budget programming and have continued to be major players with programs like *Game of Thrones* and *The Walking Dead*. The United Kingdom's ITV-produced *Downton Abbey* is yet another example of cinema-quality production value for television audiences. (*Downton* was a surprise hit, finding markets in the United States in the most unlikely of commercial avenues, PBS's *Masterpiece*, and is itself an interesting example of how television programming is marketed, finds success, and then creates a market.) Movies no longer rely on high-budget glamour, since low-budget features can turn profits. And television is now capable of delivering the kind of high-quality, high-budget production that was once only the domain of the cinema.

Movie theaters have also adjusted their tactics in order to compete for audiences. Digital sound, and now digital projection, mean a more unique experience at the theater. While larger and better home screens drive this competition, theaters are also beginning to market their other unique property: the opportunity to watch an event as part of a communal experience. Movie theaters now screen everything from opera, with the MET promoting a series of broadcast productions in "Live HD" to live concerts, sporting events, and other special "live" screenings intended to draw people to a special, communal, theater-quality viewing experience.

THE ONLINE MARKET: PRODUCTION, PROMOTION, AND DISTRIBUTION

Perhaps the two most indicative examples of the newfound home of all moving-image media are Netflix and YouTube. Netflix's service began as a DVD distribution database, an opportunity for subscribers to access more DVDs than any local blockbuster retailer could viably carry. Film students and cinephiles rejoiced to find they no longer had to search libraries and catalogs for rare and hard to find titles. Then as broadband connections got better and graphics cards improved, Netflix found another market in streaming videos. (Netflix was not the first, but became one of the most viable, in competition with sites like Hulu.) Soon Netflix, like HBO, was producing content. *Orange Is the New Black*, Netflix's critically acclaimed hit series, points to the production value, marketing ability, and popularization of a show that was Internet-produced. Netflix is not the only online service, and it may be outpaced by some new service in the near future. That entity will probably give people more options of what to watch and when and more control over how they consume the content.

Netflix is an example of high-production value and crossover content from both film and television, making those mediums so indiscreet they both now become media content. But the Internet changed moving images in other ways, too. Founded in 2005 and purchased by Google in 2006, by 2007 YouTube was an Internet institution, and its creators and managers had created a market for people who upload their own moving-image content to be paid. In that same year, Google began placing ads on YouTube. In 2011, YouTube also began creating its own content.[18] YouTube means consumers have even more control over what, where, and how they consume moving images. Furthermore, it gives them more control over how they create and share moving images. In some senses, YouTube means the home video, or the truly independent video, is now a viable commodity. In 2012 the Walker Art Center in Minneapolis hosted the first Internet Cat Video Festival, a testament not only to our human fascination with furry animals and funny home videos but also to the commercial viability (and artistic potential?) of moving-image content delivered on the Internet.

VIEWER'S CHOICE

The Internet and the app are the new remote controls. Television and film, which began with different methods of capturing and delivering moving images (and the inherent differences in content those methods would dictate), were technology-dependent mediums. As that technology has evolved, the mediums have lost many of their inherent differences and while differences remain, they are growing fewer and more fleeting. What is driving them is the remote control idea: audience choice. Giving viewers more and different options is the name of the technology game. With that comes more competition between programming styles, and the splintering of marketing and genre production to find audiences who like a certain type of program or experience.

In some senses, this myriad of choices and close control is beneficial, and whether the benefits are stronger than the detriments may largely depend on the individual consumer. With more options and more choices, viewers can create markets for better content. The current rise in faith-based films may be an example of this. More choices also mean the democratization of content. Now audiences have more direct control in "telling their own stories." Endless choices in an endlessly growing market also mean that viewers may be more aware of the glut of moving images and therefore more ready to practice discernment. These choices make viewers prey to several dangers, however, including all popular media's self-gratuitous nature and the inherent problems with humanity's temptation to pride, greed, envy, and anger. The culpability of the human heart may succumb more easily to these sins when given a myriad of choices in which to find them displayed or glamorized.

The Hunger Games series, adapted from the best-selling books by Suzanne Collins, tells the story of a society that revels in watching gratuitous violence, staging a yearly "Hunger Games" in which tributes from the various sectors of the dystopian futuristic Commonwealth compete to the death. The death sport is intended by the Capitol to appease the masses and remind them of the victory that gave the Capitol government control. Many parallels to events in the Roman coliseums are apt. The games are broadcast to all sectors, screened on both individual and corporate consumption displays. Everyone watches the games, for one reason or another. Some are disgusted by it; some revel in it. But they all watch.

The ironic thing about the films themselves is that we too watch the games. Just like the audiences in the story, we choose favorite players and cheer for their ultimate survival. And even though the film audience sees more than the games because they get the backstage story too, they still watch the fight and watch it for enjoyment. In that sense, audiences watch *The Hunger*

Games in much the same way the Capitol audiences watch the games within the story. Audiences for the films may side with Katniss (Jennifer Lawrence) and find the games brutal and unfair. However, film audiences still enjoy the thrill of excitement watching Katniss try to survive. Enjoyment of the movie is enjoyment of the Hunger Games event in which the main character is embroiled. In that sense, the film's audience and the audience in the fictional Commonwealth enjoy the sport of the games: the chase, the survival, and the romance. They—we—watch for the thrill. This points to a dangerous aspect of both moving-image media and human frailty. "The games themselves," critic Tom Hawking writes, "are very obviously a nightmarish reflection of reality TV—cameras track the contestants' every move, beaming them into the homes of slavering viewers, who lap up every brutal, bloody minute. This has been the format that's followed by pretty much every other film that's explored this idea, from the aforementioned *Running Man* to less bloody but equally sinister films like *The Truman Show*."[19]

While the games may look like reality television, and the films Hawking mentions also showcase television's sadistic potential, they are viable as cinema. *The Hunger Games* movies may look like reality television and essentially function the same way since they do what producers hope all content will do: sell. Violence sells. The Romans knew it, and all producers know it too. Television is in some ways blamed by these films, a scapegoat cinema points to in order to distract from its own potential to do the same thing. If television is to be blamed, movies must be too. If there is something sadistic about the nature of one, it cannot be separated from the nature of both. They all include moving images. They all appeal to the best and the worst in us. They all promote more watching. They all promote their own importance, their own ability to stimulate and distract, their own ability, for better or worse, to help us escape reality. And in the end they all show us only what we choose to see. With growing choices, it will ultimately be up to viewers to make their own decisions about what is worth watching (and when, and where). That means they must understand the implications of the choices they make.

NOTES

1. Art Jahnke, "Journalism Is Still Serious, Just Different," *Bostonia* no. 2 (Summer 2014): 24.

2. John Caldwell, "Convergence TV: Aggregating Form and Repurposing Content in the Culture of Conglomeration," in *Television after TV*, eds. L. Spigel, and Jan Olsson (New York: Duke University Press, 2004), 50.

3. David Thomson, *The Big Screen* (New York: Farrar, Strauss and Giroux, 2012), 520.

4. Basinger, *I Do and I Don't*, 289–290.

5. Ibid., 290.

6. Ibid., 290.

7. "Carol Burnett: A Woman of Character," Kyra Thompson, writer/director, *American Masters*. PBS, November 5, 2007, Transcript. Web, September 18, 2014.

8. John Carey, "The Evolution of TV Viewing," 2002, accessed September 29, 2014, http://www.bnet.fordham.edu/carey1/Evol%20of%20TELEVISION%20Viewi ngB.doc.

9. Allison Arngrim, quoted in "Nellie Gives Lowdown on *Little House on the Prairie*," Luchina Fisher, ABCNews.com, accessed December 26, 2012, http:// abcnews.go.com/Entertainment/house-prairie-alison-arngrim-cast-now/sto ry?id=10953217#.UNtjoJPjldQ.

10. Kendra Cherry, Albert Bandura Biography, About.com, accessed September 26, 2014, http://psychology.about.com/od/profilesofmajorthinkers/p/bio_ban dura.htm.

11. "History of Cable," California Cable & Telecommunications Association, accessed September 29, 2014, http://www.calcable.org/learn/history-of-cable/.

12. Carey, "The Evolution of TV Viewing," 4.

13. Norma McCormick, "Children's Video Sales Exceptionally Strong in 2001," *Billboard*, January 19, 2002, accessed September 28, 2014, http://books.google .com/books?id=1Q8EAAAAMBAJ&pg=PA72&lpg=PA72&dq=cinderella+2+ direct+vhs+sales&source=bl&ots=R3z41kyrSt&sig=VBv5phwp73wNn6tp T6i8sXO_gdc&hl=en&sa=X&ei=OIEpVJr9FoyZyATWzIL4Cw&ved=0CDkQ6A EwAw#v=onepage&q=cinderella%202%20direct%20vhs%20sales&f=false.

14. *Quora*, "Why Are HBO Television Series So Good?" James Altucher, re-sponder, accessed September 29, 2014, http://www.quora.com/Why-are-HBO-tele vision-series-so-good.

15. Greg Hernandez, "TV Shows Old and New Send DVD Sales Soaring," *Los Angeles Daily News*, August 31, 2003, Seattlepi.com, accessed September 29, 2014, http://www.seattlepi.com/ae/television/article/TELEVISION-shows-old-an d-new-send-DVD-sales-soaring-1122977.php.

16. Caldwell, "Convergence TV," 49.

17. Cynthia Littleton, "AMC, Sony, Make 'Bad' Budget Work," *Variety*, June 13, 2010, accessed September 29, 2014, http://variety.com/2010/television/news/ amc-sony-make-bad-budget-work-1118020572/.

18. Megan Rose Dickey, "The 22 Key Turning Points in the History of You-Tube," *Business Insider*, February 13, 2013, accessed September 29, 2014, http:// www.businessinsider.com/key-turning-points-history-of-youtube-2013-2?op=1.

19. Tom Hawking, "Are *The Hunger Games* Films Radical Social Critique—or Just More Evidence of Hollywood's Cynicism?" *Flavorwire*, November 19, 2013, ac-cessed September 29, 2014, http://flavorwire.com/426001/are-the-hunger-games-films-radical-social-critique-or-just-more-evidence-of-hollywoods-cynicism/.

CHAPTER 3

A BRIEF GUIDE TO FILM CRITICISM

Critics should be the first to notify us when the truths we hold to be self-evident cease to be true.

—*Joseph M. Williams*[1]

CRITICAL PARTICIPATION AND ARTICULATED ART

If films have been under academic scrutiny since their inception, what can be learned from this critical foundation? If there is an imperative to understand the moving image, what have critics already determined? A condensed look at the practices and discoveries of notable scholars who have written about the moving image can help audiences learn to understand the implicit and explicit messages of movies and television. It also yields a deeper understanding of why this imperative exists.

Most critical academic thought about the moving image comes under the heading "film theory." It is important to keep both the differences and the similarities between films and television in mind. Since so little "television theory" exists per se or deals with understanding the moving-image pictures, most of the history of criticism that will prove useful is "film theory." However, much of it applies to television, especially given the considerations already discussed regarding television and film convergence.

The first serious film criticism was intended to prove the viability of motion pictures as an art form. Hugo Munsterberg wrote *The Photoplay: A Psychological Study* in 1916, laying out an argument for cinema's ability to manipulate reality and create art in the mind of the spectator. Munsterberg's approach to cinema as a subject worthy of critical thought intended to "jus-tif[y] its importance to the intellectuals of the time who thought it crude and silly."[2] Gestalt theorist Rudolf Arnheim, in *Film als Kunst*, published in the United Kingdom in 1933 as *Film*, refuted the argument that "film cannot be art, for it does nothing but reproduce reality mechanically" by reasoning that the very tools of the machine do manipulate reality as they capture it.[3] Arnheim and Munsterberg were writing around the same time that film's viability as a commercial art form was drawing investors and businessmen who sought to promote film's image from Nickelodeon novelty to significant cultural endeavor by building great palaces for movie-going. The theater palaces of the 1920s had names like the Loews, the Strand, the State, the Michigan, and Radio City Music Hall. All the great art deco theaters that showed moving pictures and hired Roxy ushers to seat the viewers who came from varying social classes scattered across the country were called "movies palaces." Movies now had class. They were contenders; they were somebody.

The movie palace and the first critical writings about film were all part of an overall effort to make films a more "serious" form of entertainment, like opera, literature, painting, or the ballet. Critical praise or disparagement of particular films was therefore in some sense entirely acceptable, as it meant scholars were taking the art form seriously. That is entirely the opposite of what happened to television, which had no movie palaces and little academic "review" of shows. Movies competed with television by being a glamorous art form taken more seriously. The movies also shamelessly promoted their own glamour and their own artistic integrity by giving themselves awards. The Academy of Motion Picture Arts and Sciences was incorporated as a non-profit entity in 1927, with Douglas Fairbanks as the first president. Awards of Merit were presented to important personalities in the Hollywood indus-try at the first awards banquet in 1929, and somewhere between that time and the mid-1930s, the statuette earned the nickname "Oscar." From that time on, as the industry grew in glamour and popular culture importance, mostly because of its own promotion as such, the Oscar has become "the most recognized trophy in the world."[4] The Oscars were both promotion and propaganda. They still are celebrations of the industry, by the industry, and for the industry. Every day people get to look at the yearly, televised event with delight and envy of Hollywood's glamour and style, much the same way audiences see Hollywood's films.

Despite its self-gratuitousness, the Academy Awards are also the Amer-ican film industry's opportunity to judge any particular film's worth as art. Even though the nominations and awards are bogged down with Hollywood politics, there is still an intention to find what is worthwhile in the art of cinema and to celebrate those who have crafted cinematic storytelling in compelling ways. Oscars are not exactly altruistically given, but they still mean something in the artistic community as well as in popular culture. Film festivals around the world, especially the long celebrated ones held at Cannes and Venice, as well as Telluride, Toronto, Tribeca, and Sundance, are also political and far from altruistic. But they too are seen by the art community, and then by popular culture, as markers of what is worth celebrating in the cinematic art form.

CRITICISM = A RESPONSE

Movies are celebrated by all kinds of people, but the academic community has given the film industry, filmmaking, film spectatorship, and films themselves a closer analytical view than the popular public has. Criticism, celebration, and discussion of moving-image art are the more analytic and formal ways people respond to films. But criticism can be practiced by anyone. Movies affect us, and they elicit a reaction. We walk out of the theater and ask each other, "What did you think?" Sometimes our initial reaction changes as we learn more, listen to others, and process our own thoughts about a movie experience. We may ask ourselves why we loved it, or wonder what about it struck us or did not move us at all and was therefore somehow lacking. "Often, however," notes Timothy Corrigan, author of *A Short Guide to Writing about Film*, "the reason for our particular reaction to a movie remains unclear until we have had the opportunity to think carefully about and articulate what stimulated it. . . . Analyzing our reactions to themes, characters, or images like these can be a way not only of understanding a movie better but also of understanding better how we view the world and the cultures we live in."[5] Writing about movies stems from a desire to understand them, and in turn gives them importance as cultural artifacts. Writing about movies is an extension of a natural reaction to the experience of the film viewer, that of wanting to interact with the story by thinking and talking about it. How can we respond to what we have seen? One way is by articulating our thoughts; by thinking through our response and putting it into words.

This articulation, as Corrigan notes, is a way to help us better understand movies, and, by extension, our cultures and our world. What is it about the moving image that both lulls us into receiving its messages passively and elicits a response that requires our critical inquiry and our conscious articulation? Much of the response may depend upon a particular viewer's predisposition or the formal and content elements of a film that encourage either passivity or critical viewing. This is why some films garner more critical praise and others are largely ignored by critics. If a film does not elicit much critical thought, it is perhaps not worthy of a discussion about its artistic merit. (This has, however, changed with more critical discussion about popular culture and the growth of sociocultural film critique.)

Critical responses to films mean the viewers who articulate them are thinking about the film as a film, not just escaping into it as alternate reality or subjective fantasy. Critics are thinking about what they are watching. It should be noted that many academic film critics and theorists are film fans first, just like the general public and the everyday critic. Stanley Cavell, philosopher and Harvard professor, in his book *Pursuits of Happiness*, details a genre he terms the "Comedy of Remarriage." He offers critiques of classic Hollywood screwball comedies like *All about Eve* and *Bringing Up Baby*, juxtaposing, for instance, the theories of Kant with the films of Frank Capra. *Pursuits* is grounded in Cavell's ardent love for the films, with his knowledge of philosophy applied to them as cultural texts. Criticism starts with a desire not just to watch films but also to respond to them. Popular culture may point viewers to respond to films by spending money: buying soundtracks, posters, fan magazines, and all the merchandise a toy aisle can hold. It is this tension that viewers must resolve. We respond to films, often with our hearts (since movies are a great way to influence viewers emotionally), then sometimes with our cash (or credit), and least seldom with our heads. Critics make articulating their response to moving-image stories a practice. We all can (and should) make it a practice, too.

METHODS OF DISCOURSE

In choosing how to articulate a response to a film, critics often choose one of four larger categories that help viewers understand the role that the art form plays in shaping public opinion, portrayals of demographic groups, cultural identity, and ideology. The first category focuses on the technical mechanics of the moving-image machines. From the development of particular technologies to the idea of mass media in a mechanical age, criticism in this field explores how the machines work, and what effects may result. The second category deals largely with the qualities of the mediums themselves. Going beyond technical specificity, this critique of the medium deals with the effects of media in general. Studies potentially linking violence, or deviance, or perceived happiness to viewership all fall under this category, and it is here that the vast majority of extant television critique resides. A third category deals with the means of production, detailing, for instance, the influence of the studio system in Hollywood or of postwar economics in France. The fourth category is sometimes called "textual analysis" and offers a discussion of the film/program/moving-image content itself. Often, this analysis encapsulates both story content[6] and the formal techniques of the storytelling: the editing, camerawork, acting, etc. It is this category that is most appropriate for discussing the ideological influence of moving-image stories.

In addition to categories of critique, it is also important to delineate the two major functions of writings on film. Most writing is either a specific report or review, intending to summarize and potentially recommend a particular film, or it falls under the blanket category of cinema/television history and criticism. The former is part and parcel of Hollywood's commodification of story. All reviews are ultimately ads, whether or not that is the stated intention of the writer. They summarize and recommend, without giving a close examination. There is some gray area here, as some reviews are more insightful and more critically sound than others. The review, however, is by and large about appeal. People still often fall into a pattern of qualifying what they watch with a "thumbs up" or "thumbs down" as the ultimate assessment of a movie experience. Corrigan says cinema history and criticism, the more analytical forms of writing, aim "to explain some of the larger and more complex structures of the cinema and how we understand them."[7] This kind of writing tends toward the academic and can at times be so obtuse that most moviegoers have no desire to engage with it, or can be so steeped in cinema jargon that only those already reading about films can appreciate it. Film fans can be elitist and snobbish,[8] critics can get caught up in Hollywood politics, and theorists that delve into complex theories can be difficult to understand. But since everyone can experience movies and television, not having, for instance, the knowledge of Peter Bogdanovich's entire filmography, the inside track on who was at the Tribeca Film Festival, or how Baudelaire's theories regarding art and painting can be applied to film[9] should not stop film viewers from interacting with moving images in a critical way.

Somewhere between categorical approval or dismissal of films and critical discourse that is hard to follow is an approach to talking and writing about movies and television that constitutes the essence of what critical thought intends: it allows viewers to respond thoughtfully. It becomes a way to articulate the experience of the story. It uses the critical tools of academic writers but is as accessible as a movie review and reaches a broader audience of viewers. Much of this kind of discourse exists. Some are personal blogs, some are columns and articles in periodicals, and some are simply discussions between peers, or parents and children, or teachers and students, about the moving-image narratives they are watching. It is important to keep this in mind as more film theories are discussed. These theories are important groundwork that can help all viewers understand movies and television better.

The study of these theories can help viewers understand by aiding them in practicing an amended form of what literary critics call a "close reading" of a text, which Corrigan would put in the category of textual analysis.

Approaching film and television content with analytical eyes means a "close watching" of the film/television text. A close watching will require viewers to think as they participate in the formulation of moral judgments and the making of meaning. Not all viewership requires an articulated, written response, but approaching all viewing as an opportunity for close watching is an exercise that will strengthen critical muscles.

THE MAJOR THEORIES: TWO EARLY SCHOOLS

Those muscles should be conditioned first with the work already done by film critics. While sometimes difficult to access because of their strong academic tone and reference to complex theories, these theories are no less important in laying the groundwork for anyone interested in a close watching of movies and television. Major film theories are at times laborious, but the insights they bring are vital.

The first film critics talked about the medium, intending to support its viability as a serious art form. What flowed from there were two early schools of thought: film is important because it changes reality, and film is important because it is faithful to reality. Sergei Eisenstein, who directed notable films like *Battleship Potemkin* and *October*, celebrated film's form: the pictures themselves and their construction in editing into a moving-image story. Eisenstein believed that film's inherent power was in the juxtaposition of elements between and within images. Conflict was the essence of montage, and, as he was a product of the Bolshevik revolution and an ardent socialist, this conflict was the birth of revolution, the great human triumph. In one scene from *Potemkin*, three shots of stone lions are shown in sequence. They are three separate statues, and the camera lingers over each for only a few moments. The first lion is lying down asleep. The second is awake but still prone. The third is standing, now moving to action. Eisenstein took "dead" objects, statues of lions, and by cutting together three separate shots made it appear as if the lions were "artificially produced images of motion,"[10] a sleeping lion wakes and rises to respond. (This was, of course, symbolic of the Russian proletariat, rising to overthrow their bourgeois oppressors.) For him, the power of film was in manipulating the form.

A theorist from the postwar French film societies (and another one of the editors of *Cahiers du Cinéma*) named André Bazin represents a different approach. Bazin was interested in film's ability to faithfully represent reality. Bazin praised the long takes and deep focus of *Citizen Kane*, even though that Hollywood product had heavy camera effects. Anything that helped preserve space by not cutting in for many close-ups, or time by not cutting much at all, was more faithful to reality. Bazin posited something called the "Myth of Total Cinema." This myth, he explained, begins with the understanding that the impetus to create moving pictures comes from a deep human desire to recreate reality. Total Cinema is that fully recreated reality, "a recreation of the world in its own image, an image unburdened by the freedom of interpretation of the artist or the irreversibility of time."[11] The moving pictures in films when Bazin was writing did faithfully recreate images of reality. (Bazin would say this was trustworthy because natural light on silver halide film, and not a painter's hand, "painted" the image.) Doubtless, Bazin would have a field day with IMAX, 3D, and virtual reality (not to mention reality television). He knew, however, that a total recreation of reality is impossible. Thus, he called total cinema "a myth."

It should be noted that both of these scholars and the approaches they represent felt that these merits of film meant audiences should be more, not less, engaged in making meaning. There is a difference here between these theorists and filmmakers and Hollywood. Hollywood style dictated that audiences get lost in the world of the film and not think about the filmmaking process. The reaction of many filmmakers against Hollywood stems directly from this. Bazin, Eisenstein, and many others sought to explore what movies were capable of, and how they affected people (which is why their work is so important for people to become informed viewers). They were therefore by and large much more interested in philosophy, sociology, and psychology. Hollywood was interested in entertaining people and making money. It turns out a lot of Hollywood product can and should be studied as art, and since it affects the way viewers think, all of it should be reviewed thoughtfully, or given at least some sense of a "close watching." It is important, however, to keep in mind that Hollywood product in general was intended to help viewers suspend disbelief and enjoy the experience, and it did so often by presenting explicit meanings in an overt, albeit stylized, way.

Bazin, Eisenstein, and other theorists were less interested in the explicit messages of a story in moving images than they were with the effect of the specific choices in the telling of the tale. How do we create meaning with pictures? It is from their work that we can explore the implicit meanings. Hollywood did not want audiences to have to work too hard to make meaning. Many theorists saw Hollywood's classic style of "invisible" filmmaking in which the viewer is supposed to not notice the tools of cinematic technology, the editing, lighting, and so on, and instead be caught up only in the story, as propagandistic. They reacted by talking about how spectators create meaning anyway, and often by making films that acknowledged their own presence as a movie by foregrounding the cinematic tools: sometimes inserting people with cameras into the story and making edits noticeable to remind audiences that the movie event was something shot and constructed. The foregrounding of the process within the narrative required audiences to more actively participate in creating meaning. Active or passive participation in creating meaning could be something as small as the difference between a close-up reaction shot after a male love interest sees the female love interest pay attention to someone else and a wide shot of the same scene, where all the characters are in one shot, and the viewer must find and notice the male love interest's reaction in order to understand what is happening in the story. There are many other ways films tell us where to look and invite either our participation or our passivity in understanding the narrative. These kinds of concerns regarding active and passive viewership were themselves major fodder for critical discourse, again demonstrating the major difference between a critical essay, for instance, and a review.

THE MAJOR THEORIES: LANGUAGE, APPARATUS, AND PSYCHO/SOCIAL PERCEPTIONS

From Formalism (Eisenstein's approach, studying the film "form") and Realism (Bazin's approach, studying film's capability to capture/recreate life faithfully), the study of film turned to understanding the films more specifically themselves. This is still in the category of medium critique but is moving toward more textual analysis. Working from the film theories of Jean Mitry[12] and the linguistic theories of Ferdinand de Saussure,[13] Christian Metz (another of the postwar French film theorists) sought to find a way to understand how moving pictures could be understood by comparing them to the way language is constructed with words. His theories, which shifted and developed over time, are called "film semiotics." The word "semiotics" comes from Saussure's study of language and refers to the creation of meaning, or how we give meaning to something and have a shared understanding of its significance. Alphabet letters are a good example of this. An "a" is just a series of curving lines until we assign it significance. A red octagonal plane is just a picture and a shape until we assign it the signification "stop." Semiotic theories are theories of signs and what they signify—how we give words, pictures, and their assembly into stories some kind of meaning.

Metz's work is complex, detailed, and full of semantic nuances, but one important point that sums up much of the importance of his work is that movies seem "more like a *place* of signification rather than a *means* of it [italics original]."[14] Movies may or may not have their own "language," but the moving images used to tell stories are "places" where something can be given meaning. Moviemakers can establish that, for instance, with a reaction shot and the right soundtrack: audiences will "read" that something bad has happened, even if no words are spoken. Moving images are a place where pictures can be used to create meaning. This is critical as we are to engage in a "close watching" of a film or television text. Metz's work in helping viewers understand the signification of things in the image, especially the signification or symbolism within a story, is a major building block in becoming visually literate.

Another important theorist is Jean-Louis Baudry, who took Louis Althusser's writing about how social institutions can work as a kind of machine that instills ideology in citizens and applied that idea to film. Althusser was a Marxist who believed that social institutions like churches and schools functioned to create a mind-set in all citizens that upheld the status quo and left social classes firmly in their place. As a Marxist, Althusser saw this as a problem, since an institution like the church or the educational system, which he would call an Ideological State Apparatus, dispensed the worldview of the richest and most powerful social classes.[15] These systems functioned like machines that generated citizens with the ideological worldview the state apparatus had programmed into them. Citizens, especially working-class citizens, were passively being indoctrinated into the beliefs and values of the upper classes by way of church teaching (which may have been, for instance, in Latin instead of French or German vernacular, meaning that only those with a high degree of education could understand what the priests were saying) or the very way schools were run. These social institutions functioned like propaganda machines, creating citizens with a certain worldview. In a very similar way, Baudry argued, cinema did the same thing. Film was an Ideological State Apparatus, too, according to Baudry, and he made this link by comparing film viewing to Plato's "Allegory of the Cave."

In Plato's "Cave" the unenlightened prisoners are chained facing the wall of the cave on which shadows are projected. The prisoners cannot see that behind them is a fire, with people walking in front of it, carrying objects that look like animals. They see only what the light produces on the wall in front of them: the dreamlike shadows of animals and men. If any prisoners are freed to look at the work going on behind them, they would now realize that the pictures in front of them are not real but only the semblance of the true reality. Baudry says that cinema is in essence the cave. We sit looking at the shadows and light, but if we turn around to look at the machinery creating it we realize the shadows are only a semblance of reality. "One constantly returns to the scene of the cave: real effects or impressions of reality," he says.[16] The machinery—the projector and film—is an apparatus that constructs a reality. Because it creates meaning, it is an Ideological Apparatus. Because the stories it tells are stories of the ruling classes, it is an Ideological State Apparatus.

We believe the shadows on the wall (or screen) are real, Baudry says, because of our identification with them. We identify with the figures projected, the way that Jacques Lacan says a child identifies with itself in a mirror. According to Lacan's psychoanalytic theory, children are drawn to look in the mirror and see that the image is both their own, and that it is somehow different. The child is then affirmed in identity but confused about reality. Just so, Baudry posits, film viewers are drawn to the screen. They see people like themselves yet different, only pictures, and this, combined with the darkened, cave-like theater, makes reality less tangible. What is real? (One wonderful example of a movie playing with this concept is Woody Allen's 1985 *The Purple Rose of Cairo*, in which a character comes down "off the screen" and enters the reality of the movie.)

Some critics have said that Baudry's application of the theories of Althusser and Lacan are misplaced and that he draws connections that assume too much. But the ideas are cause for sincere reflection and perhaps have merit simply by reminding audiences that they are being passively fed ideology, and that there is some confusion between what we see on the screen and reality. Apparatus Theory is important because it foregrounds the importance of the technology and the way audiences watch moving-image stories. Screens, projectors, and reels of film are more than simple machines. They have the ability to create an environment that leaves audiences questioning what is reality and what is not. DVD players, laptops, and phone screens are extensions of those machines, with similarities and differences in the way they potentially "confuse reality." All moving-image machines may create an institutional "ideological machine," so our awareness of that potential is crucial.

The final building block is a broad range of theories that all practice textual analysis. As critical understanding of the medium broadened, it became even more interdisciplinary, and the application of psychological and social analysis to film personalities and specific film texts led to gender theories (by critics like Laura Mulvey and Molly Haskell) and racial/ethnic theories (by critics like bell hooks and Manthia Diawara). These sociocultural and psychoanalytical "film readings" tied academic understanding of how films influence audiences more to sociology and psychology. How are women depicted in films? How has it changed? What does this say about our culture? What does it say about the way individuals think about women? What does it say about our subconscious desires and affirmations? Often these critics choose particular films, especially those that are very popular or indicative of a trend, to examine those questions.

For instance, in *From Reverence to Rape*, Haskell discusses trends and exceptions in films directed by Howard Hawks, a classic Hollywood director. "Under Hawks' supervision (being forced, the story goes, to yell at the top of her lungs on a mountaintop, to deepen her voice), Lauren Bacall's Slim is one of the film's richly superior heroines and a rare example of a woman holding her own in a man's world."[17] Haskell's criticism uses (among other things) portrayals of women in film texts, like Lauren Bacall in *The Big Sleep* and *To Have and Have Not*, to discuss their deviance from or conformation to social norms.

Sociocultural and psychoanalytical critics often mined the classic Hollywood films of the 1930s and 1940s, and with good reason, as that time is often called the "golden age" of American cinema. Movies were for several decades the collective consciousness of the American public, and their sociological effects are hard to overstate. Television in many ways took on this function as well, and more and more sociocultural critics are now revisiting both contemporary and classic teievision for material. Socio-critical approaches are growing, but there are many other kinds of film theories and other highly important authors in the film criticism world, and all of them have something to say about the power of the moving image and its impact on viewers. However, this small sample of some highlights from the world of film theory and criticism is intended to help us understand the following:

- Writing and talking about film (and television) are ways to think and respond to the moving image.
- Critical analysis is different than a review or summary because it requires a "close watching" and analytical thought.
- The first critics helped establish that the moving image was a viable art form by showing how film could both faithfully capture and manipulate reality.
- Critics also established that film could be a place where things take on symbolic meanings, so we can "read" what the images are "saying."
- Other critics established that audiences need to be conscious of how movies make images and how they are different from reality.
- Critics have also taken specific films as examples of how they have shaped perceptions or depicted cultural groups.

All of these points are useful if viewers are to understand the implications of what they watch and how it affects them. This groundwork can help viewers more fully understand the effects that the movies they watch on a regular basis have on their own psyches. These are the beginnings of becoming visually literate.

NOTES

1. Joseph M. Williams, *Style: Toward Clarity and Grace* (Chicago: University of Chicago Press, 1995).

2. J. Dudley Andrews, *The Major Film Theories* (London: Oxford University Press 1976), 15.

3. Rudolph Arnheim, *Film as Art* (Berkley: University of California Press, 1957).

4. Oscars.org, About, Academy Awards, accessed October 1, 2014, http://www.oscars.org/awards/academyawards/about/awards/oscar.html.

5. Timothy Corrigan, *A Short Guide to Writing about Film*, 6th ed. (New York: Pearson Longman, 2007), 4.

6. Not all moving-image media are narratives, for example, art films or game shows. The focus of this conversation, however, is on dramatic narrative storytelling.

7. Corrigan, *A Short Guide to Writing about Film*, 8.

8. Writers David Kamp and Lawrence Levi poke loving fun at them in a volume titled *The Film Snob*s Dictionary: An Essential Lexicon of Filmological Knowledge* (New York: Broadway Books, 2006).

9. Charles Pierre Baudelaire (1821–1867) was a French poet and essayist who wrote, among other things, *The Painter in Modern Life*. Critic Stanley Cavell is one scholar who has applied Baudelaire's work to the medium of film, calling a chapter of his *The World Viewed: Reflections on the Ontology of Film* (Cambridge, MA: Harvard University Press, 1979), "Baudelaire and the Myths of Film" (pp. 41–46).

10. Sergei Eisenstein, *Film Form: Essays in Film Theory*, trans. Jay Leyda (San Diego, CA: Harvest/Harcourt Brace Jovanovich, 1949), 54.

11. André Bazin, *What Is Cinema? Volume 1*, ed. and trans. Hugh Gray (Berkley: University of California Press, 1967), 21.

12. Christian Metz, "Current Problems of Film Theory: Christian Metz on Jean Mitry's *L'Esthétique et Psychologie du Cinema*, Volume II," trans. Diana Matias, *Screen* (spring/summer 1973): 40–87, wrote a laudatory review of Mitry's book, proclaiming Mitry's working through the problems of cinema a "new era" in film theory.

13. Ferdinand de Saussure's lectures in linguistics, in which he called this study "semiotics," were published as *The Course in General Linguistics* in 1916.

14. With the previous two footnotes, Andrews, *The Major Film Theories*, 212, 214, 223.

15. Louis Althusser, *Lenin and Philosophy and Other Essays*, trans. Ben Brewster (New York: Monthly Review Press, 1971), 128–129.

16. Jean-Louis Baudry, "The Apparatus: Metapsychological Approaches to the Impression of Reality in Cinema," in *The Major Film Theories*, 5th ed., eds. Leo Braudy and Marshall Cohen (New York: Oxford University Press, 1999), 760.

17. Molly Haskell, "From Reverence to Rape," in *The Major Film Theories*, 5th ed., eds. Leo Braudy and Marshall Cohen (New York: Oxford University Press, 1999), 565.

CHAPTER 4

A BRIEF GUIDE TO CHRISTIAN FILM CRITICISM

Israel's problem with idolatry previews the caution and suspicion of the moving image prevalent in many Christian communities. The opportunities and hazards of the medium of the visual rooted in the brazen serpent would inspire and trouble those who wrestle with it.

—Terry Lindvall[1]

As a critic and an editor, I am increasingly committed here at CT Movies to trying to not just look for truths in the movies and TV we watch, but also treat them as movies and TV, treat their creators as intelligent world-builders with particular contexts and aesthetic visions, and treat readers as the intelligent, thoughtful Christians they are.

—Alissa Wilkinson[2]

WHAT'S WRONG WITH THE MOVIES?

In John R. Rice's 1938 *What's Wrong with the Movies?*, the Baptist evangelist and fundamentalist journalist vilifies cinema as a wholly bad influence on all individuals and American culture in general. He said movies "debauch the minds of children, inflame the lusts of youth, . . . [and] harden the hearts of sinners."[3] Rice's motivation stems from an understanding—and fear—of the popularity of movie-going and its potential for personal and cultural impact. Movies are pervasive and powerful. People like the movies, and a person will justify them (or at least not object to them) because "he has largely accepted the moral standards of the outside world. His attitude is not a distinctly Christian attitude."[4]

The story of Christians (specifically evangelical Christians) as a cultural group and their engagement with moving images is a complex tangle of love and hate, fear and enticement, power and vilification. It is a story that at the heart of the plot revolves around objecting to dangerous content, longing for something to watch, but fearing real engagement. How have Christians "set themselves apart," and what have the implications been? The story begins with the iconoclastic movements and cultural critics like Rice, then moves to the content review of "secular" films and content acceptance of "Christian" films based on evangelistic messages. It finally arrives at the subtitle of *Reframing Theology and Film*, a collection of Christian film essays edited by Robert K. Johnston: *New Focus for an Emerging Discipline*.

The evangelical church and its engagement with culture is shifting perceptions and changing the cultural conversation. Within our understanding of moving images, there is a vibrant emerging discipline, poised to refocus itself on lending a different, more dynamic and academically valid voice to film/television criticism from a Christian perspective. This emerging voice is a part of why understanding moving images is so necessary for all viewers, since Christians can and ought to have something valid to say about virtue: both in watching movies and television and in the moving-image stories themselves.

THREE REASONS FOR THE LACK OF CHRISTIAN FILM CRITICISM

Why is this discipline only "emerging"? Outside of the tribe itself, moving-image criticism in general only began to truly take shape in the past 60 years. The formal academic study of movies had not readily been available (or encouraged) to the general movie-going public until the advent of French-viewing societies and the first college film programs, like the dynamic ones that came to fruition in the late 1960s at NYU and UCLA, producing the directors that would become known as the "Film School Generation." Even though critics and theorists had been writing about the moving image much longer, film/television studies as a formalized academic discipline have only been around since then. In addition, evangelical Christian higher education was late in developing programs on visual media awareness and visual media production because of the history of that tradition.

Evangelicals come out of the reformation movement (as opposed to the "high church" Catholic or Anglican/Episcopalian traditions). According to Terry Lindvall, film historian and author of *Sanctuary Cinema: Origins of the*

Christian Film Industry, "For many evangelicals and conservative Protestants film flickered against the conscience as a technological form of graven images."[5] It is a tradition that extends back to the Iconoclasts of the eighth century. The Iconoclasts feared that the image—any image—could all too easily become a graven image. Throughout modern history, Christians from many traditions have struggled with and debated about what to do regarding the power of the picture.

In many Protestant traditions, this has led to a greater value being placed on the spoken word. More Protestant/evangelical colleges have radio stations than television stations, and there are several reasons: the radio was cheaper, it could broadcast wholesome Christian music and sermons, and it could avoid getting into the tricky business of dealing with images of people and things glamorized, glorified, and beamed onto screens and into homes. Obviously, there are important exceptions, including the prominence of television evangelists and the film movement Lindvall details. The point here is that in general the Protestant Christian organizations in the United States focused more on radio (audio) than movies or television (audio/video) because of the long-standing suspicions about pictures as potential graven images. Pictures carried power, and that power could be a problem.

That is why cultural critics like Rice felt they had grounds to be wary of the moving image already, and when the content of the stories they saw displayed was at times objectionable, it only proved their fears. Writers like Rice are the reason Hollywood producers formed the Motion Picture Producers and Distributors of America (MPPDA, later the MPAA) and wrote their own Production Code. They hired Will. H. Hays (former chairman of the Republican Party) and Joseph Breen (Roman Catholic journalist) to oversee their self-imposed censorship. The Hollywood community referred to the Production Code as the "Hays Code" and "Breen Office," and the self-censorship was publicly tied to the Catholic Legion of Decency and other religious organizations for social reform in order to "clean up" Hollywood's image.

Image is indicative of Hollywood's value system. Hollywood makes pictures and has always been concerned with the way those pictures, the stars that played in them, the studios, and the industry itself looked to the American public. How something looks is very important, and pictures have power because they change perception. Hollywood had earned the perception of being a place filled with debauchery because of several high-profile incidents, the most famous of which was the 1921 arrest of Roscoe "Fatty" Arbuckle for the alleged rape and murder of Virginia Rappe after a wild party. Despite being acquitted, Arbuckle was effectively blacklisted, Hollywood began to publicly clean up its act, and the Production Code was formed.

This view of Hollywood as both purveyor of dreams and seat of unmitigated vice affirmed suspicions that movies ought to be categorically rejected.

Since much of the American fundamentalist and evangelical world did largely that, their cultural understanding of the subtle and more formalistic messages of movies became a sidelined issue. Movies in total were a problem, and every evidence of star scandal or suspicious subject matter was further proof that Christians should stay away. The evangelical tradition's fear of images becoming graven images has led to a lack of real engagement in understanding the moving image, but it is only the first of two major reasons why evangelical Christianity has little to no real voice in the larger cultural dialogue of film criticism. The second is a dearth of evangelical Christian film art.

Although Hollywood is first and foremost a commercial industry, a moneymaking venture, it established itself in the 1930s and 1940s as the high watermark of the film art form. The trademark seal on every MGM movie contains the phrase "Ars Gratia Artis" in the ribbon of gold that surrounds Leo, the roaring lion. This Latin phrase means "art for art's sake." Hollywood makes a commercial product, but a portion of it at least can also be great film art. The films themselves are judged on their visual style and storytelling veracity.

Evangelical Christian films, however, were made to be judged on their capacity to evangelize. From World Wide Pictures and Gospel Films to the talking-head movies of Dr. James Dobson, the evangelical film world was full of little else besides filmed Bible stories, filmed sermons, and narratives that included a salvation message (and doubtless a conversion on at least one character's part). Lindvall and fellow Christian film historian Andrew Quicke discuss the implications of this trend in their book *Celluloid Sermons* and make plain that the movies turned out by Christians were trying to do something very different than what most of Hollywood was doing, so a comparison between them is hard to make fairly.[6]

The difference in intention between Hollywood's commercial efforts to tell a good story and the evangelical tradition's effort to tell stories that moved people to conversion points to this trend in evangelical thinking about movies.

The form, the visual style, the scriptwriting and innovative camera and editing techniques, the acting and the sound—the very things that Arnheim, Munsterberg, Eisenstein, Bazin, and all the other film critics and theorists digested for the cultural world—were and are not nearly as important as the "message." There are two things to note here: the foregrounding of content over form, and the implied understanding that all films have an overt message. (A famous Hollywood quote often mistakenly attributed to producer Samuel Goldwyn goes something like, "If you want to send a message, call Western Union," showcasing Hollywood's distaste for the idea it was proselytizing anything but "dreams.") Christian art in the evangelical tradition has been mostly a creative evangelistic endeavor and not "art for art's sake." Because of a cultural skittishness concerning images, which led to a lack of desire to focus on the beautiful in art and instead to a focus on the content/message, there are few critically acclaimed films by nominally evangelical filmmakers.

Film criticism grows out of a desire to understand and respond to compelling films. What evangelical filmmakers have by and large turned out are not compelling films but mediocre movies that often miss their evangelical mark by preaching to the choir and failing to address deeper plotlines and dynamic narratives with any sense of innovative storytelling. This is not to say that evangelical efforts have done little good (if we trust God's Word will not return to Him empty), or that there are no compelling evangelical movies (consider the power of the *Jesus Film*). The point is that the focus on content, and the paring of content down to the one intention of evangelism, have meant that the films produced have not used the medium in dynamic ways. They have not dived into other kinds of redemptive texts or undergone serious scrutiny by critics outside their group.

Evangelical audiences have been given little training in how to judge movies as movies and little understanding of the subtle ways movies construct ideology—much less enjoyment of the moving image as an art form. One reason there are few notable evangelical film critics is because there have been few evangelical films that can sustain serious critique. The values of the world of film criticism—to understand how moving image art works, what about it is laudable or dangerous, and how it affects the psyche of the audience—are not the same as the values of the evangelical film world to preach salvation. In focusing on one necessary and laudable goal, they have missed the others, and a Christian understanding of how movies work or what makes them worthwhile is therefore terribly incomplete.

SHINING A LIGHT (ON ONLY THE SUBJECT MATTER)

This lack of training in how to judge movies is part of a larger lack of understanding the form of art. In an article for *Christ and Pop Culture*, critic Alastair Roberts delineates the evangelical focus on content over form: "Evangelicals have been at particular risk of sharply separating content from form and denigrating the latter," he notes. "Our characteristic and laudable concern that the living heart of Christian faith not be neglected has often produced a wariness of those who emphasize the importance of 'externals' such as liturgies, institutions, rituals, confessional documents, and cultural forms."[7] We are wary of externals. We do not want to focus on the image. But movies are an image-centered business (in more ways than one), and ignoring the form means ignoring the way the movie works.

A reluctance to study the form of the moving image means that most evangelical writing about movies has been in the form of content reviews, not formal film critiques. A case in point are the movie reviews on the website Plugged In, an arm of Focus on the Family, whose logo labels its intention as "shining a light on the world of popular entertainment."[8] Each review contains a summary of the plot, followed by the headings "Positive Elements," "Spiritual Content," "Sexual Content," "Violent Content," "Crude or Profane Language,"[9] "Drug and Alcohol Content," and "Other Negative Elements," ending with a concluding paragraph. These categories are almost identical to the ones addressed in the 1936 "List of Don'ts and Be Carefuls" for the Hollywood Production Code: overt behavioral content, that is, pictures of things that are bad or of people doing bad things.

In one sense, this is a very valid critique. Letting parents know what to expect when choosing films suitable for their children is something the industry at large tries to do (imperfectly through the ratings system, but there are content warnings accessible with a quick Google search or at IMDB. com). That is responsible on their part, since audiences should be able to choose what kinds of pictures they wish to see and control the pictures they put in front of their family's eyes. Content critique is also valid because it points out the selling tactics of many films by noting how often gratuitous sexual and violent images appear.

It should also be noted that the Hollywood Production Code, which forbade depicting childbirth in any way (so, for instance, depictions of the Christmas story needed to be filmed carefully) or married couples sleeping in the same bed, forced filmmakers to be more creative in telling stories that still had deep dramatic impact. A good example of this occurs in *Gone with the Wind*, which bargained to keep content like Rhett's closing line ("Frankly, my dear, I don't give a damn") and the tricky scene leading up to Scarlett getting pregnant. The solution to the latter is classic Hollywood style: Rhett carries the protesting Scarlett up the grand velvet staircase. Fade out. Fade in on Scarlett, waking, stretching, and yawning with a smile. No need to show the sexual act. Any adult audience paying attention knows what happened. The Code was censorship. It was self-imposed, though, and it forced Hollywood to become subtle, and perhaps more classy. The other consequence of this kind of subtle storytelling was the ideology couched in the "sin is bad, but let's have a look at some" mentality so rampant in films of this time. Since some content was forbidden, how can we still tell the audience what *really* happened?

Reviewing content has its place. But categorical rejection of moving-image stories based on content alone creates a culture of fear and a lack of ability to critically engage the larger culture. This "setting apart-ness" has not always worked out the way Christians have intended. In *All God's Children and Blue*

Suede Shoes, author Ken Myers points out how Christianity has tried to copy or mimic popular culture trends, making an attempt to create "clean" media alternatives:

> It has not been uncommon for evangelical Christians to give up trying to come to terms with "secular" popular culture, and to boycott it altogether. But often they have simultaneously endorsed the creation of an extensive parallel popular culture . . . [which] takes all its cues from its secular counterpart, but sanitizes and customizes it with "Jesus language."[10]

When Christians have copied the forms of "secular" culture, they have often met with limited success in the Christian market, but practically none in the larger mainstream market. The reason those ventures were by and large not successful is because this kind of mimicry does not understand the implications of media forms or their subtleties. It is simply not good art.

From writers like Rice to Phil Phillips' *Saturday Morning Mind Control* to the Stand Up for Truth website's "12 Reasons Not to Fall for the *Noah* Movie Hype" (which contains a link to Ken Ham's review "suggesting that this movie might be another Hollywood con"),[11] the tradition of content rejection is hard to shake. Christians seek out "trusted" sources to try to navigate the dangers of moving-image media. Hopefully, more trustworthy critics and the development of their own abilities to critique will help audiences give assessment of more than content and move to a deeper understanding that will lead to more intentional engagement.

Christians, especially evangelicals, should also be aware of their culturally crafted tendency to look for messages. While there are few widely read evangelical film critics, there is much more writing on theological themes in film and depictions of Christian stories or overtly Christian themes. Even the Johnston-edited text that calls Christian film criticism an "emerging discipline" is titled **Reframing Theology** *and Film* [bold added]. Alissa Wilkinson, film critic at *Christianity Today,* also notes that evangelicals have a tendency to "proofread" movies the same way we have been trained to read biblical texts: "Christian critics can lean (lazily) into the idea that products of culture mainly exist as object lessons to be turned into 'truths.'"[12] Our active interaction with much of the available moving-image media is focused on looking for the "message," an overt one the movie is trying to tell us and one that is somehow tied to a Bible message or moral lesson. All films may be products of their ideology, and all stories may contain messages, but not all stories are parables. Sometimes they are just examples. Sometimes they are just the expression of ideas.

One important aspect of film critique is to do more than "find something theological to say about the film, and we'll be happy and satisfied we learned a lesson."[13] Engagement with moving-image media means we must engage with it on its own terms, not ours. It is a fine line to tread: how much should we read into what a movie is trying to say, or what it says unintentionally, and how much should we simply take it as a story told with no theological or philosophical intentions other than to give some true account of human nature or the state of the world? Simply understanding our tendency to theologize every story may be enough to keep us aware. Filmmakers are not always preaching a sermon; sometimes they are just telling a story.

FINDING AN AUDIENCE: LARRY THE CUCUMBER, MADEA, AND SUCCESSFUL FORMS

The Christian movies/television programs and critics that have achieved some level of critical success prove that mere content analysis and a lack of artistic veracity are shortcomings in the world of moving-image engagement. The umbrella term "Christian movies" or "Christian programming" could mean anything from Martin Scorsese's films to *The 700 Club*, so it is hard to nail down exactly what Christian media entails. Since there are many different subgroups of Christians within Christianity, there are also many different forms and approaches to media. There is, for example, a major difference between the approach of more liturgical traditions, especially the Roman Catholic Church, and Protestant denominations, especially the evangelical, mainline, and fundamentalist traditions. Two examples of Christian filmmakers, and one example of highly successful film criticism, will serve to showcase how paying attention to form is fruitful—yes, even necessary—to fully engage moving images.

Before we do, it is good to remember one other point. Christian critics railed against movie-going, but many Christians went anyway. Despite threatened and enacted boycotts, nominal Christian films offered as an alternative, and dire warnings against submitting to "secular" culture, many Christians from all traditions continued and continue to watch movies and own television sets. This seems to indicate that the best way to arm Christians—or anyone—to defend themselves against the dangers of moving- image stories or ideologies is not to ban them but to embrace a deeper understanding of them by empowering viewers to make critical moral judgments. Like the remote control, critical engagement and understanding means the moving image no longer lures us as some impossible-to-quantify temptress waiting in the dark of the theater or the television screen; it means the images become demystified and audiences have the potential to practice the virtue of discerning viewership.

When he set out to redraft the software that would eventually lead to the creation of Bob the Tomato and Larry the Cucumber, Phil Vischer was being led by a deep childhood desire to do "God's work—with a movie cam-era."[14] Vischer wanted to create an animation studio to rival Disney and use "my God-given creativity in combination with Hollywood's technology to make—hmm, to make what?—*to make a difference* [italics original]."[15] The original VeggieTales videos would become the most successful direct-to-video series of its time and the largest animation studio between New York and Los Angeles before succumbing to business mistakes that Vischer fully acknowledges in his book. While it lasted, however, his Big Idea Productions was a phenomenon that proved nominally Christian movies could have inno-vative form as well as content and reach a market that extended well beyond the "evangelical tribe" while still touting an overtly Christian point of view. "The Cheeseburger Song" or "Barbara Manatee" may not be "biblical" songs, but Larry the Cucumber's comic appeal sold them well and placed them be-side stories that were decidedly like parables even when they were not di-rectly based on Bible stories. Vischer personally developed the CGI software responsible for the look and feel of the cartoons, including Bob and Larry's big eyes (and no arms). The videos are technically innovative, with form that holds up to critical scrutiny. The writing was fresh, funny, and both theolog-ically and artistically sound. The programs were art. Viable, Christian art.

When Vischer lost Big Idea, VeggieTales continued to be produced, but without its creator and the team that had launched its success. VeggieTales still told overtly Christian stories (telling more stories directly from the Bible) and still used CGI imaging, but the impetus for innovation and sophis-ticated storytelling was gone. The programs have waned in popularity and in critical sophistication. Perhaps its success came from Vischer and company's touch, perhaps it was being the right program at the right time, or perhaps it was an intention to create art that was viable as art and happened to hold a Christian point of view.

Another Christian storyteller who has found broad market viability and critical acclaim (though somewhat tempered for a myriad of reasons) is Tyler Perry. Perry's hugely successful productions have been largely ignored by Hollywood, even though his relationship with Lionsgate Films meant the wide—and very successful—release of many films, including *Diary of a Mad Black Woman* and the rest of the *Madea* series. Perry's films—both comic and dramatic—had high grosses, leading some to question Hollywood's ignoring of his successes. In an article for *Forbes*, writer Dorothy Pomerantz describes, as the title indicates, "What Hollywood Can Learn from Tyler Perry." She spells out Perry's viable appeal to a potential "niche" audience, low-budget productions, multitasking duties (Perry writes and often acts in his films), branding, and crossover to other platforms (namely television in Perry's case).[16] Perry is "constantly underestimated in this town," Pomerantz points out, referring to Hollywood. His films, although ignored by some, are well constructed and successful enough to rate reviewing by all the major critics when released, and subsequent written analysis is beginning to explore the larger themes of his work.

Perry is innovative in a very different way than Vischer. Critics may call some of his formal elements "somewhat lazy filmmaking,"[17] but performers continue to be drawn to work with him, and his films hold up to scrutiny enough that critics at least take the time to review them. On Perry's own website he answers the questions, "How did you make it?" and "How did you become successful?" in a video: "There is only one answer for that. . . . It was nothing but the grace of God."[18] Even the Christian Broadcasting Network profiles Perry's Christian association, saying, "Perry's family-focused films strike a cord with American audiences as they fall in love with his faith-filled stories featuring his hilarious no-nonsense character Madea."[19] Perry's films often involve a character openly acknowledging a need to "get right with God," and family churchgoing is prevalent.

Perry has a long-standing relationship with Bishop T. D. Jakes, producing his story *Woman, Thou Art Loosed* for the stage. Perry comes from a Christian tradition that is also often overlooked in academic circles, the traditionally African American church (which often has ties to the Baptist and American Methodist Episcopal traditions). Perhaps that is why his cultural Christianity is not only less concerned with content problems like swearing but is also more palatable as Christian media to broad audiences. Perry is not overly concerned with the power of the image or with potentially difficult subject matter, and his films have retained overt Christian themes (with debatable veracity and debatable ideologies/theologies) and found success in the larger film market, leading to more critical attention.

The Roman Catholic tradition, however, has for a long time been producing and reviewing films to larger critical acclaim than the evangelical church. Many, if not most, of the more laudable "Catholic" films were not funded by the church (and there is no end to the amount of poorly made Christian films that are Catholic—as much or more than evangelical ones). They were made by filmmakers who identified themselves as Catholic and whose religious identity influenced their work. Scorsese has been vocal about the influence, and (despite a heated and called-for debate about the nature and intention of his depictions) it is seen in the overt Christian imagery of his work, including his dealing directly with the life of Christ (albeit in a very questionable way) in 1988's *The Last Temptation of Christ*. The films of Francis Ford Coppola, Scorsese's film school generation contemporary, are also often analyzed for their Catholic influence (see the baptism scene in *The Godfather*, for one). Frank Capra, Leo McCarey, and even Alfred Hitchcock came from Catholic backgrounds that influenced their works, and there are many others. Beyond that, SIGNIS, the World Catholic Association for Communication, is highly involved in the critique of moving pictures. SIGNIS is a merger between two long-standing organizations, the International Catholic Organization for Cinema (OCIC) and the International Catholic Association for Radio and Television (UNDA).

SIGNIS recognizes the dynamic power of the moving image to educate and influence but has responded by (and was formed because of) Catholics already working in the fields of "film reviews, theater management, distribution, and even production."[20] OCIC has given out awards at many prestigious film festivals, including awards first labeled the "OCIC award," then later called the "Prize of the Ecumenical Jury," at the Cannes Film Festival. Winners of the latter prize include *The Motorcycle Diaries, Paris, Texas*, and *Babel*, all of which received "R" ratings by the MPAA in the United States. The OCIC Catholic tradition is different than the cultural "setting apart" sought by the Protestant/evangelical groups, and it also points to a larger understanding of the power of moving-image stories to be worthwhile as art and viable as entertainment without focusing solely on the dangers of difficult content.

That is not to say that SIGNIS and other entities have overcome all the problems that plague the evangelical film and television worlds. "The theological interests in film that many Catholic theologians (and filmmakers!) exhibit have not received a reciprocal response from the 'secular' world of academics and the film industry, who tend to view any kind of religious entanglement as suspicious—not evidence of a serious interest but rather an evangelizing tactic to be avoided," critic Gaye Williams Ortiz observes.[21] Despite a reluctance to be embraced by the larger world of film criticism, and despite Hollywood's sometimes off- and sometimes on-again relationship with biblical themes or faith-based films, there are models of cultural engagement by Christians that promote critical understanding of movie and television form as well as content.

THE NEW(?) WAVE OF CHRISTIAN CULTURAL ENGAGEMENT

Vischer, Perry, and SIGNIS pay attention to the form of film: the filmmakers and critics understood that content was not the only aspect worth judgment. The emerging discipline of Christian film criticism understands the same. There are a growing number of evangelical academics writing about moving-image media, some of whom have been writing for years (like William D. Romanowski, author of *Eyes Wide Open: Looking for God in Popular Culture*, Lindvall, and Johnston, among others). From the foundation laid by those scholars, evangelical criticism is growing in its academic and critical veracity, showcased in the writing of critics like Roberts and Wilkinson, working at publications like *Christ and Pop Culture* and *Christianity Today*, who are fully engaged in understanding popular culture and its relationship to Christian culture. They are backed up by publications like *Crisis* magazine in the Catholic tradition.

In a review of the 2011 film *Courageous* for *Crisis*, Father Bryce Sibley critiques the evangelically produced film for much the same reason that evangelical critics did: its lack of artistic veracity (writing, acting, editing, etc.). But he also points to a tradition in Christian storytelling that serves Christian purposes without losing artistic merit. Sibley cites the literary work of writers like Evelyn Waugh, Walker Percy, and Flannery O'Connor, comparing their works to the types of books that currently fill the religious fiction sections at bookstores, which are mostly Christian romance novels:

> Like contemporary Christian fiction, these works deal directly with Christian themes (the authors in no way hide their Faith), yet they are markedly different than contemporary fiction. Why? Because they contain a real literary flair and philosophical and theological weight. They are the works of individuals who were both Christians and consummate artists. They have an intellectual, cultural, and spiritual depth that contemporary Christian fiction lacks. Contemporary Christian fiction novels are unapologetically Christian, but it takes more than a strong belief in Christ to make a good work of fiction. It takes talent and a certain amount of subtlety in dealing with the subject matter.[22]

Sibley laments the unsophisticated artistry of culturally Christian storytelling that is hard to take seriously, because the only thing it seems to take seriously is *labeling* itself as Christian:

> I look at the jackets of most of these books and they appear to me to look like a cross between a Harlequin romance novel and an edition of *Little House on the Prairie* adventures. If this is any hint as to the subject matter that lies inside, I will gladly stick with in [*sic*] the gritty realism of Graham Greene or the grotesque South of Flannery O'Connor. These novels are immanent [*sic*] enjoyable and contain a message of real human and spiritual depth.[23]

Sibley says these efforts, though well intentioned, do not even take the Gospel message seriously, "And that's the real heart of my dislike for the film [*Courageous*]—it portrays a shallow Christianity. Our two millennia old Faith has a tremendous richness to it."[24] Why should critics take Christian films seriously when they take neither their craft nor their own faith seriously?

New critics in an emerging discipline will start the process of educating viewers, filmmakers, and other critics to be more discerning. With a wealth of Christian-themed or biblical films invading the film market, this kind of discernment is necessary, but frankly, it was necessary anyway. Images do have power, and they can be purveyors of both vice and virtue. Popular moving-image media hold no special key to either Heaven or Hell, but they have an impact. As the new discipline in Christian understanding of the moving image emerges, it will help viewers intent on understanding what they watch to truly take in the implications of those stories and their storytelling. Coming from a Christian point of view, this new discipline can and will be a great asset to understanding the moving image's capacity for showcasing and encouraging both vice and virtue, in many forms.

NOTES

1. Terry Lindvall, *Sanctuary Cinema: Origins of the Christian Film Industry* (New York: New York University Press, 2007), 18.

2. Alissa Wilkinson, "Lazy Cultural Engagement," *Christianity Today*, October 1, 2014, accessed October 1, 2014, http://www.christianitytoday.com/ct/2014/october-web-only/lazy-cultural-engagement.html.

3. John R. Rice, *What's Wrong with the Movies?* 13th ed. (Grand Rapids, MI: Zondervan, 1938), 14.

4. Ibid., 9–10.

5. Lindvall, *Sanctuary Cinema*, 20.

6. See Terry Lindvall and Andrew Quicke, *Celluloid Sermons: The Emergence of the Christian Film Industry, 1930–1986* (New York: New York University Press, 2011).

7. Alastair Roberts, "Evangelicalism's Poor Form," *Christ and Pop Culture*, September 5, 2014, accessed September 5, 2014, http://christandpopculture.com/evangelicalisms-poor-form/.

8. *Plugged In*, Movies, In Theaters, accessed October 7, 2014, http://www.pluggedin.com/movies/intheaters/good-lie.aspx.

9. Words noted in the review for the 2014 *Left Behind* film are "Gosh" and "Jeez-Louise."

10. Ken Myers, *All God's Children and Blue Suede Shoes* (Wheaton, IL: Crossway, 2012), 18.

11. Amy Spreeman, "12 Reasons Not to Fall for the *Noah* Movie Hype," Stand Up for the Truth!, November 30, 2013, accessed October 7, 2014, http://standupforthetruth.com/2013/11/12-reasons-not-to-fall-for-the-noah-movie-hype/.

12. Wilkinson, "Lazy Cultural Engagement."

13. Ibid.

14. Phil Vischer, *Me, Myself, and Bob: A True Story about Dreams, God, and Talking Vegetables* (New York: Thomas Nelson, 2007), ix.

15. Ibid., 31.

16. Dorothy Pomerantz, "What Hollywood Can Learn from Tyler Perry," *Forbes*, February 24, 2014, accessed October 7, 2014, http://www.forbes.com/sites/dorothypomerantz/2012/02/24/what-hollywood-can-learn-from-tyler-perry/.

17. Roger Ebert, "Tyler Perry's *A Madea Christmas*," RogerEbert.com, December 14, 2013, accessed October 7, 2014, http://www.rogerebert.com/reviews/tyler-perrys-a-madea-christmas-2013.

18. Tyler Perry, "How to Be Successful . . .," TylerPerry.com, Scrapbook Video, accessed October 7, 2014, http://www.tylerperry.com/scrapbook/video/88/.

19. Hannah Goodwyn, "Tyler Perry's Keeping Faith Alive at the Movies," Christian Broadcasting Network, accessed October 7, 2014, http://www.cbn.com/entertainment/screen/goodwyn-i-can-do-bad-all-by-myself.aspx.

20. Signis.net, about, history, accessed November 12, 2014, http://www.signis.net/article.php3?id_article=3.

21. Gaye Williams Ortiz, "World Cinema: Opportunities for Dialogueue with Religion and Theology," in *Reframing Theology and Film: New Focus for an Emerging Discipline* (Grand Rapids, MI: Baker Academic, 2007), 79.

22. Fr. Bryce Sibley, "Why Can't Christian Films Be Better?" *Crisis*, May 25, 2012, accessed September 5, 2014, http://www.crisismagazine.com/2012/why-cant-christian-films-be-better.

23. Ibid.

24. Ibid.

CHAPTER 5

THE MOVING IMAGE AS MODERN LITERATURE

Both television and the Internet have expanded the boundaries of what it means to be a literate person in the twenty-first century.

—*Gary Edgerton*[1]

Since film and television obviously are here to stay, schools should accept the responsibility of training literate and perceptive viewers—just as they have always accepted the responsibility for the teaching of reading and writing. **The instruction of this new literacy naturally becomes the province of the teachers of English, because the core of literacy is the effort to communicate** [bold added]."

—*Harold M. Foster*[2]

YOU OUGHT TO BE IN PICTURES

Father Bryce Sibley uses literature to compare art that pursues a complex understanding of the human condition from a faith perspective (the works of Evelyn Waugh, Walker Percy, or Flannery O'Connor) to fiction that is predominantly Christian romance novels. In so doing, he is also comparing the romance novels to Christian films that have little sophistication or depth. As such he is making a parallel between literature and film. He is not the first. The mediums of literature and film have long been compared and have influenced each other profoundly. There are countless films that are adaptations from literary sources and a predominance of events and actions in modern literature, especially young adult books like the *Harry Potter* or *The Hunger Games* series, that constitute very "filmic" writing. Television has not had as much of a relationship with literature, but with the adaptation of graphic novels like *The Walking Dead* and more literary figures like Sherlock Holmes showing up in television dramas, the comparison remains important. Movies, television, and books are all related.

Moving images are used to create widely different art forms that encompass photography, dramatic arts, digital media, and even ballet or sculpture. (Since the moving image is two-dimensional but exists in motion, that gives it a third dimension, time.) The structure of narratives using moving images, though, is often most easily comparable to literature. After all, Eisenstein said film was composed of building blocks or "cells" like the words that compose sentences[3], and Metz said film could communicate with signs and symbols like a language. Academic programs for film studies are often housed either in communication or English departments. It seems the understanding of the moving image is very comparable to understanding literature.

Moving images combine many kinds of art and encompass a broad spectrum of forms. They can be abstract art or records of reality. They can be scientific documents (like footage from a Mars rover), physical experiments (like Stan Brakhage's *Mothlight*), or experiments in form (like Martin Arnold's *Passage à l'acte*). They can be home videos of a vacation or live coverage of the U.S. Senate on C-SPAN. They can be game shows or exercise videos or talking-head lectures and sermons. But even in these less narrative or entertainment-driven forms, moving images still communicate something. They still involve people (even if it is only the filmmaker/videomaker and the audience), and the people become characters. They are all still about an event of some kind, and the event constitutes plot.

Modern storytelling is (perhaps now becoming *was*) the domain of the written word. As opposed to oral traditions that came before it, literary traditions mean stories are written down in order to be passed on. Even dramatic retellings like plays are written down in a script. The academic literary tradition exists, and literature is still taught because literacy is important. In order to function well and communicate with others, mastering increasing levels of competency in reading and writing is an imperative to better one's social, financial, and personal standing. And yet, so much of how we communicate in the twenty-first century is now based on images.

READING IS FUNDAMENTAL; WATCHING IS UNIVERSAL

The summary of a report published by the National Endowment for the Arts in 2007 had three main bullet points: Americans were spending less time reading; reading comprehension skills were eroding; and those declines had serious civic, social, cultural and economic implications.[4] The report went on to spell out those implications: employers searching for a more literate workforce, better readers making better citizens, and people gaining more empathy through reading.[5,6] Reading comprehension, and not just elementary literacy, is vital. With more jobs requiring skilled labor and higher thinking skills, literacy is about more than knowing what the words say; it is knowing what they mean and the implications and inferences than can be drawn from what they communicate.

Literacy makes better citizens, but according to a 2013 Nielsen ratings report 49 percent of Americans self-reported that they "watched too much TV." The same survey stated that the number of hours per year the average American youth spent in school was 900, but the number of hours per year the average American youth spent watching television was 1,200.[7] Reading may be fundamental, but the real education of America is happening in moving pictures (many of which are supported by advertising). If we as a society are spending less time reading—and comprehension of the written word is not only valued, it is necessary for a "good" society—then it is imperative, absolutely imperative, that we learn to comprehend what we watch. In the twenty-first century, visual media culture has taken the place of literature to tell our stories. Our culture's beliefs and values, housed in its art and stories, are now predominately communicated through movies and television. If understanding the written word better will make better citizens, what will understanding the moving image create but better informed, more critically aware, empathetic citizens? Understanding the moving image is not just fundamental; it is vital.

THE STORY: ART IS IN THE TELLING

Stories come in many forms. We often study written stories in school, but stories can be told in different ways. The story—the narrative—is a vital part of our experience as human beings. "Stories are the first kinds of continuous discourse we learn," Joseph M. Williams says in his book on writing, *Style: Towards Clarity and Grace*:

> From the time we are children, we all tell stories to achieve a multitude of ends—to amuse, to warn, to excite, to inform, to explain, to persuade. *Storytelling is fundamental to human behavior.* No other form of prose can communicate large amounts of information so quickly and persuasively. At first glance, most academic and professional writing seems to consist of not narrative but explanation. But even prose that may seem wholly discursive and abstract usually has behind it the *two central components of a story—characters and their actions* [italics added].[8]

Stories are how we understand, and all writing is some kind of storytelling. The essentials of story are characters and plot, not in any specific form. Visual storytelling is therefore directly related to prose storytelling. Both convey characters and action, and the natural middle ground is filled by theatrical drama, which is the "dramatization" of the written word. Instead of reading the story, one watches it performed. But the essential is still the script, the word.

To cross over from the forms of literature to the forms of moving images, we move from characters and action embodied in words to characters and action embodied in images. "Film is capable of drawing upon most aspects of its artistic heritage to document, render, and interpret experience," say the editors of *The English Novel and the Movies*. "It does so, however, through its own particular formal and signifying properties."[9] Movies and television utilize different physical materials than novels. The form's focus is different, although the essentials of story are the same.

Therefore, comprehending stories in moving images is similar in many respects to comprehending literature. Although the forms are unique, study and critical discussion of them are comparable in significant ways. In the classic textbook *Literary Theory: An Introduction*, scholar Terry Eagleton takes students through arguments made to delineate what constitutes "literature" from other writing.[10] In these points, we find that the study of literature as an art is comparable in several key ways to the study of the moving image.

First, Russian Formalists like Roman Jacobson said literature was different from regular speech because it was a "'special' kind of language, in contrast to the 'ordinary' language we commonly use."[11] This Russian school of thought studied the form of words and how they were used. The Russian Formalist[12] movement took place in film and literature at the same time. Artists engaged in both mediums to understand how the form's unique qualities were manipulated in creating art.

Eagleton then discusses how literature is often fictional but can also be nonfictional. The same can easily be said of the forms of the moving image. *Jane Eyre* is both a fictional book and a fictional movie. *Fast Food Nation* is nonfiction literature but a fictionalized film because a narrative script based on the reports of the book constituted the film's "story." *The National Parks: America's Best Idea* is a nonfiction television documentary series made by filmmaker Ken Burns, with several nonfiction companion books based on research, photographic media, and historical data. All of these things are considered works of cultural art, fiction or not. Likewise, not all literature is linear. Some writing, for instance, the poetry of e. e. cummings's, is very abstract, but so are a great number of creative moving images, like Man Ray's surrealist film *The Return to Reason*.

One way to separate literature from other forms of writing, according to Eagleton, is literature's potential for the significance of the *way* a subject matter is discussed, rather than just the subject matter itself.[13] In other words, two writers could discuss the same subject but what would make one literary art and the other just ordinary writing is the way it was written. The same could be said for a home movie of an event, as opposed to a professionally videographed version of the same event, or that the treatment of, for example, *Citizen Kane* in visual form is what gives it artistic merit and not the fictional story based on its real-life inspiration, William Randolph Hearst. The art is in the telling of the story.

Perhaps this relationship in conveying story is why so many movies are based on published written works. Having once experienced the story in our imagination, we yearn to see it "brought to life." Some images in literature seem to have a filmic equivalent. In an essay titled "Dickens, Griffith, and the Film Today," Eisenstein once again compares the two forms, noting how he believed the innovative filmmaker D. W. Griffith's montage techniques were indebted to the close-up detailed descriptions of Charles Dickens, using an example from Dickens's story "The Cricket on the Hearth."[14] Indeed many works of fiction, especially more contemporary ones, seem to have passages that play out in our imaginations. We see the story when we read it, just like we see images onscreen (although onscreen the stories often look very different than the pictures in our imaginations). A description of a furtive glance intimates a close-up. A spoken question is answered with a nod or other nonverbal action. Dialogue is motivated by an action with a corresponding sound effect, that is, "What was that?" The strong visual imagery of literature is translated easily into moving pictures.

It seems each medium's elasticity is what makes it capable of sophisticated storytelling. Both words and moving pictures have the ability to nuance meaning and therefore can be manipulated in artistic ways. In fact, the discussion of what constitutes fine art, or really any art at all, applies both to literature and the moving image. Is a blog really literature? What makes it so? Is a YouTube video technically a "movie"? Eagleton settles on the definition of literature as "highly-valued writing" and says that value is subjective depending upon the ideology of a given group.[15] The same might be true for what constitutes a movie. A highly valued series of moving images constitutes in some way what a movie is.

WORTH A THOUSAND ABSTRACT WORDS

While the moving image is relatable to literature in a lot of ways, there are of course some significant differences. The major difference is that in literature meaning is housed in the word, and in the moving image it is housed in the picture. "A basic assumption I make is that both words and images are set signs that belong to systems and that, at a certain level of abstraction, these systems bear resemblance to each other,"[16] critic Keith Cohen says. Cohen is working directly from Metz's theory of film semiotics. A word is composed of letters, each having a sound. Together those signifiers (the different letters) mean, or signify something. Thus language in semiotic terms is composed of signs (letters), signifiers (words formed from letters), and the signified (the meaning of the word). Metz said the image could be understood the same way. One appropriate example is a picture, drawn or photographed, of a stop sign. The image is composed of signs: the red octagon, the letters S, T, O, and P. The signs together create a signifier: a stop sign. The signifier has a signified meaning: come to a halt.

To follow Metz's way of thinking, all images can therefore retain denotative and connotative meanings, just like words, and pictures can be "read." However, the inherent differences between words and pictures make such a literal "reading" impossible for pictures. Pictures do not signify in the same way letters and words do. The word "dog" is rather abstract. It could be any age, gender, or breed. A picture of a dog, however, would include those particular specifics: that is not just a dog; that is a male Beagle puppy; not only that, he looks happy and well fed.

Words can easily be abstract: "It was a gray day." On the other hand, a picture of, for instance, a landscape on a rainy October morning, is specific. It has an exact location, a distance from the equator, an atmospheric quality, trees, plants, and perhaps man-made structures. A double meaning, if one is intended, can be conveyed only by aligning a shot of the environment to the situation of a character, creating "mood." If it is the character's gray day both internally and externally, the audience must see the environment and the re-action shot of the character, in a specific situation like looking longingly out the window. Both words and pictures can convey complex ideas. But imagine how long it would take to describe the complex emotional moment in Joan's face at the stake in a still from Carl Dreyer's *The Passion of Joan of Arc*. One second of film could require pages of description to capture all its nuances.

The visual image is complex and conveys complex ideas. We overlook its implicit meanings because we do not have to take the time to comprehend them the same way we do while reading. The pictures pass by rapidly, and we get the immediate meaning necessary to create the story. We "read" a great deal subconsciously. Unless the filmmaker utilizes the form and compels or forces us to, we do not dwell long on the picture. We move on with the plot. In literature, we must read one sentence at a time, taking in description and discursive language in order to make sure we do not miss any important details or events. We have to pay attention to each word, but we do not have to pay attention to each "signifier" in a moving image.

The images do not require as much intentional thought, either. They do not require us to truly comprehend them in order to understand the story. This is deceptive. We know we can understand the plot of the movie or show, but we are not intentionally thinking through its imagery. We do not see all the signifiers and think about what they mean. Our brains do not have to do the work of reading comprehension. They do not have to, but they should.

Images do call for inspection, especially since they can convey so many layers of meaning. They are rife with signification. They are as full of ideology as the written word and profoundly affect our emotional and mental state. Mood is established not just by tone and figurative language: it can be set by a picture, often combined with music. Music's emotional capacity directly affects the spectator's mood and is a major part of the visual storytelling experience. "Of even greater importance than the film medium's unlimited range in subject matter and treatment, however," says critic Joseph M. Boggs, "is the overwhelming sense of reality it can convey. . . . This sense of reality in film is due primarily to the medium's continuous flow of sight, sound, and motion."[17] The moving image is not just a story; it is a multisensory experience.

This experience in moving picture viewing has been compared to many things. Moving images convey stories like literature does; they are a performed narrative event like theater, but they move much more like dreams. The French Surrealists thought film used the same logic as dreams: one picture after another creates a subjective, sometimes subconscious meaning. Filmmakers like May Ray and Luis Buñuel made use of film's oneiric or dreamlike states. A door could suddenly be a wall, or a window, or a fish. People appeared and did things that did not have to make sense or even be plausible. The action was an experience of our consciousness and our subconsciousness. Dreams are states of consciousness. The moving image works like a conscious state, and it affects people in a similar way. This makes the moving image tremendously powerful. It changes our very consciousness, our own mental states.

And then there is also the emoticon. A need grew out of the growth in communication by instant and text messaging to convey nonverbals as context for typed words. This was necessary because it takes a long time to convey context through words and because instant and text messaging communication is more like speech than like writing. How can the speaker or writer convey casual indifference, apology, or empathetic happiness after the word "yeah"? Exclamation points may be used. More exclamation points will indicate the level of excitement and so on. Delivery and tone also add meaning. Consider a standard telephone conversation sign-off: a "bye" or "okay, see ya." Few people simply hang up after the last necessary word in the conversation. The sign-off is said with an intonation that implies the conversation is over. Language finds a way to use more than words. Moving images do the same thing, often through use of reactions shots. The words are important, but the picture gives the real meaning, just as it does when Claudette Colbert says one thing but means quite another in *The Egg and I.*

Sarcasm, for instance, is more difficult to convey with just words. Pictures help us communicate by conveying nuance. Understanding what those pictures are indicating tends to happen intrinsically, as we are taught social customs. This is similar to the way we understand the connotative meanings of word. We learn their specific definition: *cool* means "colder," but we hear people around us using it to mean something good, and we understand it from the way other people react and its context. Then we see someone use the word and we note not only the denotative meaning but also the context and tone of delivery. Does the listener react with agreement, or is the speaker indicating he or she means the opposite of what he or she says? We see this in the picture of their faces. The context, the reaction shot, tells us more of the meaning.

VISUAL "READING" IS FUNDAMENTAL

Literacy of the written word means not only being able to take the denotative meanings of words and understand the literal meanings of phrases and sentences as they form ideas, but also improving reading levels and understanding the nuances and layers of meaning in a given text. More than just the connotative meanings of words, the themes and ideas present in literature encompass an ideology: a way of thinking, a set of cultural beliefs and values. They can also reach sophisticated forms like satire, which require very developed reading comprehension skills (as opposed to the socially learned skills of reading nonverbals like sarcasm, most of which are picked up by children long before they learn literary satire).

Most liberal arts programs require college-level competency tests for writing and mandate college-level literature studies. Learning simply to read is not enough. An intentional reading of a literary text for language usage and complex meaning is called a "close reading." A close reading is what students and scholars do to really understand *The Red Badge of Courage* or *Persuasion* or even *Gone Girl.* The close reading examines themes and forms. It nails down point of view and the use of figurative language. It breaks down narrative structure and important motifs. All of these constitute a deeper understanding of how the words work and how the story is crafted. What is the book really saying? Yes, it is about a soldier or a young girl or a murdered woman. But it is also about honor, duty, and what impels men to battle, or about modesty, humility, and love, or about honesty, lies, and the social masks people wear.

Learning to understand and increase critical understanding is thought to be a vital part of higher education and higher-level thinking skills, so close readings of text are a major part of literature classes in high school and college. If this is true for the written word, should it not also be true for the moving image? Can there not also be "close watchings" and should that not also be taught to high school and college students?

Harold Foster is one scholar who thinks so, although he is far from being the only one. His text *Visual Literacy* is intended to help secondary level educators set up programs for teaching students how to better comprehend films and television programs. Besides describing where to look for materials (the films and programs to be "read" in the classroom), Foster warns teachers to avoid labeling some films as superior, or dampen enjoyment of moving-image entertainment by examining the movie while it is playing instead of asking students to reflect after viewing. He outlines activities intended to engage students as well as hone their skills. The intention, as it is when approaching the teaching of many subject matters, is to awaken a new sense of not only understanding but also appreciation for the subject matter.

This is most important when understanding the power of the moving image. It is a power not to be feared (and categorically rejected) but to be respected and appreciated for what it is. This process is the process of demystification. When we understand the power of the images, we are put in control, or as pop-culture critics Robert H. Woods Jr. and Paul D. Patton would say, we "lead the dance" with popular media.[18] We are no longer mystified, succumbing to the messages without our conscious gatekeeping. We are instead empowered by our capacity to understand. It is true of the written word and of the moving image.

Foster points out one other fundamental reason that visual literacy is an imperative, and it relates directly to the idea that written-word literacy shaped culture and was therefore taught in schools, but this teaching is not enough:

> Future generations will grow up in a world where film and television provide stronger impact, more excitement, and flashier entertainment than schools can ever hope to do. Since film and television may provide the only sources of information that many people will willingly accept, American schools may have to change drastically to meet the needs of future generations. . . . Teachers must not allow young people to deal with media without defenses.[19]

Literacy is fundamental. It is our defense against ignorance and the fears and biases that come with it. The moving image shapes our ways of thinking and our perceptions, and we owe it to ourselves and our society to be better armed, better informed, and better prepared.

Literature has an important place in culture, and that will probably never change. But the emoticons and emojis on our cell phones and social media are a testament to our picture-conscious society. The moving image shapes our beliefs and values, and if the Nielsen statistic is true and American teenagers spend more time learning in the school of television than they do in the classroom, Foster is exactly right. We need to be able to comprehend the complex and implicit meanings in visual storytelling. Just as literacy is vital, so too is understanding moving pictures. That understanding is similar to the way we understand the complexities of the modern age's cultural keeper: the written word. If understanding literature means becoming literate, understanding pictures means learning to "read" moving pictures. Calling this "visual literacy" is a bit of a contradiction in terms, since the word "literate" relates to writing. But because an understanding of both mediums is similar in so many ways, that phrase is the most appropriate. Understanding the moving image means becoming "visually literate." This will require the acquisition of certain skills and the understanding of some production practices, but anyone who watches moving pictures is capable of learning to understand them and therefore capable of attaining visual literacy.

NOTES

    1. Gary Edgerton, *The Columbia History of American Television* (New York: Columbia University Press, 2009), 424.

    2. Harold M. Foster, *The New Literacy: The Language of Film and Television* (Urbana, IL: National Council for Teachers of English, 1979), 31.

    3. Eisenstein compared edited shots going together like reading the ideograms of Japanese haiku.

    4. The National Endowment for the Arts, *To Read or Not to Read: A Question of National Consequence*, Research Report #47, Washington D.C., 2007, accessed October 8, 2013, http://arts.gov/sites/default/files/ToRead.pdf.

    5. A section of the report titled "Reading as an Act of Empathy" even cites C. S. Lewis's *An Experiment in Criticism* as evidence that readers "identify more closely with community than non-readers" (ibid., 90).

    6. Ibid.

    7. Statistic Brain, "BLS American Time Use Survey, A.C. Nielsen Co.," accessed October 8, 2013, http://www.statisticbrain.com/television-watching-statistics/.

    8. Joseph M. Williams, *Style, Towards Clarity and Grace* (Chicago: University of Chicago Press, 1995), 20.

    9. Michael Klein and Gillian Parker, eds., *The English Novel and the Movies* (New York: Ungar, 1981), 3.

    10. Terry Eagleton, *Literary Theory: An Introduction*, 2nd ed. (Minneapolis: University of Minnesota Press, 2003), 2.

    11. Ibid., 5.

12. The Russian Formalist tradition crosses media boundaries. Jacobson comes out of the same thought of tradition as Sergei Eisenstein. Although one was concerned with literature and the other with cinema, both were a part of the same basic movement that foregrounded construction and form in making art.

13. Ibid., 9.

14. Keith Cohen, *Film and Fiction: The Dynamics of Exchange* (New Haven, CT: Yale University Press, 1979), 4.

15. Eagleton, *Literary Theory*, 11.

16. Cohen, *Film and Fiction*, 3.

17. Joseph M. Boggs, *The Art of Watching Films* (Menlo Park, CA: The Benjamin/Cummings Publishing Company, 1978), 5.

18. Robert H. Woods Jr. and Paul D. Patton, *Prophetically Incorrect: A Christian Introduction to Media Criticism* (Grand Rapids, MI: Brazos Press, 2010), xl.

19. Foster, *The New Literacy*, 49.

CHAPTER 6

VISUAL LITERACY:
A VIEWING PRIMER

An understanding of [the structural devices of film] and how they are used is one of the main skills in acquiring visual literacy. Knowing what these devices are and how they are used to elicit feelings helps the viewer to resist media influence and manipulation and to develop a more sophisticated perception of films.

—*Harold M. Foster*[1]

ACQUIRING SKILLS AND GAINING INSIGHT

Now that we have established the importance of understanding the moving image, the interrelationship of movies and television, some theories from within and without the Christian tradition, and the moving image relation to the storytelling form, we can begin to talk about the components of visual literacy. First, a one-sentence definition of visual literacy will help give us something to refer to and keep our goals at the forefront of our practice. Visual literacy can be defined as the skills necessary to understand both the explicit and implicit messages and ideologies in moving-image media. The mastery of these skills will be effective in several important ways.

The first major skill is to recognize the values and beliefs portrayed as good, worthwhile, or admirable in the main characters and their dramatic arcs and the values and beliefs portrayed as malevolent, of less value, pernicious, or immoral in main characters and their dramatic arcs. The "good guys" and "bad guys" tell us a lot about what a particular movie or show says is admirable and desirable. Heroes may make mistakes, but what redeems them? Why is that significant? What makes the villain a bad person? Does anything justify this? Should it?

Another major skill is being able to pinpoint the narrative elements that display these values and beliefs. Why is it important that the hero makes that choice in the end? What if someone else had made it? How do we know the story has come to a close? What do we learn in the first 20 minutes of a film or in the pilot episode of a show? What does that tell us about what the program values?

The third skill component is to understand how these observations about what the program portrays as good or bad are supported by elements of the moving-image form. How often is the main character isolated in a close-up so that only the audience can "see" what he or she is thinking? How often does the camera take her or his point of view?

These skills will be effective in several key ways. First, they train all viewers about specific things to look for. Instead of trying to unpack every narrative with a different approach, by looking at antagonists and protagonists and their actions (which are nearly universal), viewers will have a multipurpose tool to examine many kinds of moving-image stories. These skills will also give insight into the program's ideology, explicit or implicit and intended or not. This kind of insight leads to the recognition of the moving-image form for what it is: neither an innocent, ineffective novelty, nor a moral teacher, nor a malicious purveyor of immoral garbage, but simply a conveyor of ideas through moving-image story. This is exactly the process of demystification. When we understand the parts, the whole is no longer a mystery. We have pulled back the curtain to reveal the true wizard. We know that what scared us before was simply lights and smoke.

Visual literacy skills are effective because the recognition of ideologies in films and television programs may help us understand why we are attracted to certain narratives. Why do we like that show or those kinds of movies so much? What do we learn about ourselves from this? Do the kinds of stories we are drawn to affirm what we believe or tell us what we want to be true? This is much more a question about the human heart than the mediums themselves. A close watching of the stories that we are drawn to will also help us understand how to recognize stories that are truly edifying. Our goal, in short, is to understand how the story works by pulling out a few key components and examining them from a couple of perspectives. The yield will be better informed, more conscientious, more appreciative viewers and, in the long run, people who watch moving-image stories with greater insight and responsibility.

MAJOR DRAMATIC QUESTIONS

The first step in the "close watching" of a moving-image narrative is to pinpoint what the story is really all about. One very effective tool for doing this, called the Sentence Outline, was developed by Milan Stitt, the playwright and teacher who wrote *The Runner Stumbles*. I learned it from one of his pupils who became my writing professor, playwright Simone Yehuda. As we sat around work-shopping our initial play ideas, Professor Yehuda would make us write out a sentence outline, and suddenly we would realize why our story did not seem to be going anywhere, or why our main character did not have much focus. This tool pares down the main dramatic points of a narrative and puts them in one sentence, telling us what the story is really all about.

The Sentence Outline follows this format: This is the story of (name one main character) who wants to (the main character's goal), and after (the main character's important decision that leads to the climax) and finally (the climax of the story) because (theme, or why those events necessarily follow one another). Sentence Outlines can be written for any character in a story, but choosing one main character is essential to understanding the main subject matter and ideology of a given narrative. To see this played out, we will fill in events from a well-known example.

Star Wars: A New Hope is the first film produced in the *Star Wars* series. Although it is possible (albeit terrifically complicated) to create a sentence outline for all of the movies in the series, it is best for us to use the narrative and character information for just that film. None of the "expanded universe"—prequel, sequel, video games, or comic books—will have a bearing, just the events of that film. There is an argument to be made that the main character of that film and the entire series is the android R2-D2, but it is mutually agreed that the intended main character of *Star Wars: A New Hope* is Luke Skywalker (Mark Hamill). When we meet Luke, he is feeling trapped on his uncle's farm on a remote desert planet. He learns news that his father, whom he never knew, was once a star pilot and part of a special order of warriors called Jedi. This information comes from another Jedi named Obi-Wan Kenobi (Alec Guiness). Obi-Wan, or Ben, becomes Luke's mentor after Luke discovers that his guardians have been killed and that Ben will be going on a mission to help defeat a battle station being used to destroy other worlds.

So our sentence outline might start out like this: This is the story of *Luke Skywalker*, who wants to *learn the ways of the Force and become a Jedi like his father*. That goal can be expressed as a question: Will Luke Skywalker learn the ways of the Force and become a Jedi like his father? This question is the Major Dramatic Question, and it tells us vital information about our protagonist's intentions and values. When we examine both the theme and the protagonist's values, the Major Dramatic Question will be our most important piece of information.

Luke does train with Ben to become a Jedi. After Ben is killed in a confrontation with the film's main antagonists, Darth Vader (played by David Prowse and voiced by James Earl Jones), he still communicates with Luke through the Force. In the *Star Wars* series, the Force is a kind of supernatural "life force" shared by all things. According to Ben, a Jedi's "strength flows from the Force." Luke's ability to hear and communicate with Ben through this supernatural medium even after his death is important, because Luke's development of Force-sensitive skills is what makes him a Jedi, and that is his main goal. After Ben is killed, Luke and his friends escape from the battle station, the Death Star, and eventually come back to attack it as part of a group of fighters from the Rebellion, which has been organized to defeat Darth Vader, the Death Star, and the organization they militantly support, the Galactic Empire. The last important battle of the film is this attack on the Death Star battle station, in which Luke plays an essential part. Forced to try to hit a very small target on the Death Star while being pursued by enemy fighters, Luke must choose whether to use the technology-dependent targeting computer or use his own Force-sensitive abilities to aim. His choice to use the Force reflects his now-fulfilled aspirations to become a Jedi. (At least, it is a major step toward that goal since he acts as a Jedi would.)

The Major Dramatic Question is: Will Luke Skywalker learn the ways of the Force? Will he use the Force? When he turns off the targeting computer and makes the winning shot that blows up the Death Star, the answers is, yes, he will use the Force. That is the climax of the film, and it is at this point in a story that the Major Dramatic Question gets answered. There is a little suspense and tension that he may not have made this choice, but not much. The audience is fairly sure Luke will make the decision to use the Force instead of a computer. Why? Because some other key events in the narrative show Luke choosing the Force over technology. That key event is the crisis. This moment in *Star Wars: A New Hope* may be his listening to Ben's voice after watching his mentor being killed. In the cockpit of his starfighter plane he also listens to Ben's voice before turning off the computer. This parallel action indicates something. Ben is teaching him to use the Force, and listening to Ben is how he will fulfill his goal. So immediately after Ben's death, when he tells Luke to run instead of staying to try to avenge Ben's death, we see a key moment in Luke's development. That choice, to listen to Ben and run, indicates how Luke will act when the climax is reached.

Therefore, the Sentence Outline can be expanded: This is the story of *Luke Skywalker*, who wants to *learn the ways of the Force and become a Jedi like his father*, and after *listening to Obi-Wan telling him to run*, finally *listens to*

Obi-Wan, turns off his computer, and destroys the Death Star with the Force. The final component of the sentence outline is the theme. More than anywhere, this theme nails down the ideology of a given story simply by asking what these events mean. So what? So all this happens. Great. But why? The theme is found by inserting the word "because" into the Sentence Outline: This is the story of *Luke Skywalker,* who wants to *learn the ways of the Force and become a Jedi like his father,* and after *listening to Obi-Wan telling him to run,* finally *listens to Obi-Wan, turns off his computer, and destroys the Death Star with the Force* because _____. Why?

The key components seem to have something to do with becoming something and how that will happen. The end result of Luke's adventure is that he has learned how to become a Jedi. There is a lot more that could be said about Luke's story and its implications, especially with the knowledge that writer/director George Lucas crafted this story after studying in-depth the writings of Joseph Campbell and his *The Hero with a Thousand Faces.* Luke's journey is mythical, and his relationship to both father and mentor are archetypal. In just this story, however, the point seems to be that becoming a Jedi, and therefore fulfilling one's destiny, requires something. It requires listening to the Force. So the finished Sentence Outline might look something like this: This is the story of *Luke Skywalker,* who wants to *learn the ways of the Force and become a Jedi like his father,* and after *listening to Obi-Wan telling him to run,* finally *listens to Obi-Wan, turns off his computer, and destroys the Death Star with the Force* because *a Jedi's strength flows from the Force.*

The story is really about where a Jedi (a good guy) gets his or her strength. He does not get it from hate or revenge or man-made machines but from a universal natural and supernatural life force. That is the essential message of the film. Further stories have expanded and commented on it more, but in the 1970s, when the film was originally released, this kind of machine versus man and good versus evil story became tremendously popular.

The Sentence Outline can be used in more complex ways, too, delineating external or action-driven story (what the characters do) from internal, motivation-driven story (what the characters think and decide). It can change over time, as deeper insight into a story yields different results. It can also change from person to person, as debates occur over what the key moments of the story truly are. The point is not to find the only Sentence Outline possible, but to find one, the best one possible, for any given viewer. Audiences should not waste time wondering whether their Sentence Outline is correct; they should instead just start looking for the elements of the Sentence Outline as they watch movies and programs. What is the Major Dramatic Question? What appears to be the most important or telling decision the main character makes? Who is the story really about? All of these questions will call for a close watching and require audiences to pay real attention to the narrative. The answers to these questions themselves are housed in ideological terms, so asking them begins to make the viewers think about what the film or program is saying, even if they do not immediately come up with an answer.

MAJOR DRAMATIC SITUATIONS

Hollywood films established and perfected this kind of clear storytelling: goal, struggle, solution; question, discussion, answer. But if Hollywood movies perfected it, American television made it a social and personal institution. Instead of one Major Dramatic Question in a two-hour investment in a main character's struggle, television let audiences get to know characters by spending time with them each week, giving them hundreds of dramatic arcs, many of which are repetitive or very related.

One such example is the nine plus years of *Little House on the Prairie* on CBS. Every week Pa (Michael Landon), his family, or someone from his community of Walnut Grove overcomes some adversity. The town faces plagues, bullies, blizzards, and all manner of personal heartaches. *Little House* ran long enough that some plots were reused[2] and many were reoccurring (parent–child relationships, death and loss, financial hardship).

Each episode had its own Major Dramatic Question. We can also see the potential for one that encompasses the entire series. This is true of nearly all, if not all, dramatic television series. Some Sentence Outlines for a favorite television drama are obvious. Jack Bauer (Kiefer Sutherland) on *24* has a specific external goal. Each season he has 24 hours to foil a different terrorist plot. The goals are easy to grasp: protect the candidate, uncover the conspiracy in time, stop the bomb/nuclear devices from going off. On *Breaking Bad*, Walter White (Bryan Cranston) has a specific goal too: make sure his family is provided for (by making and selling methamphetamine) before he succumbs to lung cancer. Even Agent Mulder (David Duchovny) on *The X-Files* has a deep-seated internal goal: to find out the truth about extraterrestrial events because "the truth is out there." Mulder's partner Agent Scully (Gillian Anderson) has a related goal: to find out if the supernatural is possible. (A close watching of her character reveals this is related to her own search for faith, an interesting perspective for Christians.) Each episode of these series presents the main characters with a situation, a problem that has to be solved with a half hour or an hour's worth of storytelling.

That kind of rigorous plot work means lots of questions, lots of conflict, and, as the program develops, further and further breaks with plausible scenarios. The more need for plots that continue to raise the emotional stakes of the program, the less the show depicts any semblance of a possible life scenario. Some things about these programs are very realistic. They are all purely fiction, however, and after two or three seasons most programs begin to dig too deep for audience buy-in. The dramatic stakes can only be raised so many times, and the same plots can only happen to the same people with such regularity for a little while before implausibility gets in the way of the entertainment value. One example is the number of people that Jessica Fletcher (Angela Lansbury) witnesses dying or finds dead on *Murder She Wrote*. It becomes harder to buy into the program emotionally when the aging-author main character seems to issue a death warrant every place she goes.

David Thomson notes that television dramas "had the same characters episode after episode, but they posed as crucial dramas; they solved problems so relentlessly you wondered how problems kept arising."[3] Thomson mentions this after talking about situation comedies, or sitcoms. Sitcoms differ because there is less pretense of a real "dramatic" situation since their goal is just to make people laugh. In order to buy into the shows, however, audiences have to find the characters and the situation compelling. The "situation" in these shows is also the plot question, but it is often thematic: Will Lucy get on Ricky's show? Will the Cosby kids outsmart their dad? Will Archie Bunker's prejudice come back to haunt him? Will Roseanne's family make up after fighting? Television sitcom plots are about reoccurring kinds of problems, not major events that constitute a real trajectory. In some ways this makes them more realistic than most movies, but in some ways less. However, all plots—whether situational, weekly dramatic, or feature film—develop conflict that is expressed in terms of a Major Dramatic Question. We watch to see the question answered and the problem solved.

Determining that question gives us important insight into the nature of the program and its reflection of the human experience. If *Cosby* is about relationships between parents and children, what does it have to say about them? What does it value? How does the question often get answered? If *The X-Files* has something to say about the unexplainable and supernatural, what does it say? What does it tell us we should believe? What does it say is the truth? The answer to that question, for *The X-Files*, is perhaps that some mysteries cannot be explained. With this in mind, every episode of the notably weird, gross, potentially disturbing show is also somehow a statement of faith. That is the power of the Major Dramatic Question: it switches the conversation from content to intention. It makes us aware of ideology.

There are all kinds of implications for what it means to see stories solve problems in this weekly, episodic way, with a moral impetus for why things do or do not work out, but for now what is to be remembered is that this is what each plot does: it presents us with a question or a problem, and then it presents either a solution or some kind of answer. To do that, the storytellers must also give the audience people to root for. Storytellers also supply characters to represent, be aligned, with and perhaps cause/further the conflict that keeps the main characters from that solution or answer. The characters who further action are protagonists, also known as heroes and heroines. Those that impede action toward a solution are the antagonists, also known as villains and villainesses. The protagonist is almost always either a person or something given human characteristics (i.e., Christopher Robbin, a child, or Winnie the Pooh, a stuffed bear who is "alive," and person-like). But antagonists do not need to be living persons or creatures. The weather or nature can be an antagonist (*Twister* or *127 Hours*), and so can some internal part of a character (Mulder's battles with conspiracy and malicious aliens or his own doubts). Either kind of antagonist will also spell out an ideology by demonstrating adverse characteristics toward the people the audience is aligned with. The bad guys do not have to be "guys," but what they do is necessarily bad, and from them we learn what "bad" is.

EMOTIONAL ALIGNMENT AND PROXIMITY

Star Wars: A New Hope seems to have something to say about depending on living things instead of technology, the vast beauty of space, and the interconnectedness of living things through a Force. We can see this in the Sentence Outline and its theme, but it is latent even in the Major Dramatic Question. Will Luke learn the ways of the Force, the ways that promote living things over technology? In addition to Luke Skywalker there are other important protagonists in *Star Wars: A New Hope* (like his friends, not to mention droids), but he is the main protagonist, the most dynamic character who goes from being an uneducated but well-intentioned farm boy to hero of the Rebellion. If one person were to be chosen as the center of the story, the hero is decidedly Luke. How do we know? First, when we see him he is isolated in the frame, and the camera stays on him as the music changes. Hollywood developed this language during its golden age: the main character is revealed by a star entrance. The camera settles on them, so the audience can see their faces and get to know them, just as they get to know real people.

Theorist Béla Balázs makes a notable argument about the power of the close-up, saying that the isolation of a character in close-up is a clear way to get the audience to sympathize with a character, because in a shot like this, characters always tell the truth. The camera observes an isolated close-up as a private moment. "We have suddenly been left alone with this one face to the exclusion of the rest of the world. . . . Close-ups are often dramatic revelations of what is really happening under the surface of appearances," Balázs notes.[4] Characters rarely lie in close-up. They tell the camera exactly what is on their mind, because the camera has developed a special relationship with them, an intimate relationship. The camera is the proxy for the audience, so we, the viewers, develop this intimate trust with our main characters when we see them in close-ups. In a moving picture, we believe what characters do more than what they say because we believe what their faces say more than their words (like we do with Claudette Colbert in *The Egg and I*). Faces tell us the truth, and faces become familiar, simply by the camera moving in tight and isolating them in close-ups.

The other important film technique used to solidify audience alignment with a character is the POV, or point of view, shot. When the camera switches from observing the characters to taking the place of the characters (so we see from their "point of view"), we literally step into their place and see what they see. We become the characters. One nice example of this is a moment in *Raiders of the Lost Ark*, when Indiana Jones (Harrison Ford), running out of the temple, sets off an ancient booby trap. We hear an ominous rolling. The camera dollies behind him and stops as he turns around, a wave of terror sweeping over his face. Then comes a shot from Indy's POV as the huge boulder rolls directly toward the camera. We see what Indy sees, we become aligned with his perspective, and we are most literally on his side. This filming and editing process is referred to as "suture" because it "sews" the audience into the narrative by means of editing and subjective shot choice.

These formal techniques help us quickly gain sympathy with characters because we become close to them. We know them. One exception concerns untrustworthy main characters who take on first-person storytelling through voiceover and POV shots. These "untrustworthy narrators" are first-person storyteller characters who seem to want our intimate alliance but break this trust developed by storytelling techniques when we find out they have "lied" to the audience (for instance, *A Clockwork Orange*, or the difference in retelling events in *Rashomon*, or the Showtime series *The Affair*). It naturally follows that proximity intimates closeness, even if the close association of characters to camera and audience means the audience gets fooled by an untrustworthy main character.

A close relationship with a character elicits our sympathy and often also our empathy, even when the hero or heroine does something perceived as "bad." Carrie (Sarah Jessica Parker) on *Sex and the City* is a case in point. In season three, Carrie gets involved in an affair with her ex-boyfriend Mr. Big (Chris Noth) and cheats on current boyfriend Aidan (John Corbett). After several seasons, listening to Carrie's voiceover and getting to know her, she has earned trust with the audience. We see her during a lot of intimate moments—and not just sexually intimate. We see her when she is the most emotionally vulnerable. We see her apartment, her bathroom, her closet (which for Carrie is a very intimate space, since it contains all her shoes). The audience is on Carrie's side.

Because the audience is aligned with Carrie, they value what she values: quality high fashion (especially fashion footwear), a fun night out, and, most of all, her girlfriends. *Sex and the City* is ostensibly about sexual rendezvous, but it is really about relationships with friends and lovers. By the end of the original series, all of the women are in committed, monogamous relationships, and two of them are married. The show highly values commitment, so this plotline with Carrie's cheating is important. We are aligned with Carrie, who wants a man to commit to her, and we see from her point of view that commitment is a good thing. When Carrie breaks trust with Aidan by cheating, she in some ways also breaks trust with the audience, devaluing the thing she valued so much. Carrie is not acting honestly. She suffers admonishment from her friends and also from herself. She realizes what she is doing is wrong. At first she cannot seem to stop, but things get so bad that her presence inadvertently sends Big's then-wife Natasha (Bridget Moynahan) to the hospital when Natasha catches Carrie in their apartment, chases her down the stairs, then to Carrie's horror, trips and falls on her face. When this happens, Carrie not only sees the error of her ways, she also resolves to stop the affair and stick to it.

Protagonists do not always do good things. Carrie continues to smoke through the entire show, despite nearly everyone's disapproval. However, protagonists gain our sympathy in their mistakes and, quite often, own up to them and try to atone for them. Returning to Luke Skywalker, we see his rash judgments of Han Solo (Harrison Ford) and his first bumbling attempts at using a light-saber. As the narrative draws to a close, however, we see him taking a more mature approach and becoming more adept with Jedi skills. He is not always right, and he does foolish things. He has our sympathy, though, and we watch him learn and grow. This is important. A main character that is too altruistic is hard to relate to. Someone who makes mistakes and grows from them is not only more relatable, he or she is also capable of teaching a lesson in persistence over adversity, wisdom over rash judgment, or, in Carrie's case, an understanding that our sins will find us out and infidelity is not worth it.

After thinking through the main conflict with the Sentence Outline and the Major Dramatic Question, we turn to the most dynamic or sympathetic character, which is usually the main protagonist. What does this character value? Luke values the Jedi ways of using the Force; he values the Rebellion against the Empire; he values his relationships with friends. Those things are good things. We know this because the main character values them. What does Carrie value? Her friends, her freedom, a man who commits, New York City life, and fabulous shoes. Those become the values of the audience, too—or at least, the audience assumes those values in order to enjoy the show while watching it. We know those things are of value to Carrie, and we like Carrie, so we like those things for her sake if for nothing else. Even if we do not know a character well, if the main character values something, the audience will too. Unless it is in direct conflict with the audience's belief and values, they will assume the beliefs and values of the main characters for the duration of the plot, because they have developed a relationship with them.

On example, for instance, is the film *Thelma and Louise*. The 1989 film shot to critical acclaim and pop-culture iconicity portrays two women who kill a man, commit armed robbery, assault a police officer, destroy personal property, and run from the law so far that they are forced to choose between being taken in dead or alive. It is the female buddy-film equivalent to *Butch Cassidy and the Sundance Kid*. Like its male counterpart film, *Thelma and Louise* tells the story of two people on the wrong side of the law. They are anti-heroines. Notably, however, their actions always stem from a man choosing to violate them in some way. They take action, but it is always a reaction to one of the male characters seeking to keep them from their goal: freedom to make their own decisions.

It is hard to gain sympathy with felons (at least, we should hope so), but their situation calls for a deeper understanding of their motivations. There are plenty of movie examples like *Thelma and Louise* in which the main characters are antiheroes. How do they elicit our sympathy? By helping us get to know them better. We see not just their actions but the situations and motivations behind them. We do not have to excuse their behavior, but the film certainly asks us to understand why they make the choices they do. The close-ups, the dialogue, the POV footage, and the charisma of the characters lead us to like them. We want them to succeed in their goals.

GOOD GUYS WEAR EARTH TONES

Formal elements like camera proximity and POV can bring us into emotional alignment with characters, but there is also another formal film element that tells us a lot about the people in the story: their costumes. Movies and television are visual mediums. Characters are necessarily graphic parts of the story, and their clothes (and faces, and body types), for better or worse, matter on screen.

Luke Skywalker wears earth tones, and this too reflects his values. Luke values the Force, and the Force is a part of all living things. It is more powerful than machines. Luke is a protagonist, and he values living things over technology. He gains our sympathy and embodies this ideology through his words, actions, and even the graphic nature of his character. In the beginning of the film he wears sandy white and tan clothes. He progresses into donning a Stormtrooper uniform (itself a comment on humanity versus technology), then a Rebel pilot uniform (orange, the color of a star or gas giant planet, as opposed to the Empire's soldiers dressed either in white or black), then an outfit with black pants and a yellow/tan jacket. He has gained more mastery over technology (becoming a successful pilot) but is still identified in earth tones. Wearing both black and yellow/tan in some sense is more indicative of his underlying ideology: he brings balance between nature and technology. So perhaps Luke's ideology, and what we value therefore as well, is balance between natural and man-made things.

In the beginning of *Thelma and Louise*, both of the characters wear very feminine outfits and lots of makeup. They have pale skin. Their hair is meticulously styled. By the end of the film, they are in jeans and old shirts, with little jewelry or makeup, hair askew (more "natural"), deep tans, and dust-covered. In fact, throughout the film every time a major event takes places that develops their characters, their costumes shift further in this more "natural" direction.

The costumes indicate part of the underlying value of the film: freedom. Thelma (Geena Davis) and Louise (Susan Sarandon) go from dressing according to socially determined ideas of beauty and femininity to "freer" and more natural looks. They are no longer bound to social standards or social mores. We sympathize because we see that those standards have been arbitrarily placed on them and have become harmful to these women. We want them to be free. We see them as more free than they were in their tightly done hair and full makeup.

Thelma and Louise is a film that values freedom. We sympathize with the characters and their quest for that freedom, even if we think their actions are morally reprehensible. The ideology, that freedom is necessary and a right for all people, is reflected in the plot, the dialogue, and the art direction of the film. It reflects the deeply held cultural belief that freedom is good.

BAD GUYS DO BAD THINGS

The very embodiment of an imbalance between technology and nature in *Star Wars: A New Hope* is the main antagonist, Darth Vader. In fact, Vader is not just a bad guy; he is one of the greatest movie baddies of all time, ranking number three (just after Hannibal Lector in *Silence of the Lambs* and Norman Bates in *Psycho*) on the villain half of the American Film Institute's 2003 list of "100 Years, 100 Heroes and Villains."[5] As the personification of "the dark side" of the Force, he is the iconic representation of "bad guy." What makes him bad? The answer to this question, and the answer any time we ask this about an antagonist, tells us what the story reflects as worthy of our dislike or contempt. Stories make a moral judgment simply through a character's actions that are unwanted, unfair, harmful, or otherwise of little help or value. Even when the antagonist is internal, it is the character's poor choices, fears, pride, guilt, inhibition, selfishness, or greed that is at fault. Those things do the character harm, so they are bad.

External antagonists from nature are less convenient to judge but still stand for malicious things. A tornado, a locust swarm, or searing desert heat is, if not bad, at least dangerous. Does anyone viewing *Bambi* consider the forest fire a "good" thing? And yet, forest fires, although dangerous and potentially very harmful, are often an important and necessary part of a forest's life cycle. In movies and television shows, however, these acts of nature are rarely acclaimed for their potential benefits if they somehow bring major conflict to the main characters. We vilify storms and mountains just as we do any antagonist, although since these natural forces are not usually aimed at a specific character, we tend to treat them with something more akin to distrust than outright anger or moral judgment.

We know who the antagonists are for reasons similar to how we perceive the protagonist. A series of shots will give the main antagonist a "star entrance" as well, sometimes with ominous music. We know that character is significant and is somehow in opposition to the protagonist. This can be direct, as in a first meeting, duel, and so on, or indirect, noting their values as portrayed through their actions and dialogue, and also potentially reflected in their costume or other art direction. Darth Vader is the first major character on screen in *Star Wars: A New Hope*. He enters to music in a minor key, surrounded by dead bodies as he boards a starship by force. We immediately associate him with death, destruction, and abusive power. We also note his skull-like mask, his billowing black cape, and his machinelike presence. He does not look human. He looks like a machine of death, and that is precisely what he proves to be.

Vader's actions and appearances are clearly bad, but many antagonists are harder to judge. Often, it is only over time that we see the accumulation of a character's actions (for instance, Snape or Malfoy in the *Harry Potter* series) in order to be able to make our judgment. We withhold judgment in those cases often because we also get to know them better through close-ups and POV shots (like Snape or Vader, who get significant camera treatment, although the camera often maintains distance until they become more emotionally vulnerable). We can also get to know them because either one or more "good" character somehow sympathizes with them (like Gollum in *The Lord of the Rings* trilogy), and we see this in their reaction shots.

In fact, reaction shots are one of the easiest ways to understand what main characters think about a situation or person. Their reaction "sells" their dislike, or misgiving, or agreement. We look to the reaction shot for context. As we see one picture after another, we naturally tend to associate them together. The Soviet filmmaker Lev Kuleshov, a contemporary of Sergei Eisenstein, conducted a famous experiment in which he used footage of a noted actor (Russian matinee idol Ivan Mozzhukhin), looking earnest. He used this same shot and in one sequence cut into it a shot of a bowl of steaming soup.

In another sequence he cut in a young girl holding a toy bear. In a third, he cut in a picture of a woman in a coffin. Audiences were amazed at the actor's talent. He looks so hungry, some said. Others said he looked so happy, or so sad. The "performance" was in the mind of the spectator.[6] What we learn from this is that audiences make assumptions based on editing context. What we see just before and just after an image will be associated with it. Filmmakers can use this to add meaning to a sequence.

The reaction shot works on this principle, but in its most blatant form. Kuleshov's actor was only reacting by portraying an earnest expression. Most reaction shots are much more telling. It is a storytelling technique that can easily invite manipulation unless it only reflects the way an audience already feels about a character.

One example is Marcia Jeffries (Patricia Neal) in Elia Kazan's 1957 *A Face in the Crowd*. The main character is Lonesome Rhodes (Andy Griffith), a drifter turned media icon by Marcia's promoting him as a media personality. Marcia is in love with the volatile television personality she has created in Lonesome, and reactions tell us that at the beginning of his career he is charming and funny and that is why she, the radio and television audiences, and the audience for *A Face in the Crowd* love him, too. We know how she feels because we can see her watching him. When her involvement with him becomes so complicated that her judgment is skewed, and Lonesome's ego, ambition, and bad habits have overtaken any charm he once had (and the audience no longer sees him as a lovable character), the reaction proxy becomes the job of Mel (Walter Matthau), who himself is in love with Marcia. Mel reacts to both Lonesome and Marcia, and we are most closely aligned with his point of view. We sympathize with Marcia; we care about her. We are disenchanted with Lonesome.[7]

The idea of reaction shots giving commentary on a character's action is explicit in Kazan's film (which is perhaps one of the best critiques of media by media), but use of reaction shots is rampant in all forms of visual storytelling. Editors use reaction shots for moral judgment to the point of overt manipulation in reality television shows. A reaction shot can be taken completely out of context (and often is) to create commentary for something another character says or does. How do we know that the line a potential suitor for *The Bachelor* said was a ridiculously dumb thing to say? We see a character/contestant who is perceived as smart react to it, and this reaction shot underscores the line's inanity. The reaction shot passes judgment. The reaction shot intends to show an audience what is good or bad, dumb or funny, worthwhile or ridiculous, nice or mean.

Any character perceived as bad has the ability to be redeemed in storytelling, and what is necessary for their redemption is also a marker of what the film or television program tells us is worthwhile, morally good, and important.

Darth Vader is a villain whose machinelike person is in direct opposition to Luke's goal of bringing balance between nature and technology, but he is also redeemed by the end of the original series of *Star Wars* films. At the end of *Return of the Jedi*, after being revealed as Luke's father, now in a very altered state, Vader makes the choice to destroy his evil master, the Emperor (Ian McDiarmid) and save his son. He chooses to sacrifice his own life for someone else. This choice indicates the moral value of sacrificial love. His choice is a choice to restore his soul over his mechanical body. Vader finds atonement through self-sacrifice, a choice to love selflessly. This kind of plot is explicitly moralistic, with an ideological message that is easy to read: love redeems.

Carrie's turnaround in season three of *Sex and the City* has already been noted. She is the protagonist, though, and her partner in crime is her on-again, off-again love, Mr. Big. Big switches from protagonist to antagonist depending upon his treatment of Carrie. We want to trust him, just as Carrie wants to trust him, but if he cannot stay in a committed relationship (his marriage to Natasha fails, and throughout the show he is ambivalent about the status of his and Carrie's relationship), he is being antagonistic toward Carrie's goal to be herself and be in a successful relationship. He changes from one role to the other depending upon his actions and attitude. That change indicates the program's core values: commitment, honesty, and love. Carrie's choices, Big's choices, and the choices made by any character in a film or program that are seen as atoning or redemptive are always moral choices rife with ideological values.

OTHER FORMAL ELEMENTS

So far we have mostly talked about narrative elements: parts of the stories and characters and how they are perceived. We have backed them up with some observations about formal elements: close-ups, POV shots, suture, and reaction shots. There are a few other basic concepts regarding the moving image that will be useful for basic close watchings of films and television programs.

The first is camera angle. The camera is always the audience's proxy. We see what it sees and we are where it is, so its relative position to characters and events intimates our relationship to them. Camera position is in some ways equivalent to nonverbal communication or "body language" in a conversation. Whether the characters acknowledge the camera or not (most will not), the camera has a relationship to everything it sees. Viewers can therefore infer a lot about the nature of that relationship based on *how* the camera sees characters and events. By and large, we will sense this subconsciously, but when we intentionally examine the camera angle we often find it backs up how we already felt about a character.

If the camera is placed high, it "looks down" on events. It therefore is more empowered and makes characters look less powerful. It may also intimate that someone from the outside is watching or observing the events. The camera is inherently voyeuristic. We watch private moments all the time. Perhaps the most famous example of a film showcasing its own ability to watch others voyeuristically is Alfred Hitchcock's *Rear Window*, in which reporter Jeff Jeffries (James Stewart), stuck in a wheelchair because of a broken leg, thinks he has witnessed a murder in an apartment across a square. Jeff and his camera watch the "movie" of the murder unfold before them.

The camera can also empower characters. Placing the camera low so that it "looks up" to the subject tends to make that subject seem imposing. There are other questions to ask about where the camera looks, how it moves, and how those shots are cut and assembled that all connote importance. Who or what is in focus? What is in the middle of the screen (as opposed to "marginalized" near the edges of the frame or in the background)? What has a specific color or otherwise draws attention? If the camera is drawn to look at something, the audience can assume it was intended for us to see. It is therefore given significance. Why show us the red doorknob in *The Sixth Sense*? That must be important. What the camera sees is what we see, and we assume it was done with intention.

Elements within the picture can also take on significance because they already have symbolic relevance. Our eyes are naturally drawn to the color red. It will usually be the first color we perceive in an image. Filmmakers therefore can easily connote the importance of something by making it red (for example, the doorknob in *The Sixth Sense*, the roses in *American Beauty*, the little girl in the red coat in *Schindler's List*). Another symbol with inherent connotations is the mirror. The moving image is a very psychological medium. We can see states of being. People are often depicted as versions of themselves. When characters look in a mirror, it is always significant. Usually they are trying to "see" themselves in some way, or the audience can see there are two faces, two personas. If a character is lying to or about herself, the mirror can be either an escape into another version of herself, or proof of guilt because the character has to "face herself." It is as if the character is either putting on some kind of mask or role (like an actor preparing before the mirror) or else asking himself or herself, "Is this who I am?" There are countless examples of this, including Satine (Nicole Kidman) in *Moulin Rouge* looking in a mirror before lying to Christian (Ewan McGregor); Jake La Motta (Robert De Niro) in *Raging Bull*, practicing his act and quoting *On the Waterfront* into the mirror; and O'Brien (Siobhan Finneran) in *Downton Abbey* looking into the mirror and admitting, "Sarah O'Brien, this is not who you are," too late to stop Lady Grantham (Elizabeth McGovern) from slipping on the soap outside the tub (that O'Brien has spitefully left there) and consequently having a miscarriage.

Two other often used and very potent symbols are crosses and water. There have been entire books written on Christ figures and Christ symbols in moving images, but even just the cross is itself often used to indicate some relation to religion or Christ. In the 1927 classic silent film *Sunrise*, Janet Gaynor, playing the innocent and altruistic wife, lies sleeping as the moonlight through the window makes the sign of the cross across her bed. 1943's *Cat People*, directed by Jacques Tourneur, sees Oliver (Kent Smith) and his love interest Alice (Jane Randolph) pursued by Oliver's first wife, Irena (Simone Simon), who is cursed to turn into a giant panther and kill anyone who threatens her independence. Irena, as the panther, corners Oliver and Alice in the office where they work, which contains drafting tables, lit from underneath. Oliver backs into a corner, shielding Alice and wielding a T-square, which illuminated from beneath by the drafting tables produces the image of a cross before them and above and behind them as if they are protected from this menace by religion/the church/Christ.

Water in film is potent for many of the same reasons it is in real life. It can connote life, birth, tears, restoration, cleansing, and baptism. The Hollywood great *Casablanca* is full of water images. Humphrey Bogart's Rick spills drinks once or twice at significant times when something new is going to happen (a birth). He stands in the rain reading Ilsa (Ingrid Bergman)'s note as she leaves. The rain makes the ink on the page run, so tears seem to stream down both his face and the note. In the famous final scene, Captain Renault (Claude Rains) throws away a bottle marked "Vichy Water," a rejection of the puppet government he had been a part of and a symbol of his and Rick's baptism into the anti-Nazi fight.

These symbols are always important and easy to look for: the color red, mirrors, crosses, and water. They have been given cultural connotations, and over the history of the moving image, they have gained even more symbolic and iconic power by their use. Filmmakers are aware of them, and if viewers spot them, they can rest assured they were put there on purpose. There are many, many more symbols, but these four are always notable and often easy to detect.

Connotation extends beyond just what is in the image. Reaction shots and suture can tell viewers how the filmmaker intends for them to feel about a person or situation, but editing that utilizing this technique can move the story from literal depictions of events to symbolic representation of what a story values. The idea of suture is part of a larger connotation of editing. Cutaways and reactions can be inserted at will to give connotations to what is happening Viewers should always pay attention to the cut, and remember that it can be very arbitrary. Meaning in the moving image is constructed and can be extremely manipulated.

Visual storytellers can combine these images with symbolic meaning and their placement in a sequence to create a larger comment, analogy, or metaphor. Some films or entire series are symbolic narratives. *Thelma and Louise* looks realistic, but because the film ends where it does, we do not see the potential realistic endings: the demise of the women as their car lands at the bottom of the Grand Canyon, or, if the laws of physics were different, their successful landing on the other side, or, if they had chosen to capitulate, their turning around to go back and face the police. Audiences do not see any of those things. The last image, other than a shot of the photograph of the two women from the beginning of the film, is the car in mid-air. The film ends with a depiction of flying, giving the ending a sense of freedom. The image is focused on the triumph of that moment of freedom instead of the logical consequences audiences know will result. Because the story ends with the car mid-flight, it ends on a note of freedom instead of capitulation or death. In that sense, it moves from realistic to symbolic.

Sometimes shorter sequences in a film are symbolic. At the end of *A Face in the Crowd*, Lonesome is not aware that Marcia has revealed his real personality to his television audience. He walks out of the studio and gets into the elevator. Unbeknownst to him, he is "going down" (this image mirrors the ones of the ratings going up, depicted with liquid in a tube, earlier in the film). By the time his ride is over, he has hit bottom both literally in the elevator and figuratively with his viewing public. We see the floors light up on the elevator display as he descends, and he exits as a "zero" at the bottom floor. The images and the action intimate a deeper meaning, a metaphor. This is symbolic language, and the moving image is often used in sophisticated ways to tell the story not just with action and dialogue but also with shot choice and editing.

All these elements, both narrative and formal, can be detected by viewers as they do a close watching of a film or television program. One may find it hard to take in everything with a first viewing, especially if he or she is a fan of the program and wants to enjoy it and "see what happens" when they first watch it. However, with practice and with subsequent viewings, any audience member can begin to detect the intentions of the storytellers, the significance of what the story is truly saying, and how it is being said. An assessment of these indicators will help us make assessments about which stories have something important to say to us, and which ones are most useful for education, edification, and entertainment.

NOTES

1. Foster, *The New Literacy*, 5.

2. Like town regular Mrs. Whipple (Queenie Smith)'s son's battle with a morphine addiction in Season 2, and Albert (Matthew Labyorteaux)'s battle with a morphine addiction in Season 9.

3. David Thomson, *The Big Screen* (New York: Farrar, Strauss and Giroux, 2012), 269.

4. Béla Balázs, "The Close-Up" and "The Face of Man," in *Film Theory and Criticism: Introductory Readings*, 5th ed., eds. Leo Braudy and Marshall Cohen (New York: Oxford University Press, 1999), 305–306.

5. American Film Institute, "100 Years, 100 Heroes and Villains," accessed October 20, 2014, http://www.afi.com/100years/handv.aspx.

6. David A. Cook, *A History of Narrative Film*, 3rd ed. (New York: W.W. Norton, 1981), 137.

7. The other important reaction in *A Face in the Crowd* comes from Lonesome's television audience, who, like Marsha, think his homespun wisdom attractive until they see it is an act.

CHAPTER 7

REDEMPTIVE NARRATIVES

The shortest distance between a human being and the Truth is a story.
—*Anthony de Mello*[1]

If we can tell evil stories to make people sick, we can also tell good myths that make them well.

—*R. W. Fassbinder*[2]

Redemption is meaningless unless there is a cause for it.
—*Flannery O'Connor*[3]

Sin requires a savior, whereas evil requires only heroes.
—*Quentin J. Schultze*[4]

REDEMPTIVE VISION

As long as Christians have been studying stories, they have been assessing them for their redemptive value. There are as many views on what redemptive elements are and how they should be explored as there are Christian traditions. However, two things are clear: stories do have the ability to affect audiences for good (possibly eternal good) and bad, and the form of the story is often as important as the story itself.

Stories clearly have a profound effect upon us, and moving-image media is story in one of its most potent forms. The experience of the moving image is unlike any other, and its complex relationship with reality, its ability to evoke emotive and visceral reactions, and its ability to embody—both in content and in form—ideas, feelings, experiences, and expressions make it a story tool with undeniable power. What constitutes a redemptive film or television program? Again, it is good to remember that the apostle Paul's admonition to the church in Philippians to think on things that are worthy of praise has been evoked by Christians at every turn, and rightly so. "Whatever is true, whatever is noble, whatever is right, whatever is pure, whatever is lovely, whatever is admirable," Paul tells us, "if anything is excellent or praiseworthy—think about such things."[5]. What does that mean, though? How are audiences to discover what is noble or pure? Does this refer to the end "theme" of a story or all the parts of the story? Does it take into account cultural norms or personal experiences? What constitutes something "lovely"? Does it include story form? Elements of the photographic image? Costume design? Character choice?

The debate over this subject is what is involved in the vast majority of Christian scholastic conversation about the moving image. It would be impossible to summarize all of the extant writing about potential redemptive elements or approaches. There are arguments for how films can prove the existence of God and arguments that defend *Pulp Fiction* as well as *Sister Act* as very evocative of the redemptive narrative. The truth is many different kinds of stories can house redemptive elements and ideas about what is worthwhile in a moving-image story. For all audiences, understanding their own experience of redemption and holiness and understanding how moving-image stories can play a part in that is important. Several thoughts and approaches to what might be viewed as redemptive in story content, narrative structure, and cinematic form will be presented in this chapter. This is not an exhaustive study but a presentation of some ideas that might broaden horizons and be easily applied.

REDEMPTIVE CONTEXT

Before those approaches are explored, however, it is important to note that in order to assess a movie or television program's ability to affect the viewer for good, the viewer's personal context needs to be taken into account. An approach to film theory known as "spectatorship theory," housed in psychoanalytic studies of film, puts forth suggestions about how audiences cognitively respond to movies. However, critics of this approach argue that it fails to take into account "other factors such as class, color, race, age, or sexual preference," and therefore misses how those demographic elements affect viewer relation.[6] Jacques Derrida and other deconstructionists further argue that any thoughtful interpretation of a film is in a sense a valid interpretation because an image "can never be constrained to a single set of meanings," and the collection of potential meanings in any moving-image story "will inevitably be contradictory."[7]

In looking for shapes in clouds, people will form the meaning or signification of shapes in the cloud differently from person to person. One may see a fish, the other a sports car. Similarly, in a film one may see a satisfying "happy" ending while another sees utter defeat. Neither view is "right" or "wrong"; they are simply different interpretations, shaped by varying personal, social, cultural, and visual factors. Viewers come from different backgrounds, and their worldviews impact what they see.

In a moving image, which is also very subjective, we will see what we are disposed to see. We will look for things we know how to recognize. We will be drawn to elements for a variety of reasons, and the meanings we draw from them may be widely different from those of people around us, even though they experience the same set of moving images.

This should be no surprise. When Christ told stories (and Christ is often cited as the greatest of Christian storytellers—He certainly both told and lived stories that indelibly changed people), He told them differently to different people (attention to form), but the intended message is the Gospel, the Good News. In the parable of the sower He gave his disciples the model for understanding that audiences will receive "good words" in varying ways. The cloud's shape is specific; the story is explicit (at least, as Christ interpreted it to His disciples). We realize even if the story has one intended meaning it can still be received differently.

A farmer went out to scatter seed, Jesus relates. He scattered it everywhere. Some fell on the path and was eaten by birds, some on rocks, some among weeds. But some, we learn, fell on good soil and yielded fruit (Matt. 13:1–23, NIV). When Jesus explained the parable to his disciples, the story was interpreted as a metaphor, and while Christ was admonishing more audience members to become "good soil," he was also acknowledging that His audiences were in different states to receive stories. Not everyone hears and responds to the word in the same way. The state of the audience members, what their experience and inclinations might be, and the power of forces around them all have an impact on how they hear the story and respond to it.

Who we are and where our hearts are will have a great impact on what we find redemptive in moving-image narratives. In one of her essays, Flannery O'Connor notes that she had received a letter from a reader "who informed me that when the tired reader comes home at night, she wishes to read something that will lift up her heart." O'Connor comments, "And it seems her heart had not been lifted up by anything of mine she had read. I think that if her heart had been in the right place, it would have been lifted up."[8] O'Connor took into account that audiences want a satisfying ending.[9]

Readers want some redemption, a reminder that good conquers evil and things will work out, something that lifts up their hearts. O'Connor's intentions seem more to point to a need for understanding that things do *not* always work out, and that brokenness in our world needed to be acknowledged if we are to truly understand the power of grace. Stories like "A Good Man Is Hard to Find" and "The Life You Save May Be Your Own," two of O'Connor's most well-known, end with shocking actions by the main characters. They are tragic, and their tragedy is intended to rock complacency and make audiences question their own morality. The lack of redemption for the characters is a wake-up call for audiences. Are human beings really capable of such actions? Stories that point to the truth of the fall, of the presence of our sinful human nature, are important. They both acknowledge human fallenness, warning audiences of the culpability of every human heart, and remind us of our need for divine redemption. We have the opportunity to see redemption's cost and true power when we see how fallen human beings really are. Tragedies have great potential for admonishment: this is the real cost of sin.

Both admonishment and encouragement, hard truth and fulfilling fantasy, are useful. Which one will be seen as redemptive depends in part at least on our worldview and experience. After conversion, Christians experience the subsequent work of grace through which their virtues grow by discipline and the intervention of the Holy Spirit. In other words, with human effort—but mostly by divine grace—Christians can and should grow in the fruit of the Spirit. It is not enough to enact peace in a situation, one must become a peaceful person; it is not enough to feel joy, one must become joyful. Christians are defined by being like Christ, and in this theological tradition of holiness at least, people becoming like Christ means their human nature is changed over time. If people are growing in kindness, they may see a moving-image story differently than they used to. They may sympathize more with characters and do more to understand the forces at play in a character's potentially bad choices, while not changing the moral stance of how dangerous or detrimental the action might be. Viewers growing in their Christian walk will see narratives differently as they themselves are being changed.

In some sense, this is true for everyone since people's experiences change over time, and therefore, their perceptions will shift as they live through more life events. However, if people are developing the fruit of the Spirit—growing in love, joy, peace, patience, goodness, gentleness, meekness, kindness, faithfulness, and self-control—they are more inclined to recognize, for instance, meekness, and they are more disposed to assess different kinds of acts through those new attitudes. In all cases, what constitutes a redemptive narrative may depend very much on one's point of view.

OBJECTIONABLE CONTENT

If a narrative intends to show true redemption by showing the need for it, there is a good chance the movie or program may contain some subject matter that may not be appropriate for all viewers. As discussed, there are ways to tell the same story with less outright objectionable content. Some may argue, however, that this softens the blow of what is intended to shock. "To the hard of hearing you shout," O'Connor wrote of her often very jarring content, "and for the almost blind you draw large, startling figures."[10]

On the other hand, caution should be exercised about content, especially when it comes to those sensitive to "trigger" subject matters like heavy violence, sexual assault, demon possession, and satanic images. (This also applies when choosing material for children to see.) There is a great deal of gratuitous content that serves no purpose other than to titillate and elicit viewer compulsion. We are fallen creatures, and we can be drawn to pornography and gore-nography for the same reasons we are drawn to self-appealing or self-affirming stories: they make us feel good. There is something that seems to be satisfying or justifying in some way about them. We give in to desires, often for selfish pleasure. Depending on where viewers are in developing their own healthy habits and Christ-like heart can determine a great deal about their ability to find vice or virtue in a moving-image narrative. Different people will find satisfaction in different stories.

"Proof" of what is true or right or acceptable can and should never be gained from moving images. Movies and television can be used by artists to point out the truth, but "because it was in a movie" or "because it was on television" never justifies our actions or beliefs. If we look to movies and television programs as the reason to believe in or do something and allow them to shape or change our beliefs or attitudes, we have made those mediums our moral teachers. They can embody and reflect moral truths, but they cannot prove them.

In their book *Prophetically Incorrect*, Robert H. Woods Jr. and Paul D. Patton describe the prophetic sensibility as "thinking that resists the dominant forces of our culture while simultaneously helping others imagine alternate, hope-filled ways of thinking and being."[11] The prophets, they remind us, are good examples to look at while thinking about media. Prophets are often called to tell people uncomfortable truths. "Faithful critics, consumers, and creators of popular media today must develop a sensitivity and openness to media that shocks complacent individuals and institutions out of their self-serving agendas."[12] Stories can serve this prophetic function.

The prophets of the Old Testament, oracles, soothsayers, and in the case of *Moulin Rouge*, an enchanted sitar, have played the role of truth-teller, informing us when something is dishonest, unjust, impure, dishonorable, ugly, awful, or worthy of our disdain—the opposite of the qualities listed in Paul's letter to the Philippians. If there are things we should think about, it seems contradictory to listen to voices pointing out the opposite, but it is necessary because we need to learn the difference. Without a true picture of sin, we can never have a true picture of redemption. Just as some stories can give us visions of heaven, others must give us visions of hell. We need pictures of virtue and pictures of vice, and we need to learn to wrestle with what they mean. However, moving images should never be our sole or primary teachers of either virtue or vice. All moving-image media can do is tell stories. The viewers must decide whether the story they are watching will help them grow virtue or invite vice.

Discerning if media has a prophetic voice requires the work of the mind and heart. Fantasy can have profound benefits, and entertainment can be valuable in and of itself. However, if the qualities in a moving-image narrative help us avoid the difficult truths of life we need to face, they can become a crutch and an excuse. Stories must be kept in their rightful place as expressions and examples of things that require discernment. There are many stories intended to challenge us to reflect. They are the mirrors held up that require us to face who we are.

The films of Alfred Hitchcock did their best to showcase and expose the fallenness in American society. Hitchcock's films are full of people with questionable motives and practices (like Jeff's voyeurism in *Rear Window*). Another notable example by the Master of Suspense is the 1943 film *Shadow of a Doubt*. Hitchcock's daughter Pat said the film was "my father's favorite movie because he loved the idea of bringing menace to a small town."[13] *Shadow of a Doubt* is the story of an uncle (Joseph Cotton) with a very questionable past, who shows up just in time to lift the spirits of his namesake niece (Theresa Wright) only to make her truly question both his nature and the innocence of her "typical American family." Many of Hitchcock's films showcase America as a place where murderers may be family members, main characters may go too far, and the guy at the hotel may have deep psychological mother-issues.

Many contemporary television programs also endeavor to do the same thing: expose the brokenness of humans in our midst. *The Sopranos, Breaking Bad, Dexter*, or even *Once upon a Time* (along with too many others to count) recount visions of American family life that look one way to outsiders but hide deep, difficult situations. Some prophetic media ask audiences to question their assumptions, leaving them with cognitive dissonance or the experience of holding two seemingly contradictory beliefs. Is the family loving or dangerous? Is the father figure trustworthy or malicious?

Trying to reconcile things that seem to be in opposition is a necessary part of the Christian experience. We must reconcile that we are justified by faith but that we must also follow God's laws and do good work. King David was a man after God's own heart, yet he had his son (among others) killed. How does one become someone after God's heart if he disobeys His laws? This redemptive cognitive dissonance forces us to truly explore the nature of both ideas.

It is the same when we are left with contradictory ideas in moving images that we must reconcile. Thelma and Louise break the law; they do terrible things like hold people at gunpoint and lock a policeman in the trunk of his squad car. Yet the film invites the viewer to sympathize with their plight. We may affirm that robbery and assault are bad but are glad when they have some money and are able to get away. Every time a moving-image narrative leads to cognitive dissonance, it is an opportunity for us to explore what we believe is true or good. When we question what "lovely" really means, we start by defining *lovely*. Since we are defining it, we dwell on it. The very act of having to question the definition requires us to "think on these things." In the end, we make the decision about whether the cognitive dissonance will challenge us to dwell on what is lovely or ugly as we decide the difference. Not all stories will lift up our hearts, but if our hearts are in the right place, there is the potential that stories we may not otherwise enjoy may indeed make our hearts be lifted up.

It can be difficult to determine what may or may not be detrimental or benign. We should, however, be aware of our own areas of weakness or temptation. Until those in our care are capable of making those decisions and have developed their own ability to maintain self-control, parents, guardians, teachers, and others in positions of influence should take care about the content they expose others to. We are warned very clearly about making our brothers and sisters stumble.

Fair warning and full disclosure by those promoting a film or television show allow viewers to make their own responsible decision. Viewers themselves should exercise the right to stop watching when they realize the content is too intense or is having an ill effect. We can inform ourselves to some degree by checking in with online sites that list potentially difficult content. We should, however, not be afraid to be challenged, nor should we categorically reject a movie or television program based solely on content.[14]

Objectionable content is often the result of Hollywood pandering to fallen human nature. Sex sells. "People want to see R-rated movies," screenwriter Guinevere Turner says, "adults and children alike, and an easy way to get an R-rating is to have sex scenes or nudity. We'd be fooling ourselves if we didn't think teenagers wanted to see sex. And in creating the taboo, we create frenzy around it."[15] Making sexuality a taboo topic has given it advertising potential. Sex will sell. Violence will too, and American movies have become notoriously violent. Cable and Internet-delivery content has also stretched the boundary of what is depicted on screen for wide audiences.

The stretching of those boundaries does play with the taboo of some things that merely pander to human fallibility, but it can also mean that some stories worth telling can finally be brought to light.

It is a tricky line to walk. Think again of *Thelma and Louise*. The film is notable because it opened up discussion about rape and female autonomy. Was the violence gratuitous or necessary to tell an empowering story? It would be difficult to fully understand the situation the women find themselves in when Thelma is assaulted in the parking lot without showing uncomfortable material. In fact, part of the point is to make viewers feel uncomfortable so they can understand what Thelma is experiencing. The content is difficult but vital to the story. The way the content is handled makes a difference, too. The way action is portrayed leaves no doubt about the characters' intentions and reactions and shows only what is necessary.

However in a later scene in the film, Thelma has a sexual encounter with J.D. (Brad Pitt) that, while it is part of her character development, is mostly unnecessary. The scene in the parking lot was important because it helped the audience understand Thelma's plight. The scene with J.D. is a sex scene to help sell the movie. What constitutes objectionable or gratuitous material is subjective, and the plain truth is that we live in a violent, fallen world in which murder and rape are things that far too many people really do live with. They are true to life experience, and to deny them is to deny the stories of people who live with the consequences of those acts every day. In many ways, telling these difficult narratives and challenging taboos about discussing them gives a voice to those who are otherwise silenced and alone.

Some content is gratuitous, and some is unhealthy for certain viewers. But some difficult content is unfortunately quite necessary in order to tell the story truthfully. Viewers must first attend to the state of their own heart. If we want to be virtuous viewers, we must also endeavor to be virtuous people. Understanding differences in viewer experience and expectation, understanding our own areas of weakness or temptation, and understanding that we all see the same picture differently will help us put all moving-image stories into context. We are certainly allowed to object to some content and are always allowed to make the choice not to watch. We should also endeavor to help those around us make informed, healthy choices about what to watch. However, we must also understand that difficult stories are important for us to hear if we are to be reminded about the fallen state of the world and find empathy with our fellow creatures.

LITTLE MISS STRIPTEASE

Another film with obvious objectionable content is the 2006 film *Little Miss Sunshine*. The plot revolves around a family, each member of which has a clearly defined personal goal and all of whom fail at that goal in some way. Olive (Abigail Breslin), the young daughter, wants to win the Little Miss Sunshine pageant. Her father Richard (Greg Kinnear) wants to sell his self-help program and be a "winner." Her mother Sheryl (Toni Collette) just wants to keep the family together. Sheryl's son by a previous marriage, Duane (Paul Dano), wants to become a fighter pilot and at the beginning of the movie is not speaking to anyone. Richard's dad (Alan Arkin, in an Oscar-winning performance) wants to snort heroin and enjoy life's carnal pleasures before he dies—he also wants to help Olive know how beautiful she is, and this goal motivates him just as much as the other. Finally, Sheryl's brother Frank (Steve Carell) wants to commit suicide, since he has lost both his boyfriend and his professional prestige to a rival. Frank has already been unable to complete his goal when the film opens, since his attempted suicide failed. His goal, and everyone else's along with it, will shift to supporting Sheryl's goal of keeping the family together as the plot progresses.

The film contains images of men buying porn, Grandpa taking drugs (and, halfway through the film, overdosing on them), talk about sex, family fights, and Olive performing what she has no idea is a striptease as her talent in the pageant. There are heavy uses of objectionable language. When Duane learns he is color-blind and will never be a test pilot, he finally speaks, and the first word out of his mouth is a loud and long guttural scream of an obscenity. The film is R-rated and certainly not suitable for young audiences.

However, as we move through the film and watch people continue to fail at their personal goals, we see them shift in their thinking. Instead of being centered on their own desires and personal fulfillment and being unable to succeed under their own strength, they begin to support the family unit more fully, embodied by the yellow Volkswagen bus they must push in order to start since the transmission needs repair. Their endeavor becomes to support Olive, making sure she gets to the pageant and cheering for her as she performs her talent. The characters must each face their fallenness and their own inability to "succeed" on their own.

Scholar Quentin J. Schultze points out the Hollywood tendency to find "bad guys" to blame for society's ills: "The human tendency is to locate the source of evil outside of the self and even outside the tribe. It is much easier, probably less painful, and certainly more comforting to believe that the source of evil in the world is not one's own heart or tribe."[16] So, Schultze contends, we find evil people to vilify. The villains of *Little Miss Sunshine* are the faults of its protagonists, the character defects of each person in the story.[17] Instead of "us versus them," a mentality that means "both the problem and the solution rest in human hands,"[18] *Little Miss Sunshine* finds the problem in human nature itself. It can be read to say that we are saved by our communal love for each other—that we are each other's saviors—or it can also be interpreted to indicate that we remain in our fallenness and should help each other—that we need a superhuman savior. The second point of view is more decidedly Christian than the first, but both promote humility and selflessness.

In that sense the film does a good job of demonstrating that we are in divine need of help. Therefore, there is potential to read the film as an affirmation of Christian belief, in spite of—and in some ways because of—its objectionable content. None of these characters becomes the hero, as the hero would be a "winner" who makes everything right. They all become heroes, in a sense, when they join Olive onstage as she dances to Rick James's "Super Freak." If taking over the stage had been enough to close down the pageant, they would have overcome evil. But the pageant still exists, and they are asked to leave, and let off without facing charges (the pageant official has them arrested) as long as they agree never to enter a beauty contest in the state of California again. Evil, if it were truly embodied in the pageant official, would simply need a hero, someone to come in and save the situation. However, this is a film full of fallen creatures that can be read as pointing to the need for a savior, someone to save the very hearts of the people involved. Perhaps it says the savior is the family unit itself, perhaps not. Its ability to point out the need for a savior makes it a film with redemptive potential full of otherwise objectionable content.

The film's mature content, especially the pageant striptease, also intentionally points out flaws in what our society deems appropriate. There is no doubt Olive's dance routine to "Super Freak" has intentional sexual overtones. Both the lyrics of the song and Olive's progression from fully clothed and in a top hat to a bathing suit clearly indicate that Grandpa, who "taught her these moves," knew she was doing a striptease. Olive, being young (and clearly the most innocent member of the family), has no idea that the connotations of what she is doing are wrong. It is not sexualized in her preadolescent mind; it is just a fun dance to an upbeat song, a connection to her grandfather affirming her confidence and beauty. Olive is just having innocent fun. The pageant audience and especially the pageant official (Beth Grant) are horrified by the display. They are not, however, horrified by the other little girls in the pageant wearing highly sexualized outfits, full makeup and hair, and who are also unaware of the implications that their own costumes and looks make them into miniature adult beauty queens, even though they are not yet 10 years old. All of the girls in the pageant are sexualized. However, only Olive is seen as offensive.

Little Miss Sunshine intentionally points out these arbitrary ideals of beauty and the knowledge that all beauty pageants are overt, objectifying, sexualized displays of scantily clad women; a contest to see who can be the most appealing to someone seeking them only for pleasure. Olive's outlandish routine is intended to point out the hypocritical, self-justifying nature of the pageant world, and especially its harmful effect on young girls. The content is objectionable—a large, startling figure for the almost blind—in order to point out that all beauty pageants are just as worthy our disdain. The content must be exaggerated in order to point out what is truly objectionable.

REDEMPTIVE FORMS

Little Miss Sunshine's potentially objectionable content is embodied in its cinematic form: shots, editing, art direction, and so on. As mentioned, the yellow Volkswagen bus becomes a metaphor for the family working to support each other. In order to get the van down the road, and therefore in order to get the family down the road of life, they must all play a part. In the beginning, this is simply necessary in order to keep moving, and it is an arduous task, but as they work together they find joy in the task until the bus becomes an endearing symbol of their need and enjoyment of time together. When they work together, they truly become a family. The van is but one example of a cinematic metaphor embodying the theme of the film.

All moving-image narratives contain some formal elements: intentional shot choices, construction through editing, deliberate use of music or costumes, and so on. Understanding cinematic form is necessary to truly understand moving pictures. In a 2014 essay, scholar Crystal Downing uses the championship belt of main character Jake LaMotta in Martin Scorsese's *Raging Bull* as a metaphor for the need to take formal cinematic elements into account when understanding a moving-image story. In the film, Jake grabs the belt, studded with jewels, and hammers away at it, trying to dig the gems out. He must ruin the belt in order to separate them. But when he takes the gems to a dealer, the dealer tells him the belt left intact would have been worth more than just these gems. The entire film, Downing says, must be taken into account. "Like La Motta, then, pastors and professors tend to extract gems of insight from movies, not realizing that, no matter how brilliant, the insights are more valuable when seen as part of the film's entire visual structure."[19] Just digging out "gems" of story ruins the true account of a movie or program. The setting for the gems—the formal cinematic elements—makes them worth much more.

Can the cinematic elements and construction of a film or television program be redemptive? Moving pictures embody ideas, and if the medium is the message, then there is no doubt that some forms are more redemptive than others. Film form can embody redemption. In a musical, the form embodies transcendence. Musical stories defy reality by expressing internal states of being. Situations in which it would be plausible for characters to suddenly burst into song and dance, where, for instance, the main characters are theatrical performers and the story is about "putting on a show," are in some way realistic. However, it is still usually highly implausible. Consider the impractical plots of *Babes in Arms* or *42nd Street*. The music is "justified" but the situation is not realistic. In contrast, the "integrated" American musical (meaning songs help forward the plot instead of just being another "attraction" in a vaudeville-esque lineup of acts) includes numbers in the narrative in a way very dissimilar to our experience of real life. *West Side Story* is an often-cited example, since street gangs in New York are not known for dancing around the streets in ballet style, singing about what it means to be a "Jet" or a "Shark." The songs are a part of the story, but since in real life occasions to burst into song and dance are limited to specific settings, musicals, especially integrated ones, are by nature rather implausible. Therefore, they become metaphors, expressions of how a situation *feels* rather than how it *is*.

In the 1935 film *Top Hat*, Fred Astaire and Ginger Rogers dance one of their most famous numbers to the Irving Berlin song "Cheek to Cheek." The characters they play are lovers, separated slightly at the beginning of the dance by a temporary misunderstanding. The dance is a metaphor for their relationship (their dances almost always are) and the power of their attraction. She cannot help but love him when she is close to him as he sings to her that they are in heaven when out together "dancing cheek to cheek."[20] He professes his love by telling her that being together makes him eternally happy. There is room for discussion about whether the number and the song refer to the Christian understanding of Heaven or the cultural understanding of complete happiness, a lowercase "h" heaven. In either case, when they are dancing, they find happiness with each other. He sings and she answers by dancing with him, bringing the ideas of the song to fruition. They find "heaven" on the dance floor, in each other's arms. They find transcendence to someplace divine, a rising above their problems and cares. The audience, watching the film, is drawn into this experience by seeing the moving pictures. We are already aligned with the characters and sympathetic to them (knowing the misunderstanding is not a difficult obstacle). The camera keeps us close to them, especially in the beginning of the number. We, too, dancing with the couple, rise above our cares as we participate in the on-screen dance.

The power and appeal of the musical is its ability to give audiences this experience, and there is both a positive and negative potential in that. An escape from reality can easily become a deception. It can also be respite and encouragement, a vision of the way things can and ought to be, a vision of what we should work to achieve. *Top Hat* was a very popular film, playing in the dark days of the Depression. It gave audiences a break from a very difficult reality, and it never pretended that reality did not exist. It was just a glimpse of heaven, something lovely to think on, something worthy of praise during days filled with struggle and doubt.

The form of the moving image itself is one that casts visions, and in the case of many musicals (as well as adventure/fantasy films) the form embodies empowerment, transcendence, and joy. The camera exults, and we are swept up with it into a world where anything is possible and all comes right in the end. Is this truly possible? Can we have hope? Are there things worth celebrating and emulating? We would like to think so, and for a little while, there on the screen, those things are real to us. The pictures may not be "real" but the feelings they bring are. They are pictures of encouragement. Images of the fruit of the Spirit will define what those things look like, in case we have never known them or need to be reminded. We need to remember joy is close at hand and that faithfulness matters. We need to see what honesty looks like and what hope can do. These visions are important. They reflect a heavenly light, giving us strength on our journeys.

REDEMPTIVE NARRATIVES

Redemptive form can embody redemptive narrative, reflecting that light from one facet of storytelling through the other. Christian scholars look for redemptive narratives often by aligning stories to the meta-narrative of creation, fall, incarnation, and atonement. There is a strong justification for this, as meta-narratives—basic story structures that encompass overarching plots—are an important part of storytelling. If a story can be read to contain elements of the Judeo-Christian narrative, it may be seen as redemptive simply because of the story itself.

In his book *The Hero with a Thousand Faces*, anthropologist and mythologist Joseph Campbell details his research into a wide spectrum of cultures across the globe and throughout human history. He finds there is a story form that all peoples inherently know and use. This meta-narrative shows up in the stories of the Maori peoples of New Zealand, in Greek myths, as well as in eastern culture narratives. Somehow, Campbell posits, it is as if we all already know this story, just by being humans.

The Hero's Journey consists of important discrete stages that basically mean the protagonist or hero moves from a "normal" world to a "special" world where they must rescue something that was lost or find some kind of atonement.[21]George Lucas was heavily influenced by Campbell's work, and *Star Wars* was intentionally crafted to follow this meta-narrative plot. However, many Hollywood writers have also used this basic story form. Screenwriter Christopher Vogler puts forth a storytelling format he calls "The Writer's Journey," in which aspiring screenwriters learn to craft their script by developing characters that fit Campbell's archetypes and a plot that reflects elements of the Hero's Journey.[22] Writer Stuart Voytilla details how many Hollywood films can be seen as reflections of the Hero's Journey form in his *Myth and the Movies*. Voytilla mentions that studying moving-image stories from this perspective "provide[s] a flexible, analytical tool to understand why *any* movie's story works or fails. But most of all, the paradigm guides us to an understanding of why a story resonates on a universal level by answering our deepest mysteries [italics original]."[23] The Hero's Journey seems to reflect something universal. The most well-known Hollywood movies seem to fit the meta-narrative formula, with or without that intention.

Why is this? What is it about this story structure that is so universal? How can it so easily "answer our deepest mysteries"? Campbell posits his own reasons, but there are other indications and implications that Christians may draw. C. S. Lewis refers in his writing to the divine narrative (creation, fall, incarnation, atonement), and especially the drama that closes with Christ's return, as "the play that God wrote."[24] Creator God, from the Christian worldview, has been writing a story detailed by oral tradition, historical record, and divinely inspired prophecy in the Bible. We see through this mythic structure the divine story of God interacting with His creation, and Christ as the great turning point in that narrative. The play that God wrote is not yet finished. Christian traditions have been debating when and how Christ will return since His ascension, and the drama continues to unfold as we await the return of Christ and the presentation of the beautified Church as the Bride of Christ in Heaven. As we all participate in this narrative, we play our part, and, according to Lewis, "The playing well is what matters infinitely."[25] But we also own this meta-narrative. The story of Christ is the story we somehow know. It is the story that indelibly shapes our lives, and Christians also believe they have been given the task of sharing this Good News with others.

Perhaps, in some form or another, all people already know this story. Perhaps the meta-narrative Campbell detailed is one imprinted upon us by our Creator. Perhaps each people's history, culture, and tradition make them already a part of the divine narrative, already aware of the story of Christ in some form, and therefore all peoples can be receptive to it. In any case, there seems to be some correlation between the universally known myth Campbell speaks about and the play that God wrote.

If that is true, this story is inherently redemptive. That does not mean it cannot be misconstrued, given improper context, executed poorly, or not fully reflect the divine intention. It does mean there is some inherent worth to the shape of this story. The structure of the story and plot itself has inherent redemptive value when it reflects the play that God wrote. Some stories may only reflect certain elements (i.e., pointing out the fall or celebrating the creation), but even in those cases, Christians ready to receive those stories as reflections of God's meta-narrative will find in them some element of redemption. The story itself can reflect Godly truth.

PERSONAL OWNERSHIP

At the Baylor University Institute of Faith and Culture's 2014 Faith and Film Conference, the last event on the schedule was a screening of the 1982 film *Tender Mercies*. The director Bruce Beresford was in attendance and did a Q&A session with the audience after the film. One audience member asked about the director's take on the Christian conversion story contained in the narrative, but Beresford gave no insight into the film's "religious" intentions. The script was a close collaboration between Beresford and playwright Horton Foote, who won an Oscar for the effort. Foote deals openly with Christian themes in his work, and this story sees the conversion and baptism of a recovering, egocentric alcoholic Country Western singer named Mac Sledge (Robert Duvall, who also won an Oscar).

The film has long been a cultural touchpoint for Christians interested in film studies, yet the director avoided any overt "Christian" reading of the movie. It was a good story, a story worth telling, he said. It was clear, however, where the impetus for the question to the director came from, and it was palpable at the screening that night. Christians found some relation to the film. Here was a movie with cinematic veracity and excellent form that did not ignore, negate, or belittle Christian culture. In fact, it showed both a conversion (albeit understated), a baptism of the main character, and a "happy" ending. The end of the film does not leave the characters with all of their immediate problems solved, but Mac seems to have found a place of peace and a sense of belonging with his new family. The end of the story is a satisfying, not sugarcoated, well-earned, good place to leave the characters. Many Christians, especially Christians concerned with visual storytelling, appreciate that film. This, they seem to say, is who we are and who we can be. This tells a true story. This, in some way at least, tells *our* story. That sentiment at the screening made the event very special.

The idea that the film or program somehow tells our story is latent in all the films we deeply love. We are drawn to them because there is something in them that rings true for us. Movies we see as our stories have the potential to also be redemptive narratives. In the case of *Tender Mercies*, there is an element of recognition for many Christians, as well as many outside our tribe who may recognize something familiar in the cultural setting, experience of the characters, or subject matter. In almost any film, however, there is potential for recognition and affirmation. One can consider how important the stories of *Annie* or *Meet the Robinsons* might be to an adopted child, or the show *Gilmore Girls* for single mothers and their daughters, or how *Ordinary People, Steel Magnolias, We Bought a Zoo*, or even *Sleepless in Seattle* might be relatable for anyone going through a period of grief or loss. We are drawn to movies that reflect our experience. We relate to the characters in some way. They become "our" movies.

Sometimes it is merely in the theme and not necessarily the content. Fans of the *Lord of the Rings* films may relate to how the characters care for each other, or how they battle for freedom or struggle with power and leadership. Perhaps people who feel they will probably be overlooked and underestimated relate to the diminutive hobbits. We are drawn to the story, but when we find characters we truly love, it is often because their characteristics or their struggles somehow seem to relate to our own.

In her highly popular TED talk "The Danger of a Single Story," writer Chimamanda Ngozi Adichie says that stories are points of identity, and that all people have more than one story, more than one defining character arc. Learning stories is a way to connect, as well as to deepen understanding. When we learn more than one story about a person, we see him or her as more than just what our initial assumptions were. "Stories matter," she says. "Many stories matter." We can use stories in powerful ways because people so closely identify with them. Stories will affect how we see ourselves. When presented with only one story of life in the Midwest, for instance, *Little House on the Prairie*, perceptions of that region of America may be stilted. Old-fashioned at best, cartoonish at worst. Midwesterners, however, may see more in *Parks and Recreation* or the films of John Hughes (which often take place in or near Chicago), giving them many stories of themselves, in order to paint a broader picture and negate stereotypes. Adichie ends her talk with a reference to Alice Walker and the importance of identification with narratives, especially their ability to contain some form of redemption:

> The American writer Alice Walker wrote this about her Southern relatives who had moved to the North. She introduced them to a book about the Southern life that they had left behind: "They sat around, reading the book themselves, listening to me read the book, and a kind of paradise was regained." I would like to end with this thought: That when we reject the single story, when we realize that there is never a single story about any place, we regain a kind of paradise.[26]

The telling of the tale, the self-recognition, the ownership of the story, and the experience of challenging our own perceptions can paint a more accurate picture of the world. We may recognize in the stories we love parts of ourselves we had never acknowledged, and our perceptions of people and places may be greatly changed. Why do we love the stories we love? What do we learn about ourselves from them? What do we find in them that makes us whole, heals us, and helps us remember who we are? Stories can do those things, and if those things are a part of regaining paradise, they are redemptive indeed.

CATHARSIS

When Aristotle was outlining his *Poetics*, detailing what was best in the dramatic arts, he said an important function of tragedy was catharsis, the bringing forth of feelings of pity or fear so that they could be purged from the spectator.[27] Redemption, we have seen, may be found in the story and in the moving image and its construction through editing. Redemption may mean encouragement of virtue or admonishment against vice. Redemption may mean telling difficult stories in order to bring the truth to light. Redemption may mean telling the story God has already written on our hearts. But there is another function dramatic art—storytelling—serves that Aristotle thought extremely important.

Catharsis is important because it somehow regulates the human spirit by allowing us to really feel harmful emotions and then move on from them. There is a lot of Greek thought and science about where emotions were housed in the body and why it was important to get rid of the harmful ones. But we can think of this in a more contemporary setting: the game of football, which has been at times called a more civilized form of warfare. It consists, after all, in two opposing forces lined up to do battle for ground or territory. We trust, however, that no one will be killed on that field of battle. Our natural human tendency to compete and use aggression in that competition will be served, yet injuries sustained on the field of football battle are much fewer than those in armed combat. In that sense, watching football brings catharsis. Generally, the players and the fans are allowed to cheer and to vie for their side but after the "war" is over it is—in most cases—easier for both participants and spectators to return home in relative peace.

The same thing can happen in art. If, for instance, we watch a program in which people have to find some kind of shelter or avoid a violent adversary, we watch the show thinking about survival and safety. That is the real impetus behind all horror films since they tend to shock and scare us in controllable ways so we can arouse our latent feelings of fear and horror, control them, give them a voice, and then let them go. Instead of acting on our fears, frustrations, or desires, we give rein to them by being swept up into the story and then purge them when the story is over. Responding to *Thelma and Louise*, *Boston Globe* critic Diane White said, "For some women *Thelma and Louise* is a cathartic movie, a bit of wish-fulfillment. I know what it's like to be so brutalized and humiliated by a man that you'd like to murder him. But I didn't. Why? Because life isn't a movie. Besides, unlike Louise, I didn't have a gun handy."[28]

There can be identification with the situation on the screen. There is separation between that identification and real life. But the real emotional experience is one that can ultimately heal by giving voice to our feelings. We feel these emotions and we let them go. That is catharsis.

Catharsis is one of the many ways in which a moving image may help cause, embody, or promote redemption. Debates will rage about whether movies and television programs encourage violence and bad behavior or only reflect an already violent and morally destitute society. The truth is human beings are violent, greedy, selfish beings with temptations and frustrations all around them. However, there are many ways for the films and television programs we watch to be catalysts for a viewer's walk to become closer to God. Stories touch us, move us, make us uncomfortable, show us things that are familiar, and help us process our feelings. What we bring to them and what expectation we have for their role in our lives will make a difference. It does matter what we see, but with our hearts in the right place, more films and programs may cause the bad in us to be purged and the good in us to be lifted up.

NOTES

1. Anthony de Mello, *One Minute Wisdom* (New York: Doubleday, 1986), 23.

2. Jim Tushkinski, *"Holy Whore*: Remembering Rainer Werner Fassbinder," in *Fassbinder*, ed. Tony Rayns, British Film Institute, London, 1980, accessed October 27, 2014, http://www.jimtushinski.com/fassbinder.html.

3. Flannery O'Connor, "The Fiction Writer and His Country," in *Mystery and Manners, Occasional Prose*, eds. Sally and Robert Fitzgerald (New York: Farrar, Straus and Giroux, 1970), 33.

4. Quentin J. Schultze, *Christianity and the Mass Media in America: Toward a Democratic Accommodation* (Lansing: Michigan State University Press, 2003), 237.

5. Phil. 4:8, NIV.

6. Barbara Creed, "Film and Psychoanalysis," in *Film Studies: Critical Approaches*, eds. John Hill and Pamela Church Gibson (New York: Oxford University Press, 2000), 85.

7. See Peter Brunette, "Post-Structuralism and Deconstruction," in *Film Studies: Critical Approaches*, eds. John Hill and Pamela Church Gibson (New York: Oxford University Press, 2000), 91.

8. Flannery O'Connor, "Some Aspects of the Grotesque in Southern Fiction," in *Mystery and Manners, Occasional Prose*, 47–48.

9. As her response in the letter continues, she acknowledges that audiences want to see redemption but warns they should also see the cost of redemption. Her work focused on the latter.

10. O'Connor, "The Fiction Writer and His Country," 34.

11. Robert H. Woods Jr. and Paul D. Patton, *Prophetically Incorrect: A Christian Introduction to Media Criticism* (Grand Rapids, MI: Brazos Press, 2010), xxxiii.

12. Ibid., 88.

13. Patricia Hitchcock, "Beyond Doubt: The Making of Hitchcock's Favorite Film," *Shadow of a Doubt*, DVD, directed by Alfred Hitchcock, 1943 (Los Angeles, CA: Universal Studios Home Entertainment, 2006).

14. There is a long-standing argument that if we were to pay attention only to "PG" stories, many passages of the Bible would not make the cut. For instance, little attention is paid to the Cain and Abel narrative in most Christian children's educational materials, and stories about battles or the life of David have become sanitized in those settings. The Bible has some very clearly objectionable content. It contains narratives that are hard to reconcile (the life of Hosea, the relationship of Abraham and Hagar, etc.). The Bible, taken as a narrative, is challenging to say the least.

15. Guinevere Turner, quoted in David Keeps, "Sex Sells, Says Hollywood: Casting Directors, Writers, and Directors Discuss the Role of Nudity in Film," *The Guardian*, July 16, 2000, accessed October 17, 2014, http://www.theguardian.com/film/2000/jul/16/features1.

16. Schultze, *Christianity and the Mass Media in America*, 251.

17. There is one notable exception, the vilification of the pageant industry, but as Duane points out, "It's all a f*cking beauty contest," and their participation in it is their own fault.

18. Schultze, *Christianity and the Mass Media in America*, 251.

19. Crystal Downing, "Seeing the Medium: Martin Scorsese and C.S. Peirce," paper presented at the 2014 Baylor Symposium on Faith and Culture, Baylor University, Waco, Texas, October 24, 2014.

20. Fred Astaire and Ginger Rogers, performers, *Top Hat*, DVD, directed by Mark Sandrich (1935, Burbank, CA: Warner Home Video, 2005).

21. Joseph Campbell, *The Hero with a Thousand Faces*," 3rd ed. (Novato, CA: New World Library, 2008).

22. Christopher Vogler, *The Writer's Journey: Mythic Structure for Writers*, 2nd ed. (Studio City, CA: Michael Wiese Productions, 1998).

23. Stuart Voytilla, *Myth and the Movies: Discovering the Mythic Structure of 50 Unforgettable Films* (Studio City, CA: Michael Wiese Productions, 1999), 1.

24. C.S. Lewis, "The World's Last Night," in *The Business of Heaven: Daily Readings from C.S. Lewis*, ed. Walter Hooper (San Diego, CA: Harvest/HJB, 1984), 124.

25. Ibid.

26. Chimamanda Ngozi Adichie, "The Danger of a Single Story," TED Talks, July 2009, transcript, accessed November 4, 2014, http://www.ted.com/talks/chimamanda_adichie_the_danger_of_a_single_story/transcript?language=en.

27. Aristotle, *The Poetics*, in *Criticism: Major Statements*, 4th ed., eds. Charles Kaplan and William Davis Anderson (Boston: Bedford, St. Martin's, 2000), 29.

28. Diane White, "The Great Debate over *Thelma and Louise*," *The Boston Globe*, June 14, 1991, accessed November 4, 2014, http://www.highbeam.com/doc/1P2-7664588.html.

CHAPTER 8

TRUTH AND THE MOVING IMAGE

Of all art forms, film is the one that gives the greatest illusion of authenticity, of truth. A motion picture takes a viewer inside, where real people are supposedly doing real things. We assume that there is a certain verisimilitude, a certain authenticity. But there is always some degree of manipulation. Some degree of distortion.

—*Annette Insdorf*[1]

You tell the truth by selecting the facts that illustrate it.

—*Rose Wilder Lane*[2]

We used to believe the screen was there just to help us see the pictures, the story, and the illusion of life. But we are warier now and we guess that all these screens are the real thing, fabulous tools of course, but subtle barriers between us and life.

—*David Thomson*[3]

I think movies are real world in that they are our fears and our dreams.

—*Martin Scorsese*[4]

At the end of the 1959 film *Imitation of Life*, directed by Douglas Sirk, the great gospel singer Mahalia Jackson performs at the funeral of an African American woman named Annie (Juanita Moore). There is a great deal of irony in the use of a well-known gospel singer playing herself in a movie whose title indicates superficiality, lies and the truth, and fact and fiction within the story. After all, the story includes a character, Annie's daughter Sarah Jane (Susan Kohner), who passes as white. As well as a stunning performance by Jackson, it is an important plot moment in Sirk's subtly progressive commentary on race in America, as Sarah Jane realizes she has lost her connection with her mother and mourns both the loss of her mother and an important part of her own identity. Who is she, really? Who should she be? The entire film seems to ask the audience: what is real life and what is fake? What is the truth, especially on screen? What should our expectations for movies and television programs be?

Some moving pictures seem more real than others. Reality television and documentary filmmaking are the result of technology's progression. Digital capture, more file space, better editing software, and more affordable equipment mean it is much easier to take a camera anywhere and film all day long. This seems to indicate more "realism" in our moving-picture stories. But does it? All moving pictures contain artifice. They must cut bits of life out of the frame and be edited for clarity and length. They can never be real life. Since that is the case, it will require intentional effort to discern what about them is real or true and to navigate the moving image's lifelike presence and its inherent manipulative forms.

We may find that fiction tells the truth by being what the artist Pablo Picasso said was a "lie that makes us realize the truth."[5] We might recognize something on the screen and think, "Yes, that is the truth," about our existence, about how something feels and how things are or should be, but those images will still not be reality. The subtlety of the screen's barrier between truth and fiction has a great deal to do with how we perceive what truth or reality is, how the photographic image works in our minds, and what we want to believe. Its navigation is imperative if we are to be the masters of how movies and television affect our lives. In the end, the truth really will set us free. So finding out what is true, what constitutes truth in the movies and television, is what will ultimately determine our ability to interact with the moving image and retain control of the effect it has on us.

REFLECTING TRUTH

Edward Albee's quote about serious stories holding up a mirror and Jack Nachbar's metaphor of popular culture as a funhouse mirror speak to two vital truths about moving-image media. First, it does give a reflection of reality; there is a verisimilitude, something true about the reflection. Second, that image is not real life; it is a useful image, taken in perspective, but it is not life. Viewers can recall Dumbledore and Harry Potter standing in front of the mirror of Erised. The mirror was not real life; it was what they wanted to be real. It looked real, but it was not reality, and to stand staring and wishing did not make it so.

The moving image, likewise, has a kind of inherent truth. Unlike any other medium, it combines actual sound recordings, real people talking, and photographs "brought to life" by the magic of the animation of motion pictures. Seeing a series of similar photographs taken in sequential order shown at rapid speed gives the illusion of movement. All moving images are based on that illusion and require technology to animate the still images. The illusion is one of "bringing to life" as the pictures seem to move. It is a magic that still fascinates us, as it has since its invention. The camera itself is an astounding piece of technology, as is the phonograph, since both are able to "capture reality." One can imagine what it must have been like to sit in the darkened room when the Lumière brothers first "got the picture out of the box" and the image of a train slowing into the station loomed in front of the audience, as big as life. "Was that real?" one might ask. André Bazin's Myth of Total Cinema is relevant here and has credence. The photograph captures a reality that is unlike that of painting, which interprets it through an artist's brush. And yet, there is a good deal of interpretation in how the lenses and film stocks are utilized, where the camera is pointed, and what it chooses to show.

The moving image has also made great use of capitalizing on that interpretation, as Rudolf Arnheim argued. In telling the story, filmmakers found they could point out truth the way novelists and painters did, by making us look at life in a different way. Fictional narrative is truth presented in a different way, but truth nonetheless, and if Albee is right, it is a truth that requires us to question our own lives. That kind of questioning, as we have seen, may cause viewers to rethink their own assumptions. So perhaps the funhouse mirror is useful. Perhaps the mirror of Erised does tell us something "true," even though it is not reality. These inherent qualities in moving images, faithful recreation of reality and obvious manipulation of that reality, can be tools of truth.

When Darren Aronofsky released his 2014 film *Noah*, critics from a variety of faith traditions (Jewish, Christian, and Muslim) had a great deal (both good and bad) to say about the film, which depicts a hero from their creation/early Earth narratives. Noah is an important figure in all of those religions, and his story was one each tradition had some ownership of, so it is natural they wanted the filmmaker to "get the story right." But was that even possible? Aronofsky's film is full of extra-biblical plot and Computer Graphic Image (CGI) rock creatures. It does not seem "accurate," and yet what filmed early-Earth narrative could be? Not having been there, the only things any scholar has to go on to know the "true" story of Noah are the sacred texts that captured a story passed down for years by oral tradition, and any scientific evidence that might help account for the elements of the story. A filmed version of a Bible story never can be completely accurate.

In 2005, writer Bruce Feiler released a documentary on PBS titled *Walking the Bible: A Journey by Land through the Five Books of Moses*. The series was a companion video to his book of the same name, and in it he travels throughout the Mideast and northern Africa, researching the "real" location of the ark and searching for evidence of the 10 plagues visited on Egypt. Feiler is looking for evidence; looking for proof that the Bible is true. What he finds instead is that the narrative requires faith.

> Finding a scientific explanation for the plagues is appealing. If we can prove that one detail of the story is true, sure, the entire book is true. But I think these theories actually undermine the Bible. If the plagues can be explained by natural phenomenon, where does that leave God? I think I, like a lot of people, enjoy these theories because *it's a lot easier to think about them than it is to think about the central figure in the entire book.* The Bible reveals exactly what caused the ten plagues. God caused them. And if we're going to develop a relationship with that God, the story suggests, we have to break off from our surroundings and set off for something new [italics added].[6]

The "truth" or proof of the Bible was not as important as developing a relationship with the author of the book.

Audiences wanted something similar from *Noah*; they wanted to see the story and watch the book be brought to life. They want that bringing to life to be an accurate story. However, every filmed version of a biblical narrative is an interpretation of events. No film or television account of a Bible story can be completely accurate. What *Noah*'s audiences were asking from the screen is the same thing Feiler was asking from historical artifacts: something trustworthy. Feiler wanted proof. *Noah*'s audiences wanted accuracy. All wanted some form of verifiable truth. God and the Bible, however, are matters of faith. Moving images can try to reflect biblical truth, but they are not that sacred text, and perhaps they cannot ever reflect what is written there with justice. In movies and television, we want something more than what is written on the pages of the Bible. We want to see it brought to life, but bringing a story to cinematic life requires (among many other things) choosing locations, hairstyles, and shaping the story to appeal to an audience's sense of drama.

That is why *Noah* could never simply be the Bible story. Moving-image audiences want action and color. We watch movies and television for diversion and entertainment, perhaps to be caught up in an experience that will move us in some way. We want story. We want drama. Our experience of biblical narratives on film can never be the same as our relationship with the text itself. Films and television programs are for-profit ventures, and the moving-image medium itself comes with different expectations from viewers. Filmed Bible stories are always retellings, and it is nearly impossible to judge what films or programs "get the story right," because the story is an interpretation, heightened for dramatic effect. Even the narrative films and television programs that are most "authentic" in their capture of daily life are constructed and dramatized in order to entice viewers. Moving images are, even in their most authentic offerings, still heightened and sculpted versions of truth.

VISIONS OF REALITY

The most unrealistic television programs ever produced may be the shows that claim overtly to *be* real and belong to the genre called "reality TV." Ostensibly more realistic than fiction, these programs utilize non-actors playing themselves in "real life" situations and claim to be records of reality, something more like real-life than fictionalized dramatizations. In actuality, by stripping away the audience's agreement that they are watching fiction, reality television gets to be false and say it is true without having to explain away its inherent fictional tendencies. When watching fiction, audiences should ideally be able to willingly suspend their understanding that the story is not true in order to emotionally "buy in" to the characters and their story. Audiences temporarily agree to believe in the likelihood of the narrative in order to enjoy it. In reality television, audiences are asked to believe a supposed emotional and physical reality, without acknowledging how constructed that "reality" actually is.

The contestants on, a reality competition show, for instance, may indeed be non-actors in competition for a prize: survivors on an island, roommates in a house, potential suitors for a stunning mate, tattoo artists creating the best tattoos. However, there is more at work than just cameras recording the contest. The recording is made with intention and is heavily edited, and perhaps the parameters of the competition itself are all a part not of a record of reality but of programming content. The show has to sell. It has to find an audience. Real life does not require this. Therefore, elements of reality are shaped into a narrative. It becomes the same as any fictional narrative, although reality television is supposed to be "nonfiction." There is an inherent pernicious quality to anything that says it is real and can never be reality. "Reality television" is a contradiction in terms.

The construction of every reality television show is so conventional it could be turned into a course in elementary editing: take A-roll footage of the contest, B-roll footage of every conversation, and C-roll confessional camera footage. An editor sorts out the juiciest moments: Person 1 rolls her eyes; Person 2 falls down, screams, laughs, or cries; and Person 3 says something judgmental about anyone at any time. In the episode's opening sequence, play Person 1's eye roll, with Person 3's commentary as voiceover, and cut to

Person 2 looking shocked, disappointed, guilty, or falling down. Subjective editing tells us that all these things are happening together and concern the same thing, when in reality they could have nothing to do with each other. It is the Kuleshov experiment (where one shot of an actor is read to be different emotions depending upon which shot it is edited in next to), plus the social sciences gone mad. All reality television moments are crafted in the editing room, since these kind of moving-image stories can only be told in a world where the amount of footage or drive storage space means editors could sift through hours of normality, throw away somewhere between 60 and 95 percent of it, and construct entertainment out of the 5–40 percent necessary, depending on the show. "Trust me," says critic David Rupel, "if you watch every second of someone's life, the majority of it is quite boring."[7]

Neil Postman's *Amusing Ourselves to Death* is a stinging critique of how television's modes of communication and delivery "ha[ve] made entertainment itself the natural format for the representation of all experience."[8] In other words, some audiences now look at all life experiences and expect them to be as entertaining as the events on television. Postman's admonition is greatly reinforced by America's fascination with reality television. Some people now expect their lives to be as scintillating as the edited lives in our programming. Those are real, right? That is normal, is it not? It is a dangerous falsehood that can give people poor expectations and a strange understanding of themselves. The most fun people to watch on a reality series, for example, Honey Boo-Boo or Dog the Bounty Hunter, would be very hard to live with every day. Even these eccentric people/characters, fascinating as they are, are constructed and heightened for the camera. Living with them on a daily basis would be very different than interacting with them by watching their television show.

Reality television comes out of the documentary movement in film, which was influenced by both nonfiction cinema and nonfiction news–related programs on television (like Edward R. Murrow's *See It Now* program). In the height of the documentary's emergence in the United States, which corresponded with the social upheaval of the 1960s, two related, often confused, and not mutually exclusive schools came about: cinéma vérité and direct cinema. The former intends to watch action objectively, becoming a "fly on the wall" that brings the viewer into a real situation. Cinéma vérité strives to be more like objective journalism, observing and letting the audience experience a situation and come to their own conclusions. On the other hand, direct cinema acknowledges the camera's interaction with characters, causing them to heighten their own reality. It understands that the camera changes reality, and at its best (in films like the Maysles brothers' *Grey Gardens*) it finds the truth in the footage. Yes, there is artifice and manipulation, but there is also something real. It tells the truth by editing together the facts that illustrated the reality.

The problem with reality television is that it can never be cinéma vérité but says it is. Or perhaps the real problem is that we want it to be objective, and we do not question that it might not be able to ever tell a story without some inherent manipulation, bias, or commentary. Nonfiction moving pictures have always had this problem. Robert Flaherty's 1922 film *Nanook of the North* was largely acknowledged as the first "documentary" film.[9] Flaherty filmed near Hudson Bay, Canada, with native non-actors in their own environment. However, he famously "directed" them to, for instance, use a spear to kill prey instead of a gun. Travelogues, newsreels, and home movies all supposedly take us to real places and tell us about real things. There is something interesting in our desire to record reality for posterity or to use these records to take us to places we cannot physically go.

Currently, nonfiction film has become a haven for investigative journalism. From *Supersize Me* and *The Cove* to *The War Tapes* and the films of Ken Burns (like *The Civil War*, or *The Roosevelts: An Intimate History*), documentary filmmaking can, like other forms of journalism, seek to be as objective as possible. However, journalistic documentary films (like all forms of journalism) have relative objectivity. Even if the intention of the filmmakers is to be as objective as possible, the film is still constructed, manipulated, and edited. Because the intention is to be unbiased and tell the truth, there is a chance audiences may see these kinds of nonfiction films as the *only* story of, for instance, an event in history, instead of recognizing that the film is one perspective on a story. In the same way, audiences may see reality television and consider that as "normal life" when it is anything but. We want to believe these stories, though, because they seek to be objective. All moving images—journalistic documentary, reality television, or narrative dramatic films and programs—show us stories we choose to believe. Our expectations for "nonfiction" are predicated on the moving-image maker's intentions and our own perception of the story's authenticity. However, even journalistic-nonfiction films cannot tell a complete and wholly unbiased truth. Audiences should understand that all moving images, even the ones that look and attempt to be the most like real life, are not reality. They are stories. That means someone is telling them. They may contain truth, but they are not without some form of manipulation, bias, or commentary.

"THE UNCANNY VALLEY"

In 1970 Japanese roboticist Masahiro Mori noticed that when robots began to look and move too much like human beings, people's attitudes toward them would change. "When a robot is toylike and capable of only toylike, simple humanlike gestures," reporter Clive Thompson says, referring to Mori's findings, "we find it cute. If it starts looking and acting too human—as with, say, a rubbery prosthetic hand—we suddenly shift allegiance. We find it creepy."[10] Mori called it "the uncanny valley" between real and fake, and Thompson applies Mori's theory to the *Star Wars* robot R2-D2 (Kenny Baker). R2-D2 is not very human-like. He took on just human-enough qualities, making sounds or rotating the top part of his body, to help people perceive a personality. R2-D2 consisted of hunks of metal and plastic, operated by remote control with a guy sitting inside, and was essentially an electronic puppet. But he *seemed* real, and audiences loved him. He did not seem too real, though; otherwise he would fall into the uncanny valley: too-much-like-life-but-not-alive. The uncanny valley is life-like but false and, therefore, creepy.

R2-D2 works on the same principle that propels all animated characters. Bugs Bunny, for instance, is neither a rabbit nor a human being. He has some perceptible characteristics of both, but not so many of either that he becomes creepy. Bugs avoids the uncanny valley because he is drawn, not photographed. Other animated and anthropomorphic characters have either shifted to avoid the uncanny valley (see Bugs' development over time from crouched on all fours in his early films to always upright in the now classic shorts directed by Friz Freleng and Chuck Jones), or have failed.[11] However, audiences have little trouble accepting the "reality" of SpongeBob Square-Pants, even though their experience of the character is nothing like their experience of a real sponge. We do not want something that pretends to be real. We want something that either looks real or looks false enough to be different and still is somehow familiar.

Avoiding the uncanny valley helps storytellers sell the believability of a story. However, the uncanny valley may be useful in helping viewers separate the story world from real life. The uncanny valley is a creepy place where life-like is not alive and human-like is not human. A story that falls into it just does not seem real, or quite right. However, avoiding the uncanny valley, being too believable, may cause a moving-image story to have unintended consequences for an audience. Viewers may begin to place expectations on the real world to be like their experience of movies or television. Those expectations can greatly change what viewers value and how they interact with others and the world around them. When fiction becomes replacement for reality, our lives can fall into their own uncanny valley, places where our lives mean less than our dreams, creepy places that are full of potential for deception and lies.

In a piece performed for the National Public Radio show *Snap Judgment*, Albanian-born poet Gypsee Yo describes the effect of television programming on our perceptions of reality that lead to a change in attitudes, actions, and social states. Yo's piece begins with a tongue-in-cheek description of a "peaceful, happy" (or at least orderly) life in a country ruled by the communist proletariat. Then she describes a shift in the 1980s, when a Western agent, namely, the popular primetime soap *Dallas*, invaded the country.

Through scrambled waves, firewalls, and propaganda warnings it managed to enter the living room of every single Albanian family. What followed was heated debate in the milk and bread ration lines. "How do they manage to wash all that laundry without a washing machine?" "Did you see there's a phone in every house?" "I think I counted five—no six—rooms and a pool. What on earth is a pool?"[12]

Slowly, Yo says, people began to long for a different way of life and developed a different perception of the West. *Dallas* became more than entertainment. It became a dream of a better life.

> But the breaking point came when the infamous "A House Divided" episode aired, and the entire country was in uproar trying to find out who shot J. R. They vowed to break through the military defenses of the Cold War and go on the other side to find out. It took them nine years to do it until the Berlin Wall came down. But at the other side they sure expected to see ten-gallon cowboy hats, Mustangs, and telephones. They expected to be a part of that dream. The recovery from that dream-shattering is what is commonly known as "countries in political and economical transition." We grasped for something that wasn't really there.[13]

While Yo's tone is humorous, her point is well made. Some people want the "freedom to be something else."[14] Their perception of the world and how it works is shaped in very effective ways by the fictional programs they see in moving images. They may not be real, but they are made to look real, and people could mix up the two. Their expectations for reality become the same as our expectations for our entertainment and diversion, an uncanny valley of disillusionment, confusion, and disappointment.

Somehow, in helping us believe the pictures, movies and television can also lure people into a false sense of perception. What seems real but is false becomes a dream deferred, a promise that no one can make good. The uncanny valley for robots is one that R2-D2 avoids because he is so obviously not human. If he were more realistic, audiences might expect him to truly be human, a promise of human-ness he could never fulfill.[15] Just so, when we cannot separate movies and television from real life, they fall into an uncanny valley, a promise of reality that is merely a dream.

SELF-REFERENCE

The inherent danger of the dreams found in moving-image stories gave rise to many art movements, including what Peter Wollen calls "counter-cinema," a reaction against Hollywood's "dream factory" output.[16] Hollywood stories were false. They raised our expectations and then let us down. Life could never be like it was in the movies or on television. The "counter-cinema" movement utilized many facets to break down the Hollywood formula, and one of the most effective was the idea of self-reference. Self-reference refers to a moving-image story's ability to acknowledge its own construction within the narrative itself. Within the story, a person with a camera might appear, reminding the audience that pictures—like the moving ones they are watching—must be shot by someone. Someone is making this film or program. Even a shot through a doorway might remind an audience member that all films and programs are contained within a frame, and this frame within the frame highlights a moving image's intentional construction. If a movie or a television show uses elements of self-reference to in some way acknowledges that it is a story being told instead of just presenting a supposed picture of real life, it loses the potentially pernicious and disappointing sense of a false reality. Just as our expectation of filmed biblical narratives can never do the stories of the Bible real justice, our cinematic and televised dreams can never be a replacement for real life. There is tremendous capacity for redemption in filmic narratives, but there is also the inherent danger of implying that there is a "better" world.

A host of movies and television shows contain elements of self-reference. Scholars have debated many of them: frames within frames, allusions to Hollywood characters, filmmakers present in the story. A current rash of pop culture–referencing situation comedies also fills this role. Shows like *Community* (which has spoofed everything from *Law and Order* to Ken Burn's *The Civil War*) and *Parks and Recreation* are currently using their own ability to be constructed, manipulated moving images as part of the storytelling process. In a second season episode of *Community* titled "Competitive Wine Tasting," one of the study group of friends taking classes together at local Greenville Community College, Abed (Danny Pudi), takes a class called "Who's the Boss." The class, and its instructor (Stephen Tobolowsky), are intent on proving that the television show *Who's the Boss* did not really have a "boss." Abed, being the most astute student of popular culture on television (and also a filmmaker and film major, itself a character trait that allows for continual self-reference), takes the challenge to study the sitcom and disproves his professor's academic theory by empirical logical reasoning to aver that Angela (Judith Light) was indeed the "boss" on that show. Abed pauses before leaving the classroom and quotes the opening song to *Who's the Boss*: "There's a path you take and a path untaken. The choice is up to you, my friend." He then turns and walks away, leaving the professor to find another pop culture question worth positing.

By showcasing a character who reads meaning into a television program, breaks down its structure and story, and finds in popular media some sort of meaning beyond mere entertainment, the show *Community* makes situation comedies something worthy studying. It also mocks the "serious" study of popular culture, celebrating and mocking its own importance at the same time. *Community* says, see, all television is fake, all movies are popular culture artifacts. Emulating them (like Abed does on a regular basis) is just play-acting. It is fake. Television critiques television by using the medium itself. The medium becomes the message.

Parks and Recreation uses a less convoluted approach, namely, the documentary-style shooting of a fiction event, a "mockumentary." The documentary style allows for the perception of reality: the cameras are "cinéma vérité" watching the action but not interacting. However, characters speak directly to the camera for "confession cam" sound bites and occasionally acknowledge the camera's presence with a glance or a take, commenting to the camera, and, therefore the audience, in a filmed version of a theatrical aside. *Parks and Recreation* toys slyly with its own falsity.

In the *Parks and Recreation* season-five episode "Media Blitz," Ben (Adam Scott) finds himself having to explain his short-lived exploits as a young mayor while on the local television show *Pawnee Today*. A lower third graphic reads "Ben Wyatt: Human Disaster." The graphic looks just like the kind of lower third used in all kinds of television news and video interviews. It lists the subjects' name, the most pertinent information about them, and the reason they are talking about the issue. Ben's lower third graphic is very realistic, but it is obviously not real. No nonfiction program would label someone "human disaster."

The entire show *Parks and Recreation*, and other mockumentary-style shows, work on the same principle. Yes, audiences can acknowledge this looks just like a documentary or nonfiction news show. But we know those are actors, and from graphics like the one that labels Ben a "human distaster" we know it is not real. *Parks and Recreation* avoids confusing television with reality not by looking less real but by acknowledging its own fiction. See, this is fake. It looks real, but it is not. Self-reference helps us remember that what we are watching is just a story, not a vision of reality.

VISIONS OF A DEEPER REALITY

If movies and television can give a vision of reality that is confusing, perhaps it is because they are so much like dreams. Films have been compared to dreams for many years. There is an entire body of literature related to this topic, and there are several films and programs that deal with it directly (like the "House Divided" episode of *Dallas*, the final episode of *Newhart*, or films like *What Dreams May Come*). Christopher Nolan's 2010 film *Inception* is a dramatization that takes the comparison of movies and dreams to a deeper level, or at least to a different level than most other self-referential dream movies have done. In the film, some characters are versed in an experience called "dream sharing," which requires the proper technology to hook up each dreamer into the system (much like films and television require technology to create the dream state of watching). They take a job to implant an idea into the subconscious of a rich man's son, Robert (Cillian Murphy), as he dreams. Implanting an idea in the dreamer is called "inception." The idea being planted by the team is for the son to think his father (Pete Postlethwaite) wanted him to sell the family business, which will result in a lucrative profit for the investor paying the team. The dream sharers who go about the task all have different responsibilities in the dream world, like members of a production crew. The leader, who acts like a director, is Cobb (Leonardo DiCaprio). The problem is that Cobb is having trouble separating dreams from reality. He had spent so much time in dream worlds with his wife Mal (Marion Cotillard) that she had become confused between dream world and reality, leading to her death.[17] Now Cobb is fighting to hang on to the difference, hoping to complete this mission and obtain his payment, a visa that will allow him to reenter the United States and be reunited with their children.

If the plot sounds convoluted, that is just the tip of the dreamscape iceberg. Nolan intentionally and intelligently guides the film audience through different realities, dreams within dreams within dreams, making even the film's audience question which part was real and which was imagined. It is important to note, however, that what happens in the "imaginary" dream worlds has consequences in the real world. Mal is so confused she commits suicide, thinking that will release her into or out of a dream world (the film leaves us with that question). Cobb takes out a small top from time to time to remind himself of the difference. He explains to the inception job's architect, Ariadne (Ellen Page), that the top is a totem, a reminder of what is the dream world and what is the real world. When he spins it, he watches to see if it keeps spinning or if it eventually loses momentum and falls over. If it keeps spinning, he is in a dream world. If it topples over, he is not. The totem is his link to reality.

Inception is a movie that shows how movies work. Movies, the film says, are like dreams. They take the audience to another reality, one they can get lost in, and one in which they can become open to having ideas planted there. *Inception* both does the act of inception (planting the idea in the audience's head during the "dream" of the film) and explains that films are capable of this kind of phenomenon. It is both self-reference (pointing out to the audience that what they are watching is a dream) and dream itself.

Inception is not the first of Christopher Nolan's films to have a narrative and theme that can be seen as a metaphor for film viewership, being both self-reflective (they are films that say something about filmmaking) and also saying something about the way audiences relate to the phenomenon of the moving image. His 2006 film *The Prestige* was about a magician, and the ending can be seen as a commentary on the moving image: films are like magic tricks; this film is a magic trick.[18]

Films like *Inception* and a growing host of television dramas and comedies make use of self-reference, complicated plot, and intelligent camerawork to give audiences the opportunity to think as well as to be entertained. At times when a moving-image story gives insight into the human condition, it gives a vision that is not a reality but a vision of a deeper reality. When that vision also tells the audience what they are watching is not reality, it gives the audience a totem: a way to remind us that this was all taking place in our heads. *Inception* seems to say that what happens in our heads is also very important and can have important effects on what happens in the "real" physical world around us. In that sense, the film also means that moving images are important, powerful, and potentially transformative for good or ill.

TOTEMS

Self-reference is one totem that indicates, yes, this is a program or a movie we are watching, not real life. There are many other things that act as reminders of this difference, potential totems that help viewers note the difference between the dream world of moving image and reality. In fact, anything that reminds us that the moving-image story we are watching is something produced and performed can act as a totem to help us navigate between reality and imagination. While there is something real about all moving-image stories—people do say those words and do those things—the ideas presented are real, and the impact those stories have can be deep and lasting. Totems, however, will help us put those characteristics that make it seem real in perspective, reminding us that what we are watching is a just a story. Perhaps a powerful, important, wonderful, or terrible story, but a story nonetheless.

The opening and closing titles of any film or television show are one type of totem. Each time audiences recognize that the moving image is something produced and performed, they are reminded of the inherent falsity all movies and shows contain. Someone is telling this story. In fact, it took a whole lot of people and the efforts of production companies, manufacturers, unions, associations, and distribution arms to bring this moving-image story to viewers. There are also actors: people who assume a persona in order to tell a story or entertain. Leonardo DiCaprio assumes the name "Cobb" to play a character. He will change what he wears, how he styles his hair, perhaps the way he talks, and so on, in order to become that character in the story. But after DiCaprio has finished shooting his scene, people will stop calling him "Cobb" and start calling him Mr. DiCaprio or Leo again.[19] Telling the story by playing a character is something the actor or actress experienced, but under the guise of performance. It is the actor's or actress's life only insofar as it is a job they did and a role they took on.

Performers also serve as totems when we see them outside of character. Appearances on talk shows, awards shows, screenings, and in other media (such as interviews in magazines) feed celebrity status, but they may also remind audiences that it is the performer's job to assume different identities. Outtakes, gag reels, cameos, and any way in which characters make a kind of curtain call (acknowledging the "show" is over) help the audience separate actor from character.

When an actress or actor takes a role that break them out of their "type," this can also act as a totem, reminding us that the performer's character is not their character. Since the point of classical-style filmmaking and naturalistic acting is to make audiences believe in the characters and invest in the story, this can be a hard line for audiences to walk. It is fraught with potential identity misunderstandings and actor/character expectations. However, nothing may cure our potential misunderstanding that Norm from *Cheers* is a "real guy" (since we can be his friend on Facebook—"Norm Peterson," the fictional character, actually has at least two Facebook pages) more than seeing the real George Wendt, the actor who played Norm, appearing as Santa Claus in a Broadway production of *Elf: The Musical*, as he did in 2010. Norm would not do Broadway, but Norm is only a role. George Wendt would, and did, do a Broadway show.

Anything that becomes wholly implausible for the given situation or seems to be an obvious ploy for ratings, advertisers, or ticket sales can also act as a totem. These kinds of ploys in television shows are called "jumping the shark."[20] Whenever a film or a show tries too hard, audiences are no longer willing to enter into the agreement they all make with dramatic narratives. Why suspend disbelief when they will neither be moved nor entertained? The conscious choice to dismiss a program or movie because of its implausibility is a reminder of the artifice of all moving pictures. We recall that what each moving picture wants is our attention. In fact, the people who made the picture are working extremely hard to keep our attention. Remembering this, we come back to reality and reorient our relationship with the moving image once again, keeping our perspective about its place in our consciousness.

Artifice is a totem. Heavy art direction—costumes, makeup, location, scenery, and set dressings (say, in the films of Wes Anderson or television shows like *Deadwood*, *Mad Men*, or *American Horror Story*)—can also remind us that this is a fantastic, heightened world and therefore an imaginary one. Sometimes the things that become implausible, with obvious totems, become the more enjoyable because they are freed from the constraint of reality and therefore able to communicate the truth of an experience or of a feeling. In an introduction to his own stab at a Hollywood musical, *New York, New York*, filmmaker Martin Scorsese talks about understanding that artifice does not necessarily negate truth.

> The films that I saw in the late 40s and throughout the 50s coming from Hollywood had the stamp of the Hollywood studio on it . . . the sets themselves, the obvious sets. Sometimes the sets were painted. You could see the background. You could say, "Oh, that's a painting. It's not real." The street curbs that were supposed to be a New York street. The street curbs are too high. The extras were too well dressed somehow. It didn't look like the city I knew. But we understood it to be a different reality. A parallel universe, in a way, to the reality I knew in the streets or at home and that sort of thing. That doesn't mean that the films are any less true. . . . There was something else going on emotionally in these films that were [*sic*] very true to the human condition.[21]

When we approach films and programs with the understanding that what we are watching is not real life but can still tell us something true, we have control over how moving images change our perceptions. We keep our totems close at hand and give more credence to our own experience than to what happens on a screen. Our expectations for reality are no longer to make it match what we see in movies and on television. We know those things are false, and we appreciate them for the truth their stories can tell us anyway. We see they, like R2-D2, are not "alive," merely mechanical reproductions, manipulated and using live people, but wholly constructed and inert without technology. The things that fall into the uncanny valley—too like-life, yet not alive—will require our diligent use of totems and keeping our own consciousness in check. Otherwise we may blur the line between moving-image fiction and reality, because all moving images are to some degree fictional, and yet all can contain something that is true.

When we lose track of the difference, our expectations for both become widely skewed, leading to an unhealthy dependence upon moving images to sustain our emotional desires and a loss of investment in the physical world around us when it does not meet our expectations for life to work out just as it did in our favorite movies and shows. However, when we practice intentional separation of the real physical world around us and the dream worlds films and television inhabit in our imaginations, we will gain appreciation for each of them, understanding their proper roles in our lives. We will live in our "real worlds," and like Cobb in *Inception*, bring the truths we discover in the dream world back to our immediate present, letting our moving-image dreams become assets to our daily lives, not replacements for them.

NOTES

1. Annette Insdorf, *Imaginary Witness, Hollywood and the Holocaust*, DVD, directed by Daniel Anker (New York: Koch Lorber Films, 2009).

2. Rebecca Onion, "A Peek Inside the Mother-Daughter Collaboration That Brought Us the *Little House* Series," Slate.com, April 21, 2014, accessed November 6, 2014, http://www.slate.com/blogs/the_vault/2014/04/21/rose_wilder_lane_laura_in galls_wilder_a_letter_from_their_editorial_collaboration.html.

3. David Thomson, *The Big Screen* (New York: Farrar, Straus, and Giroux, 2012), 12.

4. See Sean O'Keefe, "Aviator" *Confessions of a Cinephile* (blog), June 9, 2013, http://seanaokeefe.wordpress.com/tag/martin-scorsese/.

5. Pablo Picasso, quoted in Alfred H. Barr Jr, *Picasso: Fifty Years of His Art* (New York: Arno Press, 1980).

6. Bruce Feiler, *Walking the Bible: A Journey by Land through the Five Books of Moses*, DVD (Boston: WGBH Boston Video, 2006).

7. David Rupel, "How Reality TV Works," The Writers Guild of America, accessed November 6, 2014, http://www.wga.org/organizesub.aspx?id=1091.

8. Neil Postman, *Amusing Ourselves to Death: Public Discourse in the Age of Show Business* (New York: Penguin Books, 1985), 87.

9. The term "documentary" would be coined a few years later, however.

10. Clive Thompson, "Almost Human: How R2-D2 Became the Most Beloved Robot in the Galaxy," *Smithsonian* 45, no. 2 (May 2014): 68.

11. There are bizarre exceptions like *Mr. Ed* or *Air Bud*, both of which somehow avoid the uncanny valley, although they may skirt close to being creepy for some audiences.

12. Gypsee Yo, "*Dallas* and Democracy," *Snap Judgment*, produced by Jamie DeWolf and Stephanie Foo, accessed October 3, 2013, http://snapjudgment.org/dallas-and-democracy.

13. Ibid.

14. Ibid.

15. The 1982 film *Blade Runner* is a commentary on this entire idea.

16. Peter Wollen, "Godard and Counter Cinema, *Vent d'Est*," in *Film Theory and Criticism: Introductory Readings*, eds. Leo Braudy and Marshall Cohen, 5th ed. (New York: Oxford University Press, 1998).

17. In the film we learn that Mal was convinced she was still in the dream world when she was in reality.

18. A magic trick has three parts, Cutter (Michael Caine) says in *The Prestige*. The first is the pledge, in which the magician shows the audience an ordinary object. The second part is called the turn, when the magician makes the object vanish. The third part of the trick is the prestige, when the vanished object returns. Through a complex plot, one supposed magician is revealed to actually be a twin whose brother dies. As Borden (Christian Bale), the remaining twin, returns to his daughter, the film plays out the third part of the trick, the return of the vanished object, the prestige.

19. When performers themselves have a hard time navigating the line between who they are and who they played on television or in a movie (take, for instance, the

lives of Desi Arnaz Jr., Heath Ledger, or the entire film *Birdman*), they prove the need for the acknowledgment that totems like opening titles should bring: she was acting. That was a role.

20. The phrase comes from a now well-known episode of *Happy Days* in which main character Fonzi (Henry Winkler) does a water-ski jump over a shark, still wearing his trademark leather jacket. The stunt was so obviously a stunt, with no real relevance to any plotline and no real dramatic tension since the situation and the genre/mood of the show meant there was nothing emotionally at stake, that it had the opposite of its intended effect, alienating viewers instead of enticing them.

21. Martin Scorsese, introduction, *New York, New York*, DVD, directed by Martin Scorsese (Beverly Hills, CA: MGM Home Entertainment, 2004).

CHAPTER 9

PUTTING IT INTO PRACTICE

Visual literacy is the acquisition of the skills necessary to understand both the explicit and implicit messages and ideologies in moving-image media. An easy list of questions and prompts can help viewers embark on a close watching of films and television programs. This list is organized by first asking questions that help audiences assess what the story is about, who the main characters are, what they value, what the program values, and how camera work can help those elements be determined. As those elements are established, viewers can begin to ask the questions that help delineate protagonist and antagonist, further assessing what qualities those characters embody and how that contributes to the overall theme of the story. The next set of questions then gives viewers insight by helping them determine how and why certain symbols might be used, and whether there are significant metaphors or symbolic sequences/narratives in the story that also contribute to the theme and ideology of the story.

Once those questions have been asked, viewers can begin to assess the story for its redemptive value. Again, this is subjective in many ways, and there are many arguments as to what constitutes a redemptive or worthwhile story, but there are some story elements, story forms, and thematic ideas that can aid viewers who are trying to assess a story's redemptive potential. Lastly, viewers can then remind themselves of the moving image's inherent difference from real life, noting specific ways in which the film or program breaks from reality. This practice will help viewers put the moving-image story and experience in perspective. The end goal is for viewers to be able to practice better habits of media viewing by becoming more informed, conscientious, and appreciative viewers capable of assessing moving images with insight and able to interact with them responsibly.

What follows in this chapter is a list of questions organized to help viewers walk through this process. The next chapters will put this process into practice utilizing four narrative television programs. Theoretical understanding of what visual literacy is cannot be worthwhile unless viewers practice it. This guide and the examples that follow it are a like a "remote control" that audiences can use to help them gain mastery over their habits of moving-image consumption and over the potential for ideological influence latent in all moving-image media.

Again, it should be noted that a close watching may be difficult to do during a first viewing of a program, episode, or movie. With practice, viewers will be able to pick these elements out whenever they are watching movies and television. However, especially as viewers begin to develop these skills, it may be necessary to watch each moving-image story multiple times in order to begin to answer the questions that need to be asked. In an age of streaming video and content creation, this is more easily done than ever, so audiences should have little trouble going back to find the potential answer to a question or prompt. It should become fairly easy, however, to begin to assess the story upon first viewing, since audiences are already paying attention to the plot.

ASSESSING THE STORY

The first pieces of information to get clear are the elements of the Sentence Outline. Therefore, a good place to begin is by asking the following:

- Who is the main character?

Main characters are usually dynamic, not static (meaning their character goes through a major change or development over time). If there is a name in the title of the movie, program, or episode, that character is probably very significant, if not the true main character of the story. If it is not easy to figure out, one way to find the answer is to see who has the most close-ups or who is more closely aligned with the character through POV, over-the-shoulder (OTS), or close-up shots:

- Who is most closely aligned with the camera through close proximity, POV, and OTS shots?

Next, we should determine the Major Dramatic Question by asking:

- What does the main character want or need? (There may be many answers to this question, but we are looking for the one that determines what the story is really all about.)

- What does he or she do in the end that seems to answer an important question or achieve (or not achieve) a major goal?

By delineating these elements, we can determine the Major Dramatic Question and the climax of the story where that question is answered. Eventually, viewers should be able to determine:

- What is the Major Dramatic Question?
  - How does the climax of the story answer that question?

Two more elements are needed to complete a Sentence Outline, the crisis and the theme:

- What does the main character do that leads us to believe how the Major Dramatic Question will be answered?

This question may be difficult to answer. Dwelling on it may become a distraction and should therefore be settled even if there is still some debate about what moment this truly is. However, ignoring this moment leaves out a key element in assuring what the theme of the story is.

The theme is determined by writing out the Sentence Outline and adding the word "because":

- This is the story of (main character) who wants to (major dramatic question) and after (crisis) finally (climax) because (theme).

Determining the theme is vital because it is the easiest way to distill the ideology of a story.

A Sentence Outline can help viewers determine the main character, the central plot, and the major ideologies of a story. In stories that are stand-alone (not having subsequent episodes, etc.), a Sentence Outline should be written for the main character, but it may be helpful to write one for several characters, especially if the narrative follows more than one major plot or character (like *Love, Actually, Crash, Babel,* or even perhaps *A Charlie Brown Christmas*). In episodic stories, it will be important to determine a Sentence Outline for both the specific episode being viewed as well as for the entire television series or film franchise. The most telling thematic ideologies will be determined when the entire series is assessed. It is usually affirmed and backed up by the Sentence Outlines for individual episodes.

ASSESSING THE IDEOLOGY

The main characters need to be divided into subgroups of antagonists and protagonists. By assessing them and how they are treated by the camera, viewers can further determine the story's ideological values. To determine the protagonists and antagonists, we can start by asking:

- Which characters have the most on-screen time?
- Which ones have the most close-ups and are most central in the frame of shots?
- Which characters are the most dynamic (change the most throughout the course of the story)?
- Which ones capture our attention the most?

Once a set of major players has been determined, we can begin to separate them:

- Which characters elicit the greatest sympathy?
- Which characters engender our diffidence, anger, or dislike?

Always asked in conjunction with these are the simple but important questions: Why or How? How sympathetic we are to a main character is important. The more closely we agree, want to agree, or want to side with a character, the more we perceive him or her as a protagonist. The main character of a film is usually a protagonist, but not necessarily, and there are many stories in which audiences are asked to be only partially sympathetic to the characters (again, *Thelma and Louise*, or *Breaking Bad*).

Viewers should note that putting characters into strictly divided categories of protagonists and antagonists, good guys and bad guys, is almost never clear-cut. Often, characters can be one or the other at different times or act in one way for a certain group or situation and in another way for others. Therefore, it may be more useful to do the following:

- Note each of the main characters.
- List each character's Major Dramatic Question.
- Make a list of qualities that determine whether they do or do not support the plot by assessing how they contribute to answering the overall story's Major Dramatic Question.
- Ask what qualities seem to define the character.

If clear qualities of a protagonist or antagonist appear, follow up by asking:

- What values are associated with each character?
- What do they "stand for"?

The next important step will help solidify each character's role as protagonist or antagonist and put each character in perspective relative to the others. As viewers determine each character's qualities, they should pay attention to how other characters perceive them. The best way to do this is to pay attention to reaction shots. Keeping track of reaction shots is one telltale way to determine ideology. How each character comments and re-acts to what someone else says or does, or what event takes place, will speak volumes about what that character values. Knowing whether that character is intended to be sympathetic will speak volumes about how that reaction shot is to be interpreted. If the characters often lie or judge others unfairly, their reaction shots may simply cause laughter or anger and solidify how the audience perceives them. A trustworthy character's sudden reaction to another main character's decision may clue the audience in that the decision is a good or bad one.

The list of main characters and what they value can therefore be assessed by noting whom the audience trusts the most and to whom they are most sympathetic.

- What qualities does each character possess?
- How is she or he seen and how do they see others?
- What does that say about what she or he value or stand for?

Answering those questions should reinforce the theme of the story. If it does not, a closer inspection should be made. It may be that the storytellers want the audience to be confused. Sometimes the point of the story is simply to express an idea, leaving the viewer with some kind of cognitive dissonance or just expressing that this kind of situation is complex and fraught with paradoxes.

However, in many narratives, determining the values of the main characters—both protagonists and antagonists—will be fairly clear and will give audiences a much clearer picture of what is good, worthwhile, and worthy of admiration of praise, or bad, harmful, or worthy of disdain in a moving-image narrative. This picture is the picture of the film or program's ideology.

OTHER SIGNIFICANT ELEMENTS

Before moving on from assessing what the ideologies of a moving image are to qualifying them, a few other important elements should be noted, as they may also contribute to our understanding of what a movie or program de-termines is worthwhile, important, and/or praiseworthy. By revisiting some common significant symbols, audiences can reiterate what is important and discover significant moments. Let us say, for instance, viewers are having a hard time determining the Major Dramatic Question. However, they per-ceive there is an important moment in the film or show. The music swells, there is a sweeping or quite noticeable camera movement, or something very significant seems to be happening because the camera lingers or the characters seem focused on the event. The presence of a significant symbol at this moment may help determine why it is important and how viewers can put it in perspective with the story and characters. So the first question becomes:

- What moments in the story seem most significant?
- What happens in them and who is present? (It may be helpful at this point to revisit the Sentence Outline and reassess the qualities/roles of the characters.)

Once these moments are determined, viewers should begin to assess them for their filmic qualities. The first questions concern the camera in relation to the event:

- Is the camera above or below the action?
- Does it seem to come from someone or something's point of view?
- How close is the camera to the action?
- Does it address it straight on or seem to take it in from an angle, distance, or through some other elements like a screen, leaves, objects, people, etc.?
- What is in focus? If it is only one object or portion of the frame, what is it or does it contain?
- Does the camera move? If so, how does it move in relation to the event, and with what kind of feeling (with speed, with slow grace, etc.)?
- Is there anything else in the shots or the editing that seems intentionally to draw our attention?
- What are the qualities of that action, event, or subject?

Answers to these questions lead to a larger assessment of how audiences are to perceive the event by understanding how they are meant to relate to it. We assume that the storytellers mean for us to perceive the event a certain way. If a moment seems significant, it is probably meant to be and understanding that moment's qualities says a great deal about the story as a whole.

The presence of a potent symbol in those moments can help give connotation to what the moment is meant to signify. Red, as mentioned in Chapter 6, is one such symbol. If someone is wearing red or red is an important element of their appearance (lips, fingernails, or a brooch, for instance), we can ask the following:

- Where is the symbol located?
- Is it associated with a certain character?
- What is it being used for or how is it being used?
- What is the character doing at this moment? Is this action in keeping with what we know about him or her? If not, how is it different? If so, what interaction is he or she having with other characters?

If the object in the frame seems to be a naturally occurring thing (like a stop sign, which is man-made, but appears on a street corner), we can ask the following:

- Where is the object in the frame?
- How close are we to it or has anything else important happened at that place in the frame that might somehow be related to this object?

If the object is not something that would happen to be in the frame regardless of planning, the same question should be asked and followed up with another:

- What is the nature of the object?
- How do characters use or perceive it?
- Why might it be important?

Answers to these last questions are usually very subjective but can also be extremely telling and important in understanding the story and what it stands for:

- What connotations does the symbol have culturally, in films, or in this specific film?
- What does it seem to signify or stand for?

Most of these questions can be asked about any of the important symbolic elements in a film or television program including but not limited to colors (like the most potent film color, red), mirrors, crosses, or water.

As viewers determine the potential for objects and qualities to take on metaphoric significance, they can also begin to look for shots, sequences, and moments that seem to have more than just a literal meaning for the plot. These can be hard to determine without talking about the unique elements of one story. However, general questions can be asked by once again revisiting the moments that seem the most significant and asking:

- Are the character's actions at this moment indicative of her or his general attributes or values?
- Are the character's actions at this moment and their significance somehow embodied in the setting, action itself, shot choice, editing, or other elements of the image?
- Are there cutaways or close-ups of significant objects, people, or places?

In other words, in the story's most important moments, what is happening and how does the audience see it?

Another element that can be examined to determine its metaphoric quality is the opening titles of a film or television program. In fact, when viewers try to determine the overarching theme of a movie or show, the opening titles can often be the best way to determine what the story is "really all about." It may be about many things, but the opening titles are designed to capture the essence of a filmed story and are therefore a distillation of the film or program's overall theme.

ASSESSING POTENTIAL FOR REDEMPTIVE VISION

The first way a film or television program's redemptive potential can be assessed is by comparing the overall theme and ideology to the moral code of the viewer. Again, this is subjective, since all people have cultural and personal beliefs and values. If the antagonistic character undermines the development of the protagonist by lying, cheating, and stealing, it is fairly easy to compare to a cultural and personal moral code, since dishonesty and theft are seen by most cultures as mostly negative things. Viewers can determine how their own beliefs and values compare by asking:

- What does this story say is right, good, or worthwhile?
- What does this story say is wrong, bad, or unimportant?

Comparing the answers to these questions, instead of just the film's or program's content, with one's own set of principles is a significant way to determine what is right, good, or worthwhile about a moving-image story. The content may have importance, but what is more important is what the film or program truly values.

Viewers may determine what is right or wrong by how a character changes or by a choice he or she makes. Viewers may assess the protagonist and ask:

- What does she or he do that redeems, protects, or saves another person or people?
- How does she or he restore something positive?
- How does a character whom the viewer perceives as having done something wrong—a protagonist or an antagonist making a poor or bad choice—then do something that either restores or changes his or her status as a "good guy"?
- Does anyone in the narrative find redemption, salvation, or find something that was lost?
- What is it she or he does? Why or for whom? And how does it change her or him?

After determining these things, viewers can once again compare what the film or program says is redemptive with their own set of beliefs. The film seems to say, for instance, a character finds redemption through self-sacrifice. Should the audience believe this? Does it line up with their own perceptions of what self-sacrifice is and what it entails?

From a Christian perspective, moving-images stories can be assessed for their redemptive value in a myriad of ways. Viewers can ask:

- Do the actions of the protagonists display Christ-like qualities or the fruits of the Spirit?
  - What qualities does the show value?
  - How do those values compare with the attributes of Christ and the fruits of the Spirit?
- Does the story reflect the narrative form of the biblical meta-narrative?
  - Does the story show some portion of creation, the fall, the incarnation and/or redemption?
- Does the story reflect the narrative of Christ?
- Does the story reflect the Hero's Journey meta-narrative, and can it therefore be seen as a Christ-like narrative?

Finally, viewers can assess whether the moving-image story somehow reflects something true to their experience or the human condition and therefore either has potential to cause catharsis or give voice to personal experience. Viewers can look for catharsis by asking:

- Could this story conjure up deep feelings and help audiences release them?

This, too, is very subjective and depends upon the viewer. It can also depend largely upon whom the audience for the film is and their own cultural and personal experiences. However, if viewers react empathetically, they may be able to perceive how the story could act as a catalyst for catharsis even if their own experience and reaction to the film are different. Viewers can assess this by asking:

- Is there anything about this story that is similar to their own lives or somehow embodies the way they have felt?

Personal ownership can tell us a great deal about our own experiences and perceptions, as well as the power of the narrative or the universality of the story experience. Personal ownership may come embodied in a specific character, story arc, moment, or thematic idea. As viewers assess a moving-image story, they should try to pinpoint what elements specifically resound with them or seem indicative of the story's larger themes. Again, the opening titles may be the best place to start, as they encapsulate what the story should entail and how it should be perceived.

PRACTICING DEMYSTIFICATION: TOTEMS

Distancing of the moving image from reality is vital, since it changes both our expectations for what a moving-image story can provide and for what our experience of the physical world around us can and should be. Totems remind us to put the moving-image story in perspective and neither wish it to be reality nor wish reality to be more like it. Totems can come in several forms:

- The opening titles and closing credits (which remind us the moving image is a scripted and crafted thing).
- Advertisements for the program or film (which remind us the moving-image story is a commercial product, designed to entice us and make us want to watch it).
- Interviews, award shows, and the presence of the actors in other media outlets.
- Outtakes, gag reels, cameos in other films or programs, and any other way we are reminded of the difference between actor/actress and role.
- Actors breaking type from role to role in different stories. (Seeing the actors out of character help remind viewers that they are not really doctors, astronauts, or vampires but only play them in the movies or on television.)

There is another major set of totems that further remove our perception of the moving-image story from our perception of reality. They include:

- Anything animated.
- CGI characters that do not look like any naturally occurring species.
- The presence of things implausible in the natural world.

The truth is stranger than fiction, and sometimes things that seem impossible can happen. However, when an object miraculously stays upright while floating through the air or a dog is somehow able to play team basketball, viewers are reminded that what they are watching is fiction.

When a movie or program creates circumstances that seem wholly implausible, especially in what seems an attempt to get viewer attention or raise emotional stakes that are already exhausted, the event acts as a totem, so viewers should ask:

- Is the film or program jumping the shark?

Other filmic elements can also act as totems. Viewers can assess the look of a film and ask:

- Do the costumes, scenery, and other art direction elements seem planned?
- Do the locations look like the actual places?

- Are the characters experiencing something that cannot or does happen in real life not except under very specific circumstances (for instance, characters who are members of New York gangs, but suddenly burst into song or ballet-style dance)?

Finally, viewers should ask:

- Is there anything else in this moving-image story that reminds viewers they are watching a film?
- Are there film crews or characters who work as moving-image storytellers? Is anything on a stage?

Anything that reminds viewers that what they are watching is fiction, or nonfiction storytelling and not reality, acts as a totem, reminding them of the difference between moving-image visions and real-life experiences.

FOUR EXAMPLES: PARAMETERS

In the ensuing chapters, four different television series will be examined using these guides. They have been chosen to cover a range of genres, formats, and target audiences. Before they are examined, however, some parameters will be set that will help us assess them more clearly and objectively.

All of the shows are series with multiple seasons and are dramatic narratives. One, *Top Chef*, on the cable channel Bravo, is a reality show with a cast that (other than the show's hosts) only appears in the season under discussion.

Another, *Modern Family* on ABC, is a fiction narrative shot as a mockumentary (in reality-television style). However, it follows standard sitcom format and utilizes a reoccurring cast of characters from season to season.

The remaining two series are both dramatic fiction with highly stylized looks and heavy production values. The AMC series *The Walking Dead* utilizes special effects and appeals to horror/thriller genre lovers, creating a huge following, sparking countless Internet rumors, and making use of subsequent merchandising tie-ins to add profits for the producers. *Downton Abbey* also uses high production values with period costumes, lavish sets, and meticulous props. The PBS-aired period drama is also known for dramatic plot twists, Internet spoilers, and an extremely dedicated fan base.

All the shows under discussion are available through DVD, streaming, and/or downloadable sources, and, as of this writing, all are still currently in production. Each program as a whole will be assessed and discussed, but for the purposes of this examination, the fifth episode of the third season of each will be examined more closely. This choice has been made for the sake of consistency, and because usually, by the third season the major qualities of a program have been determined and reinforced. Although each of these programs begins its season at different times, the fifth episode tends not to have to do the work of introducing or reintroducing major characters and plotlines since that far into the season, the major plot questions and major trajectories of characters have already been determined. People on the show are at this point being as true to their significant qualities as they are apt to be at any time during the season or series. In addition, the fifth episode often avoids special times (like sweeps week or holidays) that can play out a huge plot twist or invite a significant guest star in order to make a major play for viewers or have sideline major plots in order to have a special "Christmas episode."

The shows and episode five of each will be examined utilizing the guiding questions and calls for observation listed above. Examination of each of the programs will be undertaken at the beginning of the chapter, along with some context noting its cultural significance, fan reaction, and/or critical reception. The viewer's/reader's own experience of these programs and their own close watching and critical assessment may yield different results than the ensuing pages do. If so, it is good to remember that each viewer's perspective changes the perception of the show. Some things are perhaps universally true. Other things may be one way of interpreting or understanding the program, the elements, or the themes. However, the goal is to give examples of what it means to put visual literacy into practice.

CHAPTER 10

TOP CHEF: A STUDY IN GASTRONOMIC CRITICISM AND HUMAN BEHAVIOR

A staple on the contest-based reality show menu since 2006, Bravo channel's *Top Chef* blends two classic dishes: the cooking show and the contest reality show with progressive elimination.[1] The modern era of contest shows started with the personality-driven programs *The Real World* and *Survivor* that were themed to be about human interaction. But in the first decade of the 2000s, shows with the same basic preparation idea (the last contestant standing wins the prize) were given a genre-focusing main ingredient. In the case of *Top Chef* it was gourmet cooking. Now the numbers and kinds of contest-based reality shows are enough to fill the menu at any buffet.

The competitions are to see who is the best at a certain job or skill. They are somewhat like sporting contests for singing (*American Idol*), dating (*The Bachelor*), adventure travel (*The Amazing Race*), business (*The Apprentice*), screen makeup (*Faceoff*), tattooing (*Inked*), or even female impersonation (*RuPaul's DragRace*). These shows combine who is the "best" at a given profession/skill set with the same kind of personality contest of *The Real World* or *Survivor* by putting the contestants all together under difficult circumstances. If all reality television is life in a pressure cooker, contest reality shows boil down both talent and personality to a reduction of human behavior.

QUICKFIRE: EPISODE DETAILS

The format of these types of reality contest shows is fairly similar. Their different iterations have different names and different flavors, but the process is about the same. *Top Chef* starts off the season with 15 contestants. In every episode, the "cheftestants" compete in two events, a "Quickfire" event that helps the winner gain an advantage and an "Elimination Challenge" that sets up who will "win" that week and who will be asked to leave the contest. By the beginning of the fifth episode, three cheftestants have already been eliminated. The show judges narrow down the top contestants (the best dishes of the challenge) and the bottom contestants (the worst dishes); then they choose both winner and loser from there. The series ends with a finale cook-off and a winner when a "top chef" is announced.[2] For season 3, set in Miami, episode 5[3] contains a Quickfire to see who can make the best pairing between a cocktail made with Bombay Sapphire gin and an appetizer.

Other elements of the show stay true to the reality contest genre. The opening has pictures and names of all the contestants to remind the audience of the real people in the contest, and perhaps to celebrate their involvement in the show. The panel of judges contains an expert who is overtly critical (Simon Cowell on *American Idol*, Michelle Visage on *Drag Race*, and others); on *Top Chef* it is Chef Tom Colicchio. There is also a host (Ryan Seacrest, RuPaul), Padma Lakshmi, and guest judges who are different in every episode, some with more regularity than others. For episode 5, titled "Cooking by Numbers," the Quickfire judge is Bombay Gin mixologist Jamie Walker. The Elimination Challenge requires the cheftestants to create dishes served to the Chaîne de Rôtisseurs Supper Club with guest judges Ted Allen (a series regular) and Barton G. Weiss (owner of the Barton G. Restaurant in Miami where the challenge takes place).

ELIMINATION CHALLENGE: MAIN CHARACTERS

For every episode of *Top Chef,* the cheftestants are filmed throughout their day, with downtime footage used to complement the cooking. The editing can make the time spent cooking look comical, tense, rushed, or smooth depending on how it is put together. Any event that has some dramatic potential, like dishes falling or someone getting too close to someone else with a knife, is tagged so that it can be added in to heighten the drama. Then the editors use confession cam footage to accent the narrative being built and utilize voiceover to give the process a running, sports-like commentary. Suddenly even the event of waiting for water to boil can be given dramatic play-by-play.

Because producers want audiences for these kinds of contest shows to be in suspense about who will win, there is rarely a clear main character—protagonist or antagonist—especially early in the season. Season 3 of *Top Chef* does have some clearly antagonistic characters, but one of them, Hung Huynh (who will win the season) is seen as more self-interested than the others.[4] Episode 5, "Cooking by Numbers," however, sees little development of Hung's rise to the top, so, although he is a major player in the series for this episode, he is given less camera time than the others.

"Cooking by Numbers" starts off with Casey Thompson (who will be a runner-up) winning the Quickfire challenge. She is given a lot of screen time, and she and Dale Levitski (the other runner-up) have the most confession cam time. Dale and Casey are the episode's main characters. At this point in the season, there are still 12 contestants, so screen time for each character is limited and has to be distributed evenly enough so that everyone is still seen participating in the contest.[5] People who were major players in previous episodes will be marginalized due to a lack of time.

However, that is not uncommon for even dramatic fiction films and especially television programs. Focus swings from one story arc to another as plots develop over time. Likewise, in the contest show the major players will inevitably be those whose performance in a given challenge requires the most scrutiny. What is interesting is how often throughout a season the contests winners are given significant screen time even when their part in the action of a segment or episode is minimal. Even though his dish in episode 3 is not a winner, Hung still gets significant attention, and when the teaser for episode 4 plays over the end credits, the commentary is mostly Casey talking about Hung's rushed, careless behavior in the kitchen, played over footage of Hung hurrying and Casey reacting.

MAIN DISHES: SENTENCE OUTLINES

There are 12 contestants left in episode 5. Lia Bardeen, whose dish will win the Elimination Challenge of the episode, is an important character because she wins, but she does not have the most close-ups or screen time. Hung does not have the most time either, and neither of these two cheftestants has a dynamic arc in the episode. However, Casey and Dale, who remain main characters through the season finale, do go through more dramatic story arcs and are given more close-up and confession camera time than anyone else except Howie (Kleinberg) (whose personality is important in the episode and the season) and Camille (Becerra) (the cheftestant who ends up going home at the end of episode 5).

Casey and Dale are the two most likely candidates for being a main character, so a Sentence Outline for each of them can be constructed. For all of the cheftestants, the Major Dramatic Question revolves around winning the competition. The Elimination Challenge for "Cooking by Numbers" requires the cheftestants to split themselves into four groups. They will complete a tasting menu with four courses. Each team will take one course, and the course must be themed with a common ingredient. Because Casey has won the Quickfire Challenge (which story-wise serves as exposition), she has immunity. That means she cannot be sent home at the end of this episode.

The cheftestants throw numbers into a pot and draw for teams. Casey and Dale are initially on the second course with Howie. When Howie, by Dale's estimation, "comes out like a bulldog" trying to make sure the entire meal's menu progression is planned well, Dale offers to trade with someone in the fourth course in order to make that course a dessert option. "Finally," he tells the confession cam, "I'm, like, I want off this team now." He asks who has pastry experience. Sarah (Mair) says she has some, and Dale says he can "flex a great dessert."

A volunteer is needed to move over to the fish (second course) team with Casey and Howie, and Joey (Paulino) volunteers. In the previous episode, Joey and Howie had a yelling match in the Stew Room (the back room of the kitchen, where the cheftestants await the decisions of the judges), and when Joey volunteers there is a cut to a reaction shot of Casey, jaw set, shaking her head. "So now I have Howie and I have Joey in a group," Casey says. "And there's a lot of buildup here. And I know that this is going to be difficult. And I'm aggravated." Camille tells Dale she has some pastry experience and joins him and Sarah for the dessert (fourth) course. Hung then is sorted out to join the shrimp (first) course and Dale says, "We're team pastry." In a confession cam shot, Hung remarks, "Why do a dessert course when it's not required to do desserts?" Gourmet chefs do not always have baking experience, and as the episode plays out, the cheftestants' lack of expertise in this area becomes a major stumbling block for several characters.

These decisions, however, help solidify the episode's main characters and make the Major Dramatic Questions more specific. Each cheftestant has a Major Dramatic Question, and it reflects the one for the entire program. The Major Dramatic Question must be answered with a yes or no, so for each cheftestant it becomes, "Will I win the challenge?" or "Will I get sent home?" For this episode, the characters who win and lose the challenge (Lia wins the challenge; Camille is sent home) are important and given more screen time than in other episodes, but they are still not the most central characters. Again, the two given the most screen time are Casey and Dale. Since Casey has immunity and cannot be sent home, the Major Dramatic Question about her shifts. Her efforts will make a difference for her team. Howie and Joey can be difficult to work with, so Casey's question could become, "Will Casey still perform her best?" or "Will Casey's efforts affect Howie and Joey's chances of winning or losing?"

Dale's choices have already made a difference for his, Sarah's, and Camille's fates. While they mutually agreed to do a dessert course, Dale is the group's leader. So a Major Dramatic Question might be, "Will Dale's choice to do dessert lead to his losing the challenge?" As is the case with Casey, his choices may also affect others, so another Major Dramatic Question might be, "Will Dale's choice to do dessert affect someone else's performance?" Dale, Sarah, and Camille are taking a chance. And as any reality show viewer knows, that may have huge payoffs in a contest like this or may mean a rapid elimination from the show.

Casey and Dale have already made choices that will affect how the Major Dramatic Questions are answered, and their progress through the episode solidifies it. The Sentence Outline works best when it is about what the main characters do, as opposed to what happens to them. Their actions determine their character. In a contest, some of the actions are just the execution of something, in *Top Chef*'s case, a dish. So the initial choices and performance affect the climatic execution and judgment of the dish. That makes it hard to pin down a crisis moment, since the characters are simply completing tasks that have already been determined. Very rarely on a contest reality show is there a huge plot twist. In this episode, everyone completes a dish and gets it to the plate on time. So the plot is really determined by the characters' early decisions.

However, this lack of drama in the execution of the cooking means the focus will shift, as it often does, to the drama of interpersonal relationships. Therefore, Casey's and Dale's Major Dramatic Questions can shift to reflect their interpersonal actions more than their winning or losing the contest. Casey's becomes about keeping her course team together. Her pairing with the two "bad boys" of the competition could have given her ample cause for complaint. She says, "Nobody's really listening," to the confession cam. "We're just sort of aggravated that we're all having to work with each other right now." The camera cuts to Howie and Joey sitting on the balcony talking about how "a person with immunity should take a back seat." Already Casey has been quieter than normal. When she joins them, she says at one point, "I'm listening to you, but I don't know the quality of the product." Casey seems to be trying to keep her patience and make good decisions. A good chef will get torn apart for not setting a high standard, and Casey obviously cares. If she "takes a back seat" she would not be able to "stand behind her dish" (something each of the cheftestants say they do, meaning they take responsibility for how their cooking represents their professional work), immunity or not.

But in the execution of the meal, things go wrong. Joey uses more of the soy sauce than planned, and Casey's dish suffers. "In my mind," she says, "I just keep telling myself, 'You know, sometimes in a kitchen you're going to have to work with people you just don't want to work with.'" They are called to the judges' table (along with the folks from the dessert course) and asked why there was not "cohesion with the team" on the tuna course. Howie and Joey do most of the talking at first, and the judges note that Casey's dish was the weakest, but they ask why Joey and Howie did not taste it before it was served. Casey begins to tear up: "You guys [the judges] have laid such a guilt blanket that I can't really explain what I feel for these people right now, because having immunity is really not worth it if one of these people have [*sic*] to go home because my dish was the worst."

Casey's story arc for the episode is about trying to do her best, even though she finds her teammates hard to work with. When things go wrong, instead of blame shifting, she feels badly that her efforts may affect a teammate's fate. Therefore, a Sentence Outline for Casey might look like this: This is the story of Casey, who wants to make her team work together well so she can give her best performance, and after making a poorly received tuna tartare finally tells the judges she does not like having immunity if it means her mistakes will send someone else home because being a team leader means taking ownership of the group's mistakes.

Dale makes the choice to lead a dessert course, and his decision is motivated by not wanting to work with Howie. His team works well together interpersonally but falters in the challenge. None of the dishes from him, Sarah, or Camille are well received by the judges, and Camille's pineapple upside down cake is deemed the worst dish of the night, which sends her home. To the confession cam, Dale says, "I feel incredibly guilty. I feel that it's my fault that Camille is going home." Dale was the dessert team leader, and even though Camille made her own choices in crafting her dish, Dale still feels responsible. Therefore, his Sentence Outline might read: This is the story of Dale, who wants to work with more agreeable people than Howie, and after poorly executing a dessert course feels guilty when one of his teammates is sent home because being a team leader means taking ownership of the team's mistakes.

Although the plotlines are different, the themes of the characters are the same. This episode is about group dynamics, leadership decisions, and ownership of problems. Therefore, what Casey and Dale do, and how they react to the outcomes of their choices, reflect the episode's ideology: A good chef takes ownership of leadership decisions.

SEASONING: PROTAGONISTS AND ANTAGONISTS

Casey and Dale are the episode's clear protagonists, and this is in keeping with the roles they will play throughout the season. Editing and shot choice mean they are sometimes seen in more or less favorable ways,[6] but consistently throughout the program, these two gain audience sympathy. That culminates in Casey being named audience favorite. As the season continues after episode 5, both Casey and Dale will be given more screen time, and their reaction shots will be used more often. Their choices in this episode earn audience trust and sympathy, and this is utilized by producers throughout the season.

The protagonists' qualities are very clear: Casey and Dale both do well in the Quickfire, demonstrating competence. Casey wins, demonstrating her ability to finely execute a dish. Both of these chefs are capable of creating dishes the judges love. They are also team players who care about their teammates. Both agonize that their individual choices and performances may have an adverse effect on others. This demonstrates humility, care for others, and compassion. Casey and Dale are also leaders, and in their roles as such, they take responsibility for their actions. They both share the qualities of being competent, responsible, team leaders who care about the well-being of others.

Dale avoids being in the group with Howie, but Casey remains, even when the addition of Joey makes her group even more volatile. Perhaps this means that Casey is more patient or perhaps more stubborn. The program does not seem to indicate whether staying in the group with Howie or leaving would be better, so one choice does not seem to be valued more than the other. Dale's choice to leave could be seen as a choice to keep peace or as cowardice. Again, a judgment call is not made by the program concerning Dale's choice. (There are no real discussions or reaction shots to set against these decisions.) Instead, the poor choice seems to be Dale's insistence on sticking with a dessert menu when no one on the team is truly confident. They do say they are all capable, though, so perhaps Dale is justified in giving it a try.

Both Casey and Dale remain likable, and their reaction shots throughout the challenge indicate their intention to remain confident under circumstance they both see as less than ideal. Casey and Dale are seen as faithful professionals, capable of working under stressful, heightened conditions. *Top Chef* prizes those qualities above all others, so this adds to their likeability and audience investment.

Since all of the cheftestants have the potential to win and are working toward that end, all of them are protagonists.[7] They are furthering the plot to win a contest. However, in certain circumstances, one or more characters may function as antagonists. Our main characters are Casey and Dale who want to make their groups function well so they can win. However, when Dale leaves the second course group, he pits Casey against two potential antagonists: Howie and Joey.

Howie and Joey are hotheaded personalities. Their more emotional words and actions are the stuff reality shows feed on, so they are going to be given screen time. Since Casey's Major Dramatic Question is about keeping her group together, the bulldog-like qualities of Howie and the sometimes clashing personalities of Howie and Joey make them Casey's antagonists. Their attitude toward Casey (that since she has immunity, she should let them make the decisions), their insistence upon her involvement[8], and then mistakes in the kitchen (like Joey using too much soy sauce, and neither one tasting Casey's dish before it was served) do not help the group effort. Since Casey's objective is to make the group work, these actions are antagonistic.

The qualities associated with those antagonistic actions are rashness, stubbornness, insistence upon having one's own way, selfishness, and self-centeredness. They are in direct contrast to the qualities Casey exhibits that make her sympathetic. As the show continues, Howie at least will earn more audience sympathy. But for now, the producers help paint him as an antagonist by highlighting the actions that exhibit these qualities and comparing them to Casey's.

At this point it is important to remember that since producers are looking for the elements of story within footage being shot (not a planned script), character perception is being crafted in order to make certain cheftestants into more or less sympathetic characters. However, their qualities are in keeping with audience appeal. A good chef takes ownership of his or her decisions and exhibits the qualities of competency, responsibility, team leadership, caring for others, and, above all, faithful professionalism and excellence within the contest's structured challenges. A bad chef, or at least a worse chef, is careless of the effect his or her work has on others, insists on having his or her own way, does not plan well in working with others, and does not take ownership of group efforts. Antagonists may play by the rules, just like the protagonists, and they may execute excellent dishes, but as is the case with Howie and Joey in episode 5, they do not exhibit high levels of professionalism.

FLAVOR ESSENCE: CONSUMERISM AND COMMERCIALISM

Top Chef's ideology is about what makes the best chef, but that seems to be only partly about taste, palate, and actual cookery. While the winner of the show may have made the best food most consistently, the audience favorite, Casey, is the one who most lives up to the ideology the show's plot seems to uphold. There is, however, something else to note. While the actions of the characters indicate worthwhile personal characteristics, the overall theme of the program still values consumerism and is still supported by commercial sponsorship.

By their nature, contestant reality shows like *Top Chef* do not necessarily show the most talented or moral people. They show likable winners. The chefs on *Top Chef* are hard to qualify as the "best in the country" because the best chefs may not be competing, and because the show purposely puts the chefs into heightened situations with a strict time limit, forcing them to compete with a handicap that does not necessarily make them better or worse. *Top Chef* turns cooking—a specific kind of cooking—into a sporting event, except it is not just a race to see who is fastest or makes the best food (already a subjective parameter). It is a race to see who is fastest, looks nicest, and plays well with others, while cooking with what feels like one hand tied behind their back.

Cooking shows have been around for a long time. Julia Childs may have popularized gourmet cooking for Middle America, but *Top Chef* revels in its gastronomic self-importance. It can be safely assumed that only in a society as privileged as modern America can we celebrate fine dining so much that we turn it into a dramatic event. *Top Chef* spends lots of money to make food that only a few people eat, glamorizes overpriced dining, and rewards contestants with huge sums. This is not a show about how to feed starving populations or give Americans below the poverty line access to healthier options; it is about celebrating who makes the best fancy beef entrée or shrimp hors d'oeuvre. St. Paul comments on those whose "God is their stomach" and says their "end is destruction."[9] *Top Chef* celebrates consumption. It celebrates feeding the belly with indulgent things. In its fundamental subject matter, it cannot help but promote indulgence.

Added to that is the overtly critical nature of the show. This is not just a show about how to make a fancy dish; it is a drama about who makes the worst minute errors. Suddenly over-smoked potatoes or mediocre steaks, the kind available at any good restaurant, become life-changing issues, and chefs who are actually good at what they do are made to look like failures because of the contest's parameters and the editing for reaction. Criticism can make professionals better at their craft, and most of the chefs on the show admit that. Being "refined in the fire" is a very Christian idea, and it promotes humility.

At the same time, however, for gourmet kitchen plebeians who have no right to judge, the show makes very talented people look stupid. We, the audience, become judges too, and most of us have little competency to do so. Are audiences celebrating these great chefs or belittling them? Casey loses in the finale of season 3, but Chef Tom tells her, "I know a lot of chefs who can cook on the fly, can cook very quickly, and I know a lot of chefs who are very methodical. Doesn't mean that one method is better than the other, it's just some people are just wired that way. . . . I have no doubt that if you were to take all those dishes back to your restaurant and work on them they would all be spectacular." A nice sentiment, but in the contest she is still a loser. There is only one winner for the grand prize, and being a great chef and a likable person does not matter. This is a contest, so winning matters the most.

The errors made by the cheftestants have no dramatic stakes outside of the contest, and therefore, their emotional weight seems constructed. The drama seems forced. Outside of a television series, for most food consumers, being served a dish that is a good concept but has some bad execution is not a threatening problem; it is not even really an inconvenience. So what if the flavors are not quite balanced, or if a dish does not follow the exact recipe for eggs Florentine? When put up against the world's serious problems, *Top Chef*'s drama is inane. It is silly. We are excited, scared, upset, and angry over who made the best dish we cannot pronounce and may never eat. The American middle class may be growing in affluence, but McDonald's is still serving hamburgers. Sous vide duck with mushrooms ragout and truffle sauce[10] is not in most Betty Crocker cookbooks, and for Americans trying to pay off credit card debt and refinancing home loans, visiting a restaurant that serves it is probably at best a rare experience.

That being said, the show is relatively benign. There are certainly worse things to think about than gourmet cuisine, and in episode 5 at least, the relational aspects of the show do favor those with attributes in keeping with the fruits of the Spirit. Casey and Dale both exhibit selflessness, as both speak out about their guilt at potentially sending another contestant home. They are compassionate and show humility. Also, there is potential to read Casey's actions as sacrificial, expressing a desire to make sure she is the one to blame for her actions.

Beyond celebrating consumerism,[11] *Top Chef* does try to celebrate excellence in performance, even if the construction of its contest parameters is more about entertainment value than actual chef skills. The program is perhaps a way for those who cannot cook gourmet food to still have a "taste" of it or to gain an appreciation for it as an art form. In that sense, the show democratizes gourmet cooking, making it accessible to even those on a limited budget (as long as they have cable). That kind of democratization does celebrate what is good, pure, and excellent in the culinary arts.

CONTEST TAKEAWAYS: TOTEMS

The totems of the reality show are different from those in narrative fiction films and programs. The viewer is not lost in the story but is caught up in the "real life" drama of the situation. That drama is manipulative, however, and the lesson to learn is that perception is not reality, and drama can be manufactured in the editing room. The chefs on the show really are chefs and they really are cooking. These cheftestants are not "actors," and therefore we do not see them out of character. But as any introvert or talk show host can explain, there is a version of every person that is an on-display persona. Editors catch on to this and utilize cheftestant performance/reaction by cutting and "frankenbiting"[12] different phrases to color audience perception of character. Chef Tom notes, "The camera adds ten pounds of b*tch." What he means is that the words a character says and the things he or she does can be constructed to showcase that person at their worst. In fact, showing people at their worst makes for much better television, or at least more exciting television, and reality series highlight people's bad behavior.

Everyone acts for the camera. Therefore, whenever we see a contestant out of the context of the show—in person somewhere, on a talk show, or in his or her own cookbook or restaurant—we see a different version of them and can compare that to what was constructed by the editors of the show. Every time audiences become aware that the filming of the show crafted our view of that cheftestant's personality, that awareness leads to demystification.

Perhaps the best totems of shows like these are the extra features on the DVDs, especially the reunion shows. Reunion episodes, talk show appearances, cookbooks, and autobiographies are totems that bring us back to real life. In the reunion episodes of *Top Chef* the season's contestants revisit and rehash what happened on the show. We see them out of the context of a contest. When we watch the contestants (and judges) reacting to the "show," we see that it really is a performance, both by them and by the editors. The mystery is gone when we see the ingredients deconstructed.

Top Chef and other reality shows change our perceptions of the people on them and also change our perception of their roles and vocations. The circumstances under which these top chefs work need to be kept in mind. *Top Chef* is not really like life in a gourmet kitchen. It is a contest, with heightened circumstances (talk of too many cooks in a kitchen!) and a different set of expectations (very critical judges, time, budget, and personnel constraints). Without any experience of life in a real gourmet kitchen, audiences may lose perspective on what that kind of cooking is really like. So a totem could be any other experience that gives viewers a "second story" about what life in a gourmet kitchen really entails.

Also, by depicting in dramatic detail the minute tasks of a working chef's life, shows like *Top Chef* may turn the viewer's own life into a contest. If viewers begin to think or see life the way the program does, any action during the day becomes something to be critiqued and deconstructed. The style of voiceover over B roll can inhabit viewer daily life: "I was about to take those socks out of the dryer and suddenly I notice, hey, no one's emptied the lint trap." Dramatic close-up of lint trap full of fluff. Musical stinger. The show uses cutting, reaction shots, and music to make minute criticisms of the everyday activities of professionals. It dramatizes cooking. Imaginative viewers, or anyone who watches the shows long enough, may start dramatizing their own activities. They may see their world the way the show sees cooking. Audiences may begin to think like the shows they watch. With the right production crew, an event as ordinary as cleaning the bathroom could be a reality show contest, and in that mind-set, viewers may begin to see their own lives with contest potential. Noting the construction of voiceover, confession cam, reaction shots, and B roll will in that case act as a totem, as viewers recognize that the contests' modes of delivery are what cause the dramatic tension. Real experience of everyday tasks can therefore act as a totem when we remember that with a little production magic, even they could be constructed into dramatic television content.

Critical viewers should be alert to the obvious constructions and over-dramatizations of reality television. Our totems are seeing the construction and the contrast between reality show and real reality. Any opportunity we have to see the difference between real life and life on the screen will help us remember that one is our daily existence, the gift of being alive, and the other is a program: shot, edited, and made palatable to a wide audience of consumers.

Top Chef utilizes the tools of realty television construction to celebrate both consumerism and the culinary arts. It also, like all reality television series, is a study in human behavior. The contest itself is a platform to showcase interpersonal relations as people act out under heightened circumstances and as their best and worst moments are crafted into a narrative. *Top Chef* uses the ingredients of human behavior, culinary arts, and production, editing, and commercial sponsorship techniques, and blends them together into a dish of heightened dramatic narrative that can help us understand people better. For critical viewers, it also has the potential to help us understand the power of editing and the way in which reality contests can change the way we perceive our own daily reality.

NOTES

1. Bravo's other super hit, *Project Runway*, is the same kind of contest show but is about fashion instead of food; it is in a sense the same preparation but with a different main ingredient.

2. And wins a cash prize. In season 3 it is donated by the Glad Corporation Family of Products.

3. *Top Chef*, season 3 episode 5 "Cooking by Numbers," Amazon Streaming Video, Tom Colicchio and Padma Lakshmi, performers, (2007, Bravo Media, viewed November 2014).

4. In the introductory episode Hung says he has been called a "CPA: certified public *sshole."

5. This is especially important since viewers still do not know who the winner will be or who may act out some kind of dramatic scenario in a later episode.

6. This happens to all the characters on a reality show and is crafted by the show's producers to help keep audiences invested. Hung is perceived as self-interested

and potentially dangerous. Near the end of the season, his backstory will be given more screen time, making him a more sympathetic character, so audiences can rejoice when he wins the season.

7. If all of the cheftestants are on some level protagonists, then Padma and Chef Tom are antagonists since they thwart all but one cheftestant's efforts to win the contest. There is a way to read the show that gives Chef Tom more of an antagonist role. It does not seem to be his nature, however, but rather his role as critic and judge that causes him to be critical of the cheftestants and at times seem "mean" as he judges the execution of their work.

8. At one point they insist on her joining them for group discussion, interrupting her in the middle of eating a sandwich. She says she will come out when she is done, then appears walking onto the balcony to sit with them, still holding food in a napkin in her hand.

9. Phil 3:19, NIV.

10. Hung's winning dish in the finale.

11. This show promotes consumerism in many ways. Season 3 is sponsored by the Glad Corporation Family of Products (like plastic-wraps and food containers), and the contestants are escorted around in Toyota RAV4s, something the show highlights by zooming in to a close-up of the Glad lid being placed on a container, or the Toyota RAV4 decal on the back door of the vehicle as a contestant is shutting it. Product placement is all over the show, overtly expressed in close-ups and zooms to product labels.

12. "Frankenbiting" is the process of a choosing what phrases people say and cutting those words into a situational context in order to showcase a character's nature or highlight an emotion. In "Cooking by Numbers" Casey's confession cam comment—"Joey starts taking it personally, as if Colicchio were attacking him. Like he was insecure about the dish he was going to make"—is followed immediately by a frankenbite "[beep]" and B roll of Joey saying, "Whatever. I'll [beep] go home," before returning to Casey's next comment, "sort of angry and cussing, which is a waste of time."

CHAPTER 11

MODERN FAMILY: NOT NORMAL IS THE NEW NORMAL

When the ABC sitcom *Modern Family* premiered in the fall of 2009, *New York Times* reviewer Ginia Bellafante called it the "best new half-hour of funny television." She said what made the show significant was that it brought back a genre that had been out of favor since *Murphy Brown*: the family sitcom. "The workplace had become the new household, the cubicle the new bedroom and young careerist upstarts the precocious toddlers of the urban nursery."[1] The return of the family sitcom required a socially relevant twist, though.

Taking nods from shows like *Arrested Development, Modern Family* is an updated look at the contemporary, or modern, idea of what constitutes a family. There is a dad, Jay Pritchett (Ed O'Neil), and his two adult children, Claire (Julie Bowen) and Mitchell (Jesse Tyler Ferguson). Jay is remarried to a much younger woman, Gloria (Sofia Vergara), who has a son of her own, Manny (Rico Rodriguez). Claire is married to Phil Dunphy (Ty Burrell) and they have three children: Haley (Sarah Hyland), Alex (Ariel Winter), and Luke (Nolan Gould). Mitchell is in a committed relationship with Cameron, "Cam" (Eric Stonestreet), and they have an adopted daughter, Lily (Aubrey Anderson-Emmons).[2] The three generations of Pritchetts and Dunphys (and one Tucker, Cameron) have the same kinds of relationship issues that all families have. The parents want the children to grow into responsible adults and be safe; the children want freedom with encouragement from their parents.

The twist in the premise of *Modern Family* is foregrounded: this is an extended, not-quite-traditional-but-maybe-just-as-traditional-as-any family. Therefore, the show uses the same kinds of plots that have been around since other famous family sitcoms like *The Cosby Show* or *I Love Lucy*. However,

Modern Family puts a unique spin on these standard family plots, often trying to highlight more contemporary views on subjects (or one could say
"modern views" even though they are really more postmodern and actually
rather conservative). This is accented by hinting at what Bellafante says has
been the other block to family sitcoms: reality television is effective not only
"because of its prevalence but also because its commitments to unchecked
domestic lunacy render the entertainment value of mere dysfunction, the
family sitcom's lifeblood, obsolete."[3]

The effect of reality television style and its "unchecked lunacy" may
also explain two other traits that mark the series: it is shot mockumentary
style with lots of cutaways to on-camera confessionals, and it sparkles with
quick-witted dialogue. If other "modern family" shows on television include
Here Comes Honey Boo Boo and *Family Guy*, what separates *Modern Family*
is how much more it looks like real life (hence, reality / mockumentary
style) than those extreme portrayals of family life. However, it still contains
well-written one-liners, malapropisms (Phil is famous for them), and other
entertainment elements that showcase its obvious fiction.

For all its new twists on old ideas, *Modern Family* sticks fairly close to
a lot of conservative notions about the home. Jay and Gloria, and Phil and
Claire, are married and work to make their marriages last. At the beginning
of the series, both Gloria and Claire are stay-at-home moms; Mitch and Cam
are committed to each other.[4] The show therefore promotes monogamous
relationships.[5] The larger family consists of three nuclear families, which,
despite some not-so-traditional characteristics, are two parents and their
children or child. The main topics of the show are child–parent relations,
sibling relations, children growing up, working parents trying to tend their
families, Mom's gift for Dad for Christmas, and so on, all with a quirky twist.
Will Dad learn how to walk a tight rope? Will the blood-related practical
Pritchetts win the bet, or will the related-by-marriage-to-the-Pritchett-fam-
ily dreamers actually get a pumpkin to fly the length of a football field?[6]
These are situational plots just like Cliff Huxtable having to hold a funeral
for a fish or Lucy dressing like Carmen Miranda. Despite the "modern" twist,
Modern Family is still about preserving the family and loving each other.
"Perhaps that's why," says Bruce Feiler in the *New York Times*, "a study last
year listed *Modern Family* as the third-most popular show among Republi-
cans. In its fundamentally conservative vision, *Modern Family* turns out to be
not so modern after all."[7]

FOCUSING ON THE FAMILY: MAIN CHARACTERS

Because it foregrounds family, *Modern Family* is decidedly an ensemble piece.
While each episode may feature more prominent roles or dynamic character

development for different family members, screen time for characters is divided more equally than on other types of programs. The "A" plot of the program entails overlapping storylines that will also continue into other episodes. In season 3, episode 5, titled "Hit and Run," Claire decides to challenge longtime town councilman Duane Bailey (David Cross) and run for a council seat.[8] Phil tries to prove to Claire he can handle more of the parenting duties if she decides to run for office and accidentally gives Luke a black eye and gives Alex nighttime allergy medicine, so she is drugged and sleeps through the group family dinner. Haley tries to beg $900 from her siblings to pay off some fake IDs that never materialized. Mitch and Cam discuss when someone should take an aggressive stand against an aggressor (be they guys who take children to violent movies or hit-and-run drivers). Jay tries to keep an account with the son of a client who has taken over his dad's company, and Gloria tries to get anyone, especially Jay or Manny, to take her advice. All of these plots overlap and in some way comment on each other.

In order to try to pin down the ideology of *Modern Family* by finding the themes in "Hit and Run," viewers can follow the most prominent story arc(s) and the most dynamic character(s) for the episode. On many well-written programs, following almost any story arc will support the themes of the main one, as writers often try to make them related. This is true of "Hit and Run," so if a viewer discovers the most prominent arc and compares it to the others, common themes will be found.

The episode has two pre-opening sequences. The one that begins the episode finds Claire and Phil headed through the parking lot to the local grocery. On the way in, Claire spots Duane, the council member who turned down her petition for a new stop sign at a dangerous intersection. Duane is canvassing for votes in the upcoming election.

Claire:	Oh, don't look. There's that jerk, Duane Bailey.
Phil:	Aw, yuck.
Claire:	I should say something to him, shouldn't I?
Phil:	I gotta be honest. I was just working off your tone. Who is Duane Bailey and why do I hate him?
Claire:	Honey, he's that guy, that councilman who shot down my stop sign, the big phoney.
Phil:	Yeah. . . .

Claire is the first person to speak and is the most active member of the family in the scene. This scene is more about her than Phil. It also immediately pits her against a known antagonist from another episode, Duane. This is reinforced by the dialogue with Phil that reminds the audience who Duane is and that he is an antagonist.

The next sequence sees Mitch and Cam having an altercation with another man in a movie theater when Cam thinks the man is taking children to see a violent movie. This proves to be a misunderstanding, as Mitch and Cam were actually in a different theater than the one they thought, and this theater happens to be screening *The Muppet Movie*, not a violent thriller. Later in the episode, Mitch and Cam will be rear-ended (hence the episode's title) and disagree over whether or not to chase the assailant, just as they argued in the theater over whether Cam should confront the other man or not. Mitchell avoids confrontation; Cam finds it necessary. Their plot will prove to be a subplot, but it serves a purpose and solidifies a theme.

Claire's plot with Duane, however, will prove to be the episode's most dominant one, and she will be the most dynamic main character. Aiding it are Jay's plot to win over the new client and Gloria's to get people to listen to her advice. The theme for each of them will be about depending upon their family. This is the underlying theme of many, if not most, family sitcom episodes and is most often at play in *Modern Family*.

FAMILY ASSETS: SENTENCE OUTLINES

Claire's Sentence Outline revolves around her deciding to join the race for town council. She makes the decision to do so, and that is her dynamic action through the episode. Sentence Outlines for other members of the family will help inform Claire's and, again, solidify the common themes.

After seeing Duane in the parking lot, Claire and Phil come home and discuss the meeting while putting the groceries away. When Claire laments that "ridiculous people" like Duane end up in office, Phil suggests that she run. Claire pauses and considers. She says she "would be lying if I said I'd never considered it," but she wonders how things will work at home. She is a stay-at-home mom. Phil tries to assure her he can handle more of the parenting duties and attempts to do so when she later goes to the city offices to pick up the necessary forms to enter the town council race.

When Claire runs into Duane at the office building, he tells her he has won six straight elections, so she should not "quit her lack of a day job." When she tries to retort, Claire is interrupted by a phone call that informs her that Haley has lost $900 to a man who is supposed to be providing her and her friends with fake IDs. Claire tells Duane she is not a bored housewife, Later at the family dinner she confronts Haley about the money and sees Luke's eye and Alex nearly passed out from her allergy medicine on a couch. How can she run for office when her absence means the family falls apart? "I take my eye off the ball for one minute, and I've got one in a coma, one with a black eye, and one running a crime ring."[9] Claire's Major Dramatic Question seems at first to have something to do with her being able to run for town council and still be a mom.

After Jay, Phil, Mitch, and Cam leave to go confront the man who took Haley's money, Claire and Gloria talk as they make cupcakes in the kitchen. Throughout the episode, Gloria has been trying to get anyone, especially Jay or Manny, to take her advice, so she actively tries to get Claire to open up. When Claire asked Phil why Luke's face was bruised or why Alex was nearly passed out and Phil gave her a false answer, Claire simply re-asked the question and then Phil capitulated. In the kitchen, Gloria tries the same thing. "Why are you not running for office?" she asks Claire. "Because my family needs me; you saw what just happened in there." Gloria repeats the question. "That doesn't work with me," Claire responds, but Gloria overpowers her, yelling the question a third time and Claire responds, "Because I don't want to lose!" The truth is out. Claire's obstacle in answering her Major Dramatic Question (will Claire run for town council?) is not her family needing her; it is the thought of trying to do something outside the home but failing. Claire does not want to be a failure. Gloria responds by telling a ridiculous story about a beauty pageant loser, making the point that the important thing is to try.

In spite of her obvious differences in culture, style, and approach to family situations, Gloria (who is Colombian-American and much younger than Jay) is still an important part of the family. This is significant for a couple of reasons. First, her presence and importance in this scene supports the notion that family helps each other overcome life's obstacles. Second, her presence as someone with obvious differences gives her a different kind of insight. Those two themes underlie all of the plots on *Modern Family*: family helps each other over life's difficulties, and the unique differences of each family member are their assets. What makes them different makes them stronger as a family.

Claire's conversation with Gloria is pivotal. When the men return with Haley's money (thanks to Mitchell, who stayed by the car and was therefore able to tackle the kid who took Haley's money when he tried to run away), Gloria announces that Claire has decided to run for office.[10] The Major Dramatic Question is answered, and the main plot of the show is resolved. Therefore, Claire's sentence outline might look like this: This is the story of Claire who wants to run for town council and after admitting her fear of failure to Gloria finally decides to join the race because admitting one's fears helps overcome them, or because family can help someone overcome fears.

Claire's story through the season will be about her starting a new venture outside the home. However, this episode is mainly about her making the decision to do that. Her character development happens because of interactions with the family. Since all of the other family members also have arcs that support themes of overcoming fear (Mitchell confronting an antagonist) or seeing family as an asset, Claire's theme is part of an overall ideology that is very much about the importance and role of family in personal development.

Even Jay's story arc supports this. Jay wants to keep a client, and the new executive is the former executive's son. Jay has a hard time relating to the "kid" who wants the designed closets to be "wow!" but uses no concrete language to tell Jay what that means. When Jay comes home from work, Gloria tries to get him to talk about his day. She wants to feel important and contribute to the family by giving good advice. Manny does not want her advice with his schoolwork, and now Jay does not know what to do about his client. Manny blames the client's reaction on the "Beiberization of America," which Gloria explains in broken English: when the beavers, "build the dams all over the country so there's no floods, is the beaver-ization of the Americas." Manny replies to his mother and stepfather, "I'm finding there's less and less we can talk about," and leaves the room. Gloria cannot seem to help, and Jay is still at a loss as to how to win over his client. After the men return and Claire's new candidacy is announced, Gloria asserts she is very helpful and asks Manny and Jay why they do not want her advice and help more. Claire encourages her father, "Dad, you should listen to her. She might really help you." She then whispers, "She could be an asset." The episode ends with Gloria presenting the young client with Jay's promotional closet specs and the young client staring at Gloria's low-cut dress, saying, "Wow!" Jay responds to the confession cam, "Same exact closet." Gloria is an asset. She gets the truth out of Claire and helps Jay's business, even if it is by using her sex appeal. This reinforces the theme of family helping each other, and what makes each one unique is what makes each of them an asset.

A Sentence Outline could be written for each character in the episode, since all have their own plotlines. However, the same themes would arise, solidifying the basic ideology. Feiler's comment that the "modern" family is still traditional and has a "fundamentally conservative vision" becomes clearer when the underlying ideologies are made plain.

BAD GUYS BREED PUGGLES: PROTAGONISTS AND ANTAGONISTS

If there is a primary protagonist for *Modern Family*, it is the entire Pritchett-Dunphy-Tucker clan. Each of the main characters on the show gets prominent screen time, close-ups, and plotlines. In fact, *Modern Family*, more than some other family sitcoms, does not align itself primarily with either the children or the parents but with each character in turn. The mockumentary style means each character has moments of one-on-one with the audience. (In this episode, Luke gets a sidebar in which he reveals that he has saved over $1,000, but it is "not exactly liquid"—because he has frozen it in a block of ice.) Because of this, character traits give way to family traits to encompass what the program asserts are worthwhile values embodied in its protagonists. There are "family characteristics" that the show decidedly promotes: (1) family supports and helps each other as each member develops or faces obstacles, and (2) differences between members are potential assets. The program also promotes other traits exhibited by the family as a whole.

If the family is the protagonist, antagonists will be anything or anybody that threatens the family's ability to function. This could include certain people who thwart the growth of family members or forces from within and without that lead to conflict. For Claire, the main character of "Hit and Run," there is a decidedly antagonistic character who represents to a certain extent qualities that *Modern Family* deems bad or wrong. That person is "puggle-breeding"[11] town council member Duane Bailey.

At the city offices, Claire stops at the receptionist's desk for directions. Duane walks by, complimenting the receptionist in a playful manner by saying, "Beyoncé, when did you start working here?" He then introduces himself as someone running for office to Claire. "You've got to be kidding me," she says. "You saw me in the parking lot two hours ago." Duane may compliment others, but he does not compliment Claire. He makes fun of her, mocking her in the parking lot scene. Not only is Duane unkind, he is not even genuine. He does not remember her when he sees her again. He introduces himself and moves to shake her hand, announcing he is running for reelection. When he realizes who she is, he withdraws his hand and his countenance changes. He was being kind only to get her vote. He may therefore only be complimenting the receptionist to flatter her and win her vote.

On the way to the elevator Duane asks, "Do you know why I breed puggles?" Puggles are a metaphor for his character. "It's because they're lovable, but they're also tenacious hunters who won't quit until the kill is complete." Duane appears lovable. He smiles and shakes hands. He bats his eyes and laughs. These things may win over Phil, who earlier started to laugh at a joke Duane made about Canada before Claire cut him off, but Claire is not taken in by him. Duane wants to appear harmless, but when he meets an opponent, he is vicious. "Look, lady," he tells Claire, "you're going down." Moments later, after Claire has repeatedly pushed the button to call the elevator (so she can go to the fourth floor and retrieve the necessary paperwork to join the council race), Duane explains that the car is not coming because this is a staff elevator. "Here," he says, holding out his ID card to swipe it, "allow me to. . . ." He then withdraws his hand and the card and finishes, "not get that for you." He walks away, calling, "Have a nice day!" over his shoulder as Claire stares off in frustration.

Duane is mean and deceptive. He focuses on appearances more than on true qualities. Those characteristics are decidedly bad and are in conflict with the program's overall ideology. Duane is selfish and he demeans Claire's role as a stay-at-home mom, as well as her desire for a stop sign in the neighborhood.

Duane represents political bureaucracy, focusing on campaigning instead of the issue that directly affects the Dunphy family (the stop sign); he is pretentious and false, and when meeting opposition, he becomes extremely aggressive. Duane is a politician. Therefore, his place as an antagonist and his politician-like qualities mean *Modern Family* does not value pretension, condescension, aggression, or political maneuvering for personal gain.

Duane does have one characteristic that the show values: humor. Duane is clever. However, humor seems to be a means for him and not an end. Humor has the potential for gaining power or attention: whoever is being funny gets the camera's notice. Duane is funny, but he uses his cleverness for personal gain and to belittle others. Therefore he "belongs" on the show, since he speaks the same clever language. His humor does not make him a protagonist; it makes him able to communicate with others in the comic sitcom world. He is a "bad guy" because he is an aggressive bureaucrat who belittles Claire.

FAMILY VALUES: REDEMPTIVE POTENTIAL

The Pritchett-Dunphy-Tuckers are a decidedly mixed family, with members from different ethnic backgrounds and cultures. Jay and Gloria have a wide age gap, and Mitch and Cam are a gay couple with an adopted daughter. There is also a mix of types. Haley is "flirty," more interested in boys and parties than her younger sister Alex, the academic overachiever. Luke, the youngest sibling of the Dunphy family, seems clueless at times but proves to be more clever than he lets on (as is the case with his saving money). Manny is a young renaissance man, more interested in art and culture than watching football with Jay. The family is more than a mix of backgrounds and experiences; it is a mix of personality types and cultures. Therefore, one trait of this family is accepting their differences and valuing different personal experiences and traits. The family shares the trait of valuing diversity and acceptance.

The family also values honesty and responsibility. Claire demands to know what really happened to Luke and Alex and why Haley lost $900. Mitch and Cam tell Lily they are not fighting, then admit to fighting to the rest of the family. Lily also catches them in their fib about not seeing *The Muppet Movie* without her. (They stayed for two of the musical numbers but only admit it when she finds out.) Lying is bad. Trust requires honesty. Claire is also truly concerned about Phil taking on more parenting duties. There is a prominent shot of her reacting when Haley tries to escape punishment by saying that "disappointing my family and friends is punishment enough," and Phil responds, "Nice try. You're grounded for two weeks." Claire's smile indicates her acknowledgement of Phil taking responsibility as a parent and punishing

Haley for her behavior. Viewers undoubtedly—and rightly—should weigh what "responsible parenting" means on the program, but the show clearly esteems what is required of a responsible parent, even if the definition of "responsible" is up for discussion.

Claire and Phil, and in fact all the parents on the show, make mistakes in their parenting just as the children make life mistakes and the couples and siblings make relationship mistakes. Everyone in the family has to ask for forgiveness at some point, and everyone has to forgive someone. Therefore, the show also values forgiveness and reconciliation as fundamental to human relationships. *Modern Family* clearly values family members sharing personal things with each other and caring for each other. It highly values familial love.

It also highly values humor. As a sitcom, one of the major appeals of *Modern Family* is its comic situations and fast-paced, witty dialogue. Even the younger children make quick rejoinders and say precociously clever things. (Lily and Luke do this as much as any of the children, and they are the youngest until Joe is born.) The Pritchett-Dunphy-Tuckers value intelligence and wit. They all engage in clever dialogue and congratulate each other on saying or doing witty things. Phil says unintentionally awkward things all the time but in an attempt to be clever. In "Hit and Run" he tells Claire, "If you want to fly I don't want to be the one to hold your feet to the ground. I want to be the one to push you off the cliff." At the end of the episode when Claire says Gloria might be an "asset" to Jay, Phil repeats the word as he stands by Luke. Luke notices the word "asset" and emphasizes the first syllable to note how much it sounds like a cuss word. Both chuckle and Luke comments, "Heard it." Cleverness is valued, even by the children. And potentially infantile humor is valued by the adults. This is a family that values humor and wit, even when certain family members fail at being funny or witty. As mentioned with Duane, however, humor is the language *Modern Family* uses. Being clever gains attention; it means one is a part of the conversation. That means it is a highly valued characteristic by the characters on the show and its potential audience who watch it in order to be entertained. *Modern Family* preaches humor as a value to its choir of viewers who tune in because of the comic script.

Viewers may not agree with the singular actions or behaviors of certain characters, but the wide Republican audience for the show is explained when the fundamental values of the show become apparent. The show does promote "family values," and they are more conservative in principle than the show's family itself may be politically. Viewers should make their own decisions regarding whether those values are "redemptive" and overcome anything potentially objective about the characters' values, choices, or lifestyles. However, the idea that the show promotes familial love, forgiveness, honesty,

and acceptance does at least in some measure line up with values fundamental to the Christian tradition. There are no large themes of self-sacrifice and
no Hero's Journey plot. There may be catharsis through humor for a viewer
facing family struggles or, in the case of this episode, afraid to try a career/
opportunity outside the home for the first time. There may also be ownership of the story for those who relate to the family's differences, humor, and
interactions.

IN THE ACTION: FORMAL ELEMENTS AND SYMBOLS

Modern Family is a scripted, fictional narrative, but it is filmed in the style
of a documentary, just as the sitcoms *The Office* and *Parks and Recreation*
are. That means the camera is often handheld, swinging around to "catch"
action or reaction. The camera is supposed to be a direct cinema-style "fly on
the wall" that goes unnoticed by the characters who are the subjects of the
story. The other element taken from documentaries and reality shows is the
use of the confession cam as characters "break the fourth wall"[12] and directly
address the camera, usually only singularly or in pairs, to distill important
information or insight.

Placing a handheld camera in the midst of the family's everyday life puts
the viewer among them. Documentary-style shooting puts the audience in
the same space as the actors because the camera is in that space. This is very
different than theatrical styles where the events in the camera frame could
just as well be taking place on a stage. Often on *Modern Family* the cameras
are placed in the middle of the action, zooming between close-up and medium shot. There is shot-reverse-shot editing, meaning either that the scene
is filmed multiple times or that more than one camera is used. (With the
show's budget and extemporaneous nature, one can assume it is filmed with
multiple cameras.) The cameras do not usually travel; they just pan, tilt, and
zoom to reframe the subjects. Most of the time the cameras are moving. The
shots are kept in almost perpetual motion, so what the audience notices is
usually a significant stop by the camera or in the action. These formal elements heighten the show's quick-witted dialogue and the general mood of
perpetual motion life in the twenty-first century.

The subtle camera work makes viewers used to the motion, however, and
sets up a special relationship making them a part of the family as they sit
comfortably and observe the hilarity. Viewers have no need to go looking for
the joke; the camera will find it. However, they are told almost constantly
to be active listeners, since many subtle verbal jokes are not presented in
a way to make them sound like punch lines, and there is no laugh track.
These formal elements make the show more "realistic," since the there is no
live studio audience (which makes viewers acknowledge the presence of an

audience). The use of real locations for exteriors and realistic interiors also adds to the feeling that the audience is simply watching a reality show about a real family.

There does not seem to be a larger metaphor in this approach, but it does support the themes of family and being a part of a group. Everyone is accepted in the Pritchett-Dunphy-Tucker family, even the audience who dwells in their midst (or this film crew, which seems to be ever-present in their lives but is never acknowledged).

In "Hit and Run" there is at least one potent symbol worth noting. When Claire and Phil first run into Duane out campaigning, Duane points out that he loves puggles because "they are a different mix of breeds, just like America." He then makes a coy, lovable face, and slyly points to the American flag pin on the lapel of his vest. American flags are potent symbols themselves, but the flag pin has become a symbol of politics that pander to conservative America. The flag pin is an attempt by politicians to align themselves with "American values," and Duane is doing just that. The pin reinforces his identity as a bureaucrat.

FRAMES WITHIN FRAMES: TOTEMS

Modern Family follows standard sitcom format, and, as one would expect, it uses the general television totems in clever ways. The opening titles are literally frames. While having the names of actors and production team members flash at the bottom of the screen frame, the last image of the opening scene is minimized and put into a frame as the camera zooms out to reveal the Dunphy family standing posed and holding a picture frame. Then the same action is repeated with each family in their own picture frame as a family portrait, ending on a full group portrait where the picture frame is flipped over to reveal a title card for the show. If one of the techniques of visual self-reflexivity is to let the viewer know where the frame is—therefore calling attention to the camerawork—*Modern Family* cleverly lets the audience know that the entire show is a composed picture of a family.

Another totem is seeing the cast outside of their roles on the show. Any full cast appearance at an awards show or on late night television breaks the spell that the actors are the characters. Sofia Vergara may be Colombian and have a thick accent, but she is not really married to Ed O'Neil. And most tellingly perhaps, Eric Stonestreet (who plays the very gay Cameron) is straight. The actors are acting.

Another potential in-show totem is the mockumentary-style camera setup, which acknowledges that the actions of the family are being filmed. The camera's presence in the middle of situations is actually very much like the standard shot coverage used in most motion picture narratives. The confession cam breaks the fourth wall and acknowledges that the show is being filmed. However, it does so in the style of a reality television program, making the show still look like a potentially real family. Although there is self-reference, it only furthers the idea that the Pritchett-Dunphy-Tuckers are just like real people, or potentially are real people rather than fictional characters.

Modern Family is realistic enough to fall into the uncanny valley and be confused with real life. As a narrative, it certainly heightens reality, exaggerating characters and situations for comic effect. However, it rarely jumps the shark, and while the family is certainly quirky and the situations rare, they are never completely implausible. Therefore, the opening titles and any acknowledgement that *Modern Family* is a fictional television show are very important.

Whether one appreciates the humor or agrees with the values of *Modern Family*, viewers should still use caution in assessing the family, their behaviors and values, and the situational plots as "normal." *Modern Family* is a good example of the funhouse mirror. When audiences acknowledge its intention purely to entertain, they can put into perspective its ideology and values. *Modern Family* showcases "not normal" as the new normal. However, it is a fictional television program: a clever, entertaining show with potentially redeeming values about family. It offers a portrait of American family life, but it offers it as something that helps us laugh at our own foibles. The characters on the show make mistakes and have to overcome them to function as a family. That is the ideology the show truly promotes. As such, and not as a definitive picture of what an American family is or ought to be in outward characteristics, *Modern Family* is a fictional "lie" that reveals a deeper truth about what family really means, a "true" picture of family.

NOTES

1. Ginia Bellafante, "'I'm the Cool Dad' and Other Debatable Dispatches from the Home Front," *The New York Times*, September 22, 2009, Web, accessed November 7, 2013, http://www.nytimes.com/2009/09/23/arts/television/23modern. html?_r=0.

2. Eventually, Jay's and Gloria's characters will also have a son, Joe, whose full name is Fulgencio Joseph Pritchett (uncredited in season 4, Pierce Wallace in season 5).

3. Bellafonte, "'I'm the Cool Dad.'"

4. Mitch and Cam get married in season 5, a timely plot choice as it follows the 2012 Supreme Court ruling against California's Defense of Marriage Act.

5. It also portrays a gay couple that has moved on from the nightclub scene to raising a family. The show's appeal resets both of these things: monogamous gay couple and family-centered gay couple as cultural norms. This means on some level they are already normal enough to be accepted, but also acceptable enough to become

more normal. The show both reflects and promotes the idea of a gay couple raising a family.

6. Both plots appear in season 5 of the show.

7. Bruce Feiler, "What 'Modern Family' Says about Modern Families," *The New York Times*, January 21, 2011, Web, accessed December 18 2014, http://www.nytimes.com/2011/01/23/fashion/23THISLIFE.html?pagewanted=all&_r=0/.

8. *Modern Family*, season 3 episode 5 "Hit and Run," DVD, directed by Jason Winer, (2011, Twentieth Century Fox, 2012).

9. Gloria responds to Claire by pointing out that technically Haley was "running a crime ring" while Claire's "eye was still on the ball."

10. Gloria announces Claire is running for "mayor," but Claire corrects her.

11. A puggle is a half-pug, half beagle.

12. Breaking the fourth wall means acknowledging the audience. In theater, breaking the fourth wall means turning and looking at or speaking to the audience. In film and television, it means looking at or speaking to the camera.

Chapter 12

The Walking Dead:
Perspectives on Undeath

After *The Walking Dead* premiered in 2010 on the AMC network, *The Washington Post*'s review included a sidebar that describes "Why zombies cast a spell over America" by calling a fictional apocalypse "the great social do-over. Unlike nuclear war or alien annihilation scenarios, a zombie epidemic leaves the world intact while offering the scant survivors a chance to reboot and reorder civilization. Of course, this never ends well."[1]

The dramatic television series is about a group of survivors trying to find a way to live after an epidemic renders most of humanity mindless, consuming corpses. They "reboot" the world, and, as the new start to humanity, they showcase physical, emotional, and moral struggles that will determine the values of a new civilization. The question for viewers is: will this end well? Will the social do-over instill hope in humanity or despair?

The show has won awards and attracted huge audiences. In fact, *The Walking Dead* is part of a rash of zombie narratives that have found great popularity and success in contemporary visual storytelling. Perhaps this fascination comes from some collective cultural mindset. In the review itself, columnist Hank Stuever connects the social dots of our fascination: "So much of our collective culture feels zombified," he notes. "Just look around at all the zombies. Everywhere. Mobs lined up outside the Apple Store, groaning with desire to devour Steve Jobs's *braiiiin* [italics original]."[2] Contemporary Americans are mindless consumers. We are the zombies. Robert Kirkman's 2005 graphic novel on which the show is based understands itself as social commentary on this issue and solidifies Stuever's point. Mindless consumerism is a modern plague. Kirkman is intentionally making a statement about

American consumerism. The back cover of his graphic novel contains a leading paragraph that reads:

> How many hours are in a day when you don't spend half of them watch-
> ing television? When is the last time any of us REALLY worked to get
> something that we wanted? How long has it been since any of us really
> NEEDED something that we WANTED? [emphasis original][3]

Social commentary metaphors have been around for a long time and can
develop as society changes. Vampires have represented different threats to
humanity at different times, so their iteration has changed depending on
the social evils they represent. Likewise, in the 1950s, which saw both communism and nuclear war as great threats, narratives developed about giant
lizards (*Godzilla*) or giant radioactive ants (*Them!*) to help audiences by giving them tangible evils. The zombie is a modern-day tangible evil. Mindless
consumption, brainless inactivity, and needs that feast off others are plagues
on our civilization.

However, the problem with making the zombie apocalypse into a television series is that after the end of the world there are only so many plotlines
to be had, which might explain why the first season of *The Walking Dead*
is largely regarded as the best. The award-winning AMC series has high
production values and a fascinating premise, but cherry-picking the source
material (Kirkman's best-selling graphic novels) rendered some of the subsequent plotlines as lifeless as a twice-killed corpse. The strength of the show
rests in its premise and the two major issues both the graphic novel and the
television show wrestle with: How does one survive the zombie apocalypse
emotionally and physically, and what is the cost of consumption? For all
its gore and emotional pitching, *The Walking Dead* does ask some excellent
questions.

The premise of the novels and the show is the basic zombie apocalypse:
an unnamed epidemic has caused millions of people to turn into reanimated,
flesh-eating corpses. The government had told people to go to cities for safety,
but since the zombification was caused by a contagion, more people only
meant more rampant sickness and an uncontrolled outbreak. Some strag-
glers, including a policeman, Rick Grimes (Andrew Lincoln), who woke up
from a gunshot-induced coma and went in search of his family, have banned
together to try to survive.

The general rules of the zombie genre apply, with some show specifics.
The undead are mindless, flesh-eating entities, whose bites cause victims to
turn into zombies too. They can only be killed with a blow to the head, so
destroying a zombie's non-brain preserves the other person's brain, so to
speak. On *The Walking Dead*, zombies eat all flesh, not only brains, and any

corpse will reanimate unless its brain is destroyed. In other words, everyone has the disease, and dying only makes a person undead until killed the second time.

The beginning of season 3, episode 5, titled "Say the Word," starts off with the show's main character, Rick Grimes, reeling from the death of his wife Lori (Sarah Wayne Callies) at the end of the previous episode.[4] Rick is the acting leader of the group he found, which included his missing family, his untrustworthy best friend (who met his demise in season 2), and some others who have joined along the way. They are holed up in a prison.

One of the original group, Andrea (Laurie Holden), who had to be left behind during season 2's finale escape, has survived, and she and her katana-bearing friend Michonne (Danai Gurira) have made their way to the bunkered town of Woodbury. Woodbury is run by a man known as the Governor (David Morrissey). In "Say the Word," Michonne's distrust of the Governor grows to the point that she leaves the town. Andrea does not see a reason to leave, so she and Michonne part on bad terms.

In the episode before this, Lori had died while giving birth during an attack by a "walker" (as zombies are called by Rick's group). That attack also caused the death of group member T-Dog (Iron E. Singleton) and the supposed death of Carol (Melissa McBride). Rick and Lori's son Carl (Chandler Riggs) is left caring for the baby (named Judith). At the beginning of the episode, in the first scene after the opening titles, Rick stands in shock as Carl holds the baby for the group to see. Then, he grabs an ax and runs back into the prison compound buildings. The baby needs formula, so Maggie (Lauren Cohan) and Daryl (Norman Reedus) go out of the compound to look for some, as Glen (Steven Yeun), Beth (Emily Kinney), Carl, the baby, and Herschel (Scott Wilson) stay behind.

FOLLOWING THE LEADERS: MAIN CHARACTERS

In both the graphic novel and the television series, the main character of *The Walking Dead* is Rick. Although he is the central protagonist and "hero," the ensemble nature of the program and the premise of the show, which requires its protagonist to struggle to survive in more ways than one, mean screen time and sympathy are shared by a handful of major characters. The protagonist group is composed of the survivors that the audience is rooting for. Rick is their leader, however, and even though he has only a few scenes in "Say the Word," they are key ones in his overall character trajectory.

Lori's death was a significant event. She had been a main character in the drama for the past two seasons, and Rick's relationship with his wife had been a big part of both the show's plot and his character development. Her death raises a vital question about Rick. Now, faced with the death of his wife, will Rick remain human? Will he even remain sane? Throughout the series, Rick and the others are trying to regain a sense of safety and normalcy, but they are constantly in crisis mode, fighting for survival against the never-ending attacks of the undead. No place is safe. How can they survive physically? And because of the brutality and moral questions they face, how can they remain human?

While Rick is the series protagonist, "Say the Word" gives significant screen time to another character, whose importance in the protagonist group has been growing and will continue to do so as the show progresses. Michonne first makes an appearance in the finale of season 2. When season 3 picks up, she has teamed up with Andrea as they navigate through the area on their own. Michonne is a loner and a survivor, who seems less in crisis mode than most of the others because she seems more capable of surviving in the post-apocalyptic world. When Andrea finds her, Michonne is leading two walkers whose arms and lower jaws have been cut off. She leads them on chains, like guard dogs, and will not talk about who the bodies were when they were first alive. (They are, of course, significant people in Michonne's life before the apocalypse, something audiences will find out later.) Michonne is both capable and awe-inspiring. She seems to be holding her own, not running pell-mell from one crisis to another.

In "Say the Word," Michonne becomes more trustworthy than Andrea. Andrea's judgment had always been a little suspect,[5] and even though Michonne is a relatively new character, the camera work and storytelling clearly mark her as a protagonist. She has significant close-ups and point-of-view shots, as well as several important "hero" shots (dramatic low-angle and, at one point, a high-angle shot where she stands surrounded by dead walkers and flicks the blood of the last zombie victim off her sword). Michonne is also dressed as a protagonist, in a leather vest and dreadlocks, carrying her samurai-like katana on her back after she takes it back from its confiscated location in the Governor's apartment. Michonne is like an action figure and looks like a force to be reckoned with. The camera treats her like one, too, giving her lots of reaction shots. There are plenty of them in "Say the Word," and they work well to establish Michonne's trustworthiness. She observes the Governor, whom the audience knows is hiding things, and talks frankly only to Andrea. In fact, she does not talk much at all. Her conversations with the Governor are terse, and she does not really speak to anyone else except Andrea.

Michonne also takes a look around the Governor's apartment after recovering her sword and discovers a notebook with names, including the name "Penny" written more boldly than the others and followed by pages of hash marks. Michonne later confronts the Governor about this. She has figured out he is keeping zombies around for some reason. One of those zombies is a little girl. Michonne sees the picture of the Governor with a wife and small girl. Penny (Kylie Szymanski) is the Governor's daughter. Michonne has discovered he is keeping her, in hope (the audience will later find out) of somehow finding an antidote and bringing her back to life.

Therefore, Michonne is someone who finds and tells the truth. In "Say the Word" she does both of those things and gains audience trust. Michonne will prove to be right in not trusting the Governor, so her instincts as well as her actions in this episode become significant when the Governor later lays siege to the prison compound where Rick's group is living. By that time, Michonne will have joined Rick's group and is clearly on the protagonist group side as they face the Governor's forces. Michonne is insightful and trustworthy, and she wants the truth. Those are her qualities as a protagonist. (She is also a protector and fearless fighter, both of which are assets in the world of zombie survival.) The camera work tells the audience she is a main character in this episode, and the plotline solidifies it.

SURVIVAL OF THE SOUL: SENTENCE OUTLINES

Throughout the series, Rick is fighting for physical survival, but that is a metaphor for the real dramatic arc of the show: Rick's most important fight is to regain and then retain his humanity. As the episode begins, Rick stands in shock. A wide-angle shot outside the prison puts the camera close to Rick's face and distorts the world around him. The shot then pans from a close-up to a POV, racking focus from foreground to background, as Rick sees an ax on the ground. Suddenly, he picks up the ax and goes screaming through the prison hallways, slashing at zombies we do not see because they are behind the camera. Rick's rage is blind. In his fight to deal with Lori's death he takes out his rage on anything in his way. The camera does not turn around to see where he is going or whom he is fighting. Viewers do not see that because Rick really does not see it either. Eventually he finds the boiler room where Lori died and the bullet that killed her. He sees a trail of blood leading off down a hallway and finds the zombie that has devoured her corpse. He nearly slashes the zombie open but cannot bring himself to do it, and instead just stabs the bloated stomach over and over.

At the end of the episode, the phone in the boiler room rings. Rick slowly picks up the receiver and "says the word," his first in the episode and his first since Lori's death, a scratchy "Hello?" What viewers will learn in the next episode is that Rick's subconscious decides to deal with Lori's death by letting him talk to her on the phone. His hello is answered at the beginning of the next episode with Lori's voice in response. In talking to her, he will somehow regain his sanity and his will to live, as well as his capacity to care for both Carl and Judith. Rick did not get to say goodbye to Lori, so he plays out a scenario in which Lori can talk to him from beyond death and help him take care of his son, accept his new daughter, and go on without her.

Therefore, Rick's Major Dramatic Question is about staying human. Externally, it is about physical survival for himself and his group; internally, it is about retaining his humanity, which includes his capacity to care for others. A Sentence Outline for Rick that extends to plot points that are outside "Say the Word" might read: This is the story of Rick, who wants to remain human and, after saying goodbye to his wife, finally is able to love his children because love is what makes us human. In "Say the Word" Rick takes an important step toward being able to say goodbye to his wife, so an episode-specific Sentence Outline might read: This is the story of Rick, who wants to be able to take care of his son and daughter, and, after stabbing the stomach of the zombie that ate his wife's body, finally picks up the phone and through his imagined conversation says goodbye to his wife because grieving for loved ones is part of the healing necessary in order to be able to love.

In both cases, the theme is about human emotion more than physical survival. Lori dies but retains her humanity. She comes back as a voice on the phone in Rick's subconscious. She is the only character on the series whose spirit (instead of body) somehow comes back to life instead of reanimating as a corpse. Rick is fighting to survive, but physical survival is really secondary to emotional survival. What *The Walking Dead* promotes is the idea that real humanity lies in our capacity to connect with others in love. Rick's storyline is about just that.

Michonne's Sentence Outline likewise reflects something about true survival, including emotional life. What happens in "Say the Word" is that she must choose between her own survival instincts and her friendship with Andrea. Michonne cannot stay in Woodbury because she knows it is a dangerous place. But Andrea, her friend and partner, stays.[6] After the Governor's men catch Michonne, he confronts her. Then the Governor talks to Andrea, continuing to convince her that he and the men who help him run the town "are not barbarians." Andrea comes back to her room with Michonne. "We need to talk," she says, and Michonne responds, "We need to leave." Michonne argues that the walls that protect the town also contain some evil and keep people trapped. Andrea argues that they are safe here, and, after eight months on the run fighting for survival, Woodbury offers them a sense of a normal life. Andrea does not see the danger, and she does not want to leave. "You need to trust me," Michonne says. "And you need to give me more to go on," Andrea answers. Michonne does not give specifics but tells her, "This place is not what they say it is."

We see nothing more of their conversation, but in their next scene both Andrea and Michonne are walking toward the front gate of Woodbury, large doors that connect to a barricade that surrounds the town, making it very literally a gated community. They approach the gate, but the Governor's henchman Merle (Michael Rooker) stops them. The two women argue again about whether they are "allowed" to leave and whether they should. Merle allows them to leave, which seems like a victory to Andrea, but Michonne is suspicious. The two argue again. Michonne wants freedom; she is suspicious of the Governor. Andrea is afraid Michonne is "gonna disappear" and wants the security of staying. Michonne asks if she will come or stay. Andrea rejects the ultimatum, finally urging Michonne to stay nonverbally by indicating with her head to go back. Michonne walks around her to leave through the gate, muttering, "You just slowed me down, anyway."

Michonne is often cold, her face betraying little emotion. But it is clear she cares about Andrea. Perhaps Michonne's cool demeanor belies an exterior she wears to protect herself emotionally in the brutal world she is trying to survive. Andrea is someone who Michonne could trust, but since Andrea refuses to trust her and come with her, the link between them is broken. A Sentence Outline for Michonne's external physical struggle might read: This is the story of Michonne, who wants to survive by not being trapped, and, after being unable to convince Andrea to go with her, finally leaves Woodbury by herself because she travels fastest when she travels alone. Survival is of utmost importance, and Michonne knows she cannot emotionally survive in the false, pretentious (and patriarchal) Woodbury. Since she is finding out secrets about the Governor, Michonne's physical survival is also in question. It means leaving Andrea and losing a human relationship, but Michonne chooses to leave because she believes it is the only way to survive.

It is important to note she does not force Andrea to come with her. She tries to persuade her through reason, evidence, and relational trust. However, if Andrea will not go, Michonne is not going to force her, since freedom is also something Michonne highly values and one reason she cannot stay in Woodbury. If Michonne's Major Dramatic Question is really about freedom and trust, a Sentence Outline for her story in "Say the Word" might read: This is the story of Michonne, who wants to remain human, and, after asking Andrea to trust her but is rejected, finally rejects Andrea and leaves because freedom is vital for remaining human.

Rick needs to connect with people in order to retain his emotional humanity. Michonne has to break a relationship in order to retain her personal autonomy, which is vital to her humanity. Both of these main characters are fighting to remain physically and emotionally "alive" in a world where fighting death is arm-to-arm combat fraught with moral pitfalls. Rick has had to kill in order to help others live, shutting down his feelings in order to focus on survival. Now, he fights to be able to feel anything, so he can grieve his wife and take care of his children. Michonne has had to be alone in order to survive. Now she must reject the only real human connection she has so as to remain physically alive and be free of another's control. These themes are indicative of the predominant ideologies of *The Walking Dead*: the struggle to survive both physically and emotionally, themes that use language and ideas that indicate the struggle is also moral and spiritual. *The Walking Dead* is about what makes people human, and what happens when loving people becomes a morally contentious battle.

BRUTALITY VERSUS HUMANITY: PROTAGONISTS AND ANTAGONISTS

If Rick and Michonne are the protagonists of "Say the Word," the clear antagonist is the Governor. In the episode's pre-title sequence, we see him brushing the hair of a young girl, who is revealed to be his now zombified daughter (the Penny in the notebook). The Governor is a man of secrets and lies, putting on a party for the townspeople, even though his scientist lackey Milton (Dallas Roberts) thinks they should shut down the generators and save power so he can work further on his experiments in "curing" zombies. What the Governor wants is to fool people into trusting him and to bring the reanimated dead back to full life. He, like Rick, is dealing with loss. Like Michonne, he truly trusts no one but himself.

The clear difference between the Governor and both Rick and Michonne is that he uses underhanded tactics—lies, false fronts, telling the townspeople they are safe, even though he keeps walkers penned up inside the city gates—for selfish gains. He is not really concerned about anyone else but himself. He even keeps Penny alive in her reanimated state, trying to hang on to her. This, in contrast to how Carl and Maggie deal with Lori's death (killing her corpse after she dies in childbirth), proves to be an ultimately selfish move. The Governor will not let Penny go. He keeps her alive for his own sake. "Keeping" his daughter does not heighten his capacity to love others, because it is motivated by selfish desire. It is not best for Penny to exist as a monster. Carl and Maggie know this, and they therefore do not allow Lori's corpse to become a zombie. Keeping the dead alive is selfish, as it does them no good.

The Governor is also controlling, unwilling to let anyone work outside his authority. Michonne will not stand for this. She sees he is not genuine and sees his selfish behavior toward his daughter's zombie corpse. Michonne values truth and freedom; the Governor, secrecy, lies, and control. The ideology of *The Walking Dead* shines through in the comparison: the values that make us human include our capacity to love selflessly and sacrificially and the freedom to make our own choices.

At the end of "Say the Word," the Governor escorts Andrea to a fight between Woodbury toughs (one of whom is Merle), staged in a makeshift arena lit by torches. The fighting area is ringed by toothless walkers on extendable chains. Andrea calls the bout "barbaric," but the Governor says the townspeople "need entertainment," and that staging a bout with zombies "shines a light on the monster under the bed." Is this a metaphor for *The Walking Dead* itself? What might make *The Walking Dead* so fascinating is that this struggle to be human is indeed metaphoric. The emotional subtext of the show is about emotional capacity and connections between people. The people we cheer for the most are the people who come back to the land of the living emotionally. They all value humanity: both physical life and, more importantly, the capacity to love others. Viewers may cheer for Rick to connect with Lori, but they also watch fascinated as a bullet rips through an undead skull or a limb gets hacked off. By watching such brutality, is the audience siding more with Rick, aching for him to keep his humanity, or with Andrea, calling the violence barbaric but watching it anyway? Does it expose the monster under the bed or glorify gore?

The Walking Dead is gory through and through. It celebrates blood, guts, and violent action on purpose, spending a great deal of camera time and production effort on the explosion of zombie brains as a boot smashes them, as blood drips down the shaking hand of a protagonist. Big guns and everything from axes to baseball bats to shards of glass are handy tools for survival. If the show seeks to make viewers appreciate humanity, it comes at a cost—just as it does for characters on the show. By watching *The Walking Dead*, viewers are subjected to brutal violence as a spectator sport. The show itself is the gladiatorial arena. Does it let off steam or does it promote brutality? Andrea says, "If you want to blow off steam, go for a run." But she watches the fight. Audiences hear her say this, but while they see Rick, Michonne, and the others struggle to kill bodies but connect with people, they still flock to *The Walking Dead*, like Romans to the Coliseum, so they can watch the undead and alive alike get smashed, slashed, and shot.

THE RESURRECTION OF THE SPIRIT: REDEMPTIVE POTENTIAL

The Walking Dead is a suspense/horror program. Zombies, like werewolves and vampires, are fantastical horror creatures. They are symbolic and metaphoric in nature. Their presence is always indicative of something to do with life and death and what both truly mean. If stories have the potential to serve as warnings, *The Walking Dead* is a reminder of what the resurrection of the body but not the spirit might entail. The series is a depiction of Hell.

"Christ promised the resurrection of the dead," Herschel says in season 2, episode 13; "I just thought he had something a little different in mind." The show, like the graphic novel it is based on, is a social commentary. Zombies represent mindless evil and mindless consumption. Christian belief about resurrection holds that the dead rise perfected, their spirits glorified. On *The Walking Dead* corpses—the things without perfected spirits—rise again in unnatural life. Christianity teaches a second birth: one of the body; one of the spirit. Zombie narratives preach a second death, one of the spirit and one of the corpse. Those left behind in a zombie apocalypse (the term is so apropos) must live in a world where the perfected spirit cannot return (except perhaps through memory, as may be the case with Lori's voice on the phone to Rick). They are instead living among that which has not gone to Heaven. In this existence, "survival" is a toss-up between physical survival and emotional/spiritual survival. In order to survive physically, people might need to sacrifice their care for others, abandoning or mercy-killing family members. One must be violent and brutal in order to survive, and those who have the easiest time surviving are those who operate selfishly and mercilessly, like the Governor living in comfort. This existence is a place where growing in the fruits of the Spirit will prolong one's emotional survival but not one's physical survival.

The afterlife world of *The Walking Dead* has great potential as a morality tale. It values love and freedom. It certainly draws large, very startling characters that showcase the brutality of a life in desolation, a life without the spirit. However, it also glorifies that brutality by celebrating it with long shots of violence and gore, fights in gladiator arenas of afterlife and second death. Whether viewers are most affected by the redemptive themes of love and humanity or by the brutal gore-nography might truly depend upon the state of their own hearts and their own temptations and habits. *The Walking Dead* may be a space viewers mentally inhabit and retain their capacity to love; they may find the moral quandaries of the protagonists good fodder for thought and discussion. Rick's or Michonne's struggles may help them think about the things that are true or worthy of praise. But there is also a latent danger that by celebrating brutal violence, *The Walking Dead* will undermine all of its own character ideologies, asking viewers to mindlessly consume the gore depicted on the show until they too become more like flesh-loving zombies.

GRAPHIC IMAGES: FORMAL ELEMENTS AND SYMBOLS

The formal filmmaking elements of *The Walking Dead* betray these competing ideologies. The idea that zombies are mindless consumers is highlighted by the graphic novel, which is itself a commercial piece of literature to be "mindlessly" consumed. However, the themes of the novel and its depiction of gore make it more thought-provoking and less celebratory of the brutality depicted in the heavy art direction of the AMC series. The look of the show is filtered, with extreme lighting used in many scenes. *The Walking Dead* is a highly stylized and cinematically planned program.

The look of many of the shots reflects the art of the drawings that make up the original graphic novel. *The Walking Dead* is a comic-book-style moving-image story, with fantastic metaphoric realities and very planned shots. The shots themselves even lock down the cinematic space in the frame, making it look more like the still cells of the graphic novel. In fact, there are many moments where the directors recreate shots that are the equivalent of still frames. More action happens between cuts than in shots themselves, a style utilized by graphic novels to give the illusion of motion. Characters in a graphic novel appear already in motion or indicate a change in motion. The filmed version of that idea simply lets a motion already begun continue in the frame. Significant changes in action are often dictated by a cut. Often, actors walk into frame and hold a pose to deliver lines, producing the effect of a comic-style cell. This happens when the Governor talks to Michonne, and when Rick picks up the phone. A still of the scene with a dialogue bubble or a subtitle would give the same information as the moving-image shot itself.

Utilizing this graphic-novel style is in keeping with *The Walking Dead*'s source material as well as the stylized attributes of the genre. The show also uses the cinematic language of suspense to solidify its genre as a suspense/horror story. Characters look off frame, followed by POV shots in which viewers must also "search" for the potential danger. Sounds come from off-camera, and the camera often leaves things out of frame, a Hitchcock-perfected technique that leaves viewers wondering what danger is lurking just off screen. The camera also dollies and pans behind objects, as viewers too are hiding from danger. Sudden cuts to screams or loud noises startle viewers. All of these techniques are the language of suspense/horror, a genre that has the potential to help viewers cathartically face their fears (as the Governor's comment about "shining a light on the monster under the bed" seems to indicate). But they can also simply titillate viewers with thrills and violence. The construction of the show supports the themes of the story by showcasing it like the graphic novel in a planned fiction form that asks viewers to actively consider the story and its themes, but it also celebrates and titillates audiences with its suspense and gore. These two ideologies compete through the cinematic techniques to both manipulate viewers and yet ask them to think.

CONSUMPTION AND COMMERCIALISM: TOTEMS

It is the nature of fantasy stories that the premise of the program has already in some way jumped the shark: it is just not plausible. Viewers know any death on screen is staged and zombies are not real creatures. The first reminder that *The Walking Dead* is fake should be that it cannot ever be real.

A second totem reminding viewers that *The Walking Dead* is a fictional dream state instead of a real-life scenario is the fact it has won so many awards for makeup, including two Emmys. It is a good idea for audience members to remind themselves that the actors are made to look dirty and sweaty. Great effort is made to achieve the weathered clothing that costumes the actors, and blood spatters are precisely dotted over their faces.

To add to that, the zombies eating flesh are actors eating props. All the zombies are combinations of actor, CGI, and in-camera special effects. It helps to imagine that after "cut!" is yelled on the set, zombies and heroes alike take a coffee break. All of the performers take off their costumes and makeup and go home at the end of the day. The reminder of this is, of course, the opening titles. The names of the people who make the program always help remind viewers it is a show.

Slow pans through the filtered and heavily stylized opening titles also help accent the intentional art direction. The look of *The Walking Dead* is not realistic. All the style effects also remind us that it is a production, a story. Even the filmic language of suspense only serves to heighten the filmic manipulation, calling our attention to camera and editing and reminding us of its unreality.

The last totems to note are those bizarre pieces of merchandise aimed at *The Walking Dead* fans. If anything can break the illusion that *The Walking Dead* is somehow real, it is the fact that one can play *Walking Dead* Monopoly or drink coffee out of a *Walking Dead* mug. The merchandise calls attention to the fact it is a show, a brand, and a product. *The Walking Dead* is as real as Monopoly money. It is all fantasy, all pretend.

The Walking Dead presents a vision of a new civilization. Those truly human in that new world are the ones who are able to retain their humanity. The discussion of what makes us human and what retaining our humanity requires has great potential for critical thought and moral questioning. However, this ideology of the program may be lost as viewers are asked to celebrate the violence. The protagonists endure violence, but viewers celebrate it. And if *The Walking Dead* reminds viewers that mindless consumption is an enemy, it also allows fans to mindlessly consume its presence, its ideologies, and its associated merchandise. Viewers of *The Walking Dead* may find themselves fighting to retain their own humanity as they both cheer and fear the resurrection of the body but not the spirit. If *The Walking Dead* gives perspective on undeath, it does so at a significant cost.

NOTES

1. Hank Stuever, "TV Review: AMC's 'Walking Dead' Feeds Our Zombie Love Alive," *The Washington Post*, October 31, 2010, accessed October 31, 2013, http://www.washingtonpost.com/wpdyn/content/article/2010/10/29/AR2010102900331.html.

2. Ibid.

3. Robert Kirkman, creator, writer, *Walking Dead, Compendium One* (Berkeley, CA: Image Comics, 2005).

4. *The Walking Dead,* season 3 episode 5 "Say the Word," DVD, directed by Greg Nicotero, (2012, Starz/Anchor Bay, 2013).

5. Andrea sided with Shane (Jon Bernthal), who lost his humanity both internally and externally in season 2. As season 3 progresses, Andrea's character will develop more, but even more so than Rick; she has audience sympathy but not necessarily their trust. In "Say the Word" she begins to regain it at the end when she calls the Woodbury gladiator fights brutal. However, she once again trusts a man, the Governor, who proves to be a killer, and in so doing chooses him over Michonne, who is decidedly a protagonist. That makes Andrea, for this episode at least, an antagonist.

6. Michonne and Andrea have functioned as a couple. There is nothing explicitly romantic or sexual about their relationship, but they have been surviving together and have developed a strong bond. They are partners in survival.

CHAPTER 13

DOWNTON ABBEY:
SOCIAL PROGRESSIVISM MEETS
PERIOD (MELLOW) DRAMA

U.K. network ITV's 2010 super-hit *Downton Abbey* has turned into a PBS show (aired through the *Masterpiece* series) that even people who do not watch PBS are hooked on. It is a primetime soap opera with higher production values than many A-list features and is a weepy[1] with clever class sensibilities, making it the not-quite-guilty pleasure of Anglophiles everywhere. The success of the show is nothing short of a public television phenomenon. "According to PBS, the third season finale of *Downton Abbey* boasted 8.2 million viewers," Chris Harnick of *The Huffington Post* reports, "a series high in the US. . . . Over its third season on PBS, the Masterpiece/Carnival co-production drew more than quadruple PBS's primetime average."[2]

Downton Abbey melds the same kind of premise as *Upstairs/Downstairs* with the drawing room drollness and social commentary of *Gosford Park* (which also starred Dame Maggie Smith and was written by series creator Julian Fellows). It keeps successful elements from both, namely, the disparity between the lower-class servants from downstairs and the upper-class nobles in the drawing room and startlingly high production values. The first episode of *Downton* finds the Crawley family, headed by the Earl of Grantham, Robert (Hugh Bonneville), reeling from the news that the *Titanic* has sunk, killing the heir to the family title. This cousin is the heir since Robert and his American-born wife Cora (Elizabeth McGovern) have no male children. Their three daughters, Mary (Michelle Dockery), Edith (Laura Carmichael), and Sybil (Jessica Brown Findlay) are all coming of age. (Sybil, the youngest, is presented in London in the first season.) Their grandmama Violet Crawley, Dowager Countess of Grantham (Maggie Smith), is a stalwart of tradition, but she does not see why Mary cannot receive money as an heir, even if she cannot receive the title. When the next heir in line, a middle-class lawyer named Matthew Crawley (Dan Stevens) arrives with his mother Isobel (Penelope Wilton), he is at first coldly received by the family, who preside at the earl's estate, a turreted house christened Downton Abbey.[3]

Downstairs at Downton the butler Mr. Carson (Jim Carter) rules, with housekeeper Mrs. Hughes (Phyllis Logan) as second-in-command. Order and status are very important among the servants, as first footman Thomas (Robert James-Collier) and lady's maid O'Brien (Siobhan Finneran) well know; they are always competing for either some kind of promotion for themselves or some demotion for someone else. In the first two seasons, Thomas and O'Brien spend most of their time annoying Lord Grantham's valet (a friend from the South African War), Mr. Bates (Brendan Coyle), much to the chagrin of head housemaid Anna (Joanne Froggatt), who is in love with the luckless Bates. The kitchen is run by the implacable Mrs. Patmore (Lesley Nicol), who takes her own turn bossing around kitchen maid Daisy (Sophie McShera) and spouting hilarious lines of dialog.[4]

Plots interweave upward social mobility, historic events (series 2 is built around World War I), potential romance, and personal vendettas. When chauffeur and socialist Tom Branson (Allen Leech) falls in love with young Lady Sybil, the two find that changing times make for a new kind of future. The plots between upstairs and downstairs are mixed, with servants and nobles and middle-class lawyers all knowing each other's dirty secrets. The specific historical, political, and geographical settings help define the show as social commentary. However, *Downton Abbey*'s appeal is not all in its premise. It is also due to gorgeous visuals and surprising—sometimes-painful—plot twists. In the third episode of the series a visiting Turkish diplomat, Kemal Pamuk (Theo James), ends up dead, naked, in Lady Mary's bed. The plot twists have only become more bizarre and brilliant from there. *Downton* may be political commentary, but perhaps the sociocultural themes are only additional dramatic production elements just like costumes or locations, settings that help clarify or contextualize the personal dramas.

Melodrama is defined as a story with such extravagant theatricality that the twists and turns of the plot override character development. The idea, largely lambasted by critics as sentimental and shallow shock value, is that in melodrama the audience is more concerned with the improbable but provoking plot than with seeing character development and letting that drive the nature of the story. Soap operas, with their tropes of multiple marriages, comas, newly discovered twin siblings, mistaken identities, and bouts of amnesia, represent perhaps the height of melodrama. The genre has been around for ages, however, and includes many "women's films" from the golden age of Hollywood[5] as well as many stage productions from the late nineteenth century.

At first glance, *Downton Abbey* has the appearance and emotional temperament of a melodrama. Pamuk's death, according to series creator and generally recognized series auteur Julian Fellowes, was based on a real incident. It seems implausible, but it was based on a true event. Fellowes's writing seems to override the famous Mark Twain quote that "the truth is stranger than fiction, but it is because fiction is obliged to stick to possibilities." The plots of *Downton Abbey* are not really obliged to stick to possibilities, even when based on nonfiction events. The story arcs may seem implausible, and audiences must accept them in order to invest in the show in any way. This means viewers are always flirting with suspending disbelief, as the plots are on the edge of what is plausible.

The show gives audiences a "marvelous setting and the chance to wallow in the social mores and accouterments of another age," *Los Angeles Times* writer Mary McNamara says. But "Even with its high-lather soap factor, no one would consider *Downton Abbey* a guilty pleasure—it's *Masterpiece*, for heaven's sake, the television equivalent of graduate school."[6] If it is a plot-twist melodrama, it is higher-quality melodrama for two reasons: high production values and complex treatment of both character and plot. That in itself makes it more acceptable both ideologically and artistically, and the character development and high production value seem to indicate that *Downton*'s melodramatic qualities are at least more sophisticated.

Downton's truthful fiction is very heightened. Every moment must contain some supposed life-changing dramatic event. And with half a dozen or more plots interweaving simultaneously, there is not just something at stake in every moment; there are entire lives and loves being won and lost in one character choice or turn of events. In season 3, episode 5, at least seven plots or subplots see some development.[7] The main "A" plot of the episode is undeniably Lady Sybil giving birth and her subsequent death from eclampsia. However, it is also revealed in this episode that Bates is innocent of his ex-wife's murder (and Anna, by this time his wife, has found the evidence to prove his innocence); that Matthew (now married to Mary and taking his place as the heir) begins the first steps of revitalizing Downton's investment in the community; that Edith receives an offer to write a column for the London publication *The Sketch* (an opportunity that will change the entire trajectory of her character); and that Isobel hires the reformed or reforming housemaid Ethel (Amy Nuttall), despite Ethel's tarnished reputation. Thomas continues to flirt with footman Jimmy (Ed Speleers), and Daisy continues to bully the new kitchen maid Ivy (Cara Theobold) because she is upset over footman Alfred (Matt Milne) paying more attention to Ivy.

Even with plot-driven emotional highs and lows running as rampant as footmen on their afternoons off, the characters do develop. Over the course of the series, characters never remain static. Each person in the house has her or his own moment of crisis and change. The true natures of certain characters at times are questioned.[8] The daughters' characters in particular go through significant external and internal changes. Mary becomes a mother and wonders if the "soft" part of her has died when Matthew dies at the end of series 3. Edith becomes a writer and a mother but must keep her out-of-wedlock child a secret. Sybil gains independence by becoming a nurse, then marries, moves to Ireland, and dies just after giving birth to her daughter. The women do not just experience plot twists; they experience change and growth over time. There is more than just plot arc to *Downton;* there is definite character development.

NOBILITY AND NOTORIETY: MAIN CHARACTERS

Downton Abbey utilizes almost no POV shots and limits close-ups to very intimate moments. This keeps audiences at a distance and forces characters to share their private moments with others besides the audience. There are predominantly multi-person shots, which sometimes shift and draw focus from one character to another, but the shots very seldom leave a character in a close-up without some shadow or shoulder of another character entering in. Each character in turn has a moment of insight or isolation that the camera can capture. These moments are spread around. Of the three Crawley daughters, Mary gets the most screen time, but Edith certainly gets her share. Sybil's time on screen is less, but in this episode it is just as dramatic. The sisters command screen attention much like their birth order might suggest and as their characters play out: Mary is in charge, she has authority; Edith will defy expectations and rebel against being overlooked and told what to do, demanding the attention she is not given outright; and Sybil will remain the innocent, the only sister who openly loves and praises the other two. As Mary tells Edith after Sybil's death, "She was the only person who thought that you and I were such nice people." All are important. Mary may only get more screen time because she is the eldest daughter who both marries and eventually gives birth to an heir. Their treatment by the camera reflects this. It is almost as if the camera pays attention according to their place in the family, reflecting the situation instead of dictating the story.

In some ways, this indicates the real "main character" of the show, the house itself. After all, the series title highlights the estate, not the people, and exterior shots of the house frequent each episode and the opening titles. It could be said that the main character of *Downton Abbey* is Downton itself, and the main plot of the show is simply the lives of the people who inhabit it, and how they affect what Downton Abbey was, is, and will be. Mary gets more screen time because her character arc deals so directly with the fate of the estate. If that is the case, perhaps *Downton Abbey* becomes a social metaphor, and the estate is a microcosm of British society. This would not be the first story, in print or on screen, to make use of such a device. *Gosford Park* and another period drama (this one with literary credentials), *Howard's End*, are two other examples that seem to focus on social commentary and use a place as a metaphoric microcosm of English culture. Stories of this kind are simply in keeping with the traditions of British literature, a natural extension of the way English social discourse works. The estate stands for something, and what it stands for is English society. If that is the case, every member of the household represents some part of how British society plays out.

The house may be the real protagonist and may be a metaphor for something larger. However, the audience is invested in the personal lives of the people who inhabit the house. In season 3 episode 5 the A plot revolves around Sybil's labor and the birth of her child. As her father, and as the person most closely associated with what Downton Abbey stands for, Lord Grantham becomes the most key dynamic character of the episode. Sybil and Tom (once the chauffeur, now her husband) are at Downton, and Sybil is in the last stages of her pregnancy. The episode opens with local and family physician Dr. Clarkson (David Robb) visiting Sybil as she rests in bed and assuring her family that she is coming along fine. Over dinner, Robert (Lord Grantham) tells the family he has invited Sir Philip Tapsell (Tim Pigott-Smith), a noted obstetrician and a member of the nobility, to stay with them through the birth. There is some discussion over making sure Dr. Clarkson is not left out. Cora (Lady Grantham) and Mary are decidedly for Dr. Clarkson's participation. Robert does not want Sir Philip to feel unwanted or untrusted.

As things develop, Dr. Clarkson (whom Cora invites to Downton anyway) reveals his fears that Sybil may have eclampsia. Sir Philip thinks this is nonsense, an unwarranted disruption and unnecessary fear. When Dr. Clarkson insists, heavy discussion ensues. Robert must choose whom to trust, but Cora and the Dowager insist he must consult Tom, as Sybil's husband should have a say in the decision making. Dr. Clarkson insists a cesarean section procedure is necessary but cannot guarantee that Sybil will live through it. Tom, beside himself to make a choice and fearful of his wife undergoing surgery, defers to Robert. Robert stalls, still debating but wanting to trust Sir Philip's advice that the fears are unwarranted and a natural birth is the best idea. In not making a decision, Robert by default sides with Sir Philip. The baby is born naturally and is healthy. The whole house goes to bed, only to be woken later as Sybil undergoes tremendous pain. Tom, Mary, and Cora remain at Sybil's side. Matthew and Edith stand looking on helplessly, Sir Philip stands in shock, and Dr. Clarkson paces back and forth, knowing all too well what is happening. Robert moves between the doctors and the bed, and the entire family watches as Sybil's breath, then her heart, stop.

Later, as Cora sits with Sybil's body, Mary comes in to ask her mother to go to bed. Cora tells her she will in a while and asks Mary to tell Robert to sleep in the dressing room. When the Dowager comes the next day, she witnesses Cora blaming Robert for Sybil's death and tells him, "When tragedies strike we try to find someone to blame and in the absence of a suitable candidate we usually blame ourselves." Despite the Dowager's insightful and caring insistence that Sybil's death was not her father's fault, Robert does blame himself. The fallout of Sybil's death has consequences for the entire household, but the family consequences that require immediate attention involve Robert and Lady Cora as they find themselves in conflict during a difficult time.

In this episode, the character forced to make the most important decision, with the most devastating consequences, is Robert. Since viewers are asked to have sympathy for nearly every character at times, and often with Lord Grantham in spite of his mistakes, we are aligned with him. Robert is a protagonist throughout the series, often turning into an antagonist against himself when he follows conflicting ideals. Robert makes many mistakes, usually motivated by his own faulty desires. He is a tragic hero and, in this episode especially, one with a fatal flaw. Robert chooses to bring Sir Philip to Downton because he wants Sir Philip's opinion and presence, since a nobleman should be an expert, and his opinion and experience are specialized. Lady Cora trusts Dr. Clarkson, despite the local physician's past mistakes, because he knows the family. Robert trusts high birth, nobility, and supposedly superior training. Lady Cora trusts the working-class doctor, familiarity, and practicality.

Therefore, as Robert chooses between trusting these two characters and the plot plays itself out, his Major Dramatic Question is revealed: Will Robert trust Sir Philip instead of Dr. Clarkson? The answer, as Robert stalls on giving the word for Dr. Clarkson to perform the surgery, is yes. The result is that Robert blames himself for Sybil's death. Robert's Sentence Outline might therefore be: This is the story of Robert, who wants to believe that Sir Philip is right and, after not giving Dr. Clarkson permission to perform a cesarean section on Sybil, finally blames himself for Sybil's death because people blame themselves when they feel their judgment is clouded.

Since Lady Cora will become Robert's antagonist when she blames him for Sybil's death (although she is decidedly a protagonist in this episode, vying for Dr. Clarkson and the values he stands for), a Sentence Outline for her helps solidify the real theme of their story. Lady Cora, like Robert, wants Sybil to go through childbirth in the safest way. She believes Dr. Clarkson is the best expert to have on hand. When her insistence that Dr. Clarkson's advice be heeded goes unfollowed, Lady Cora blames her husband.

Therefore, her Sentence Outline might read: This is the story of Lady Cora, who wants to believe Dr. Clarkson is right since he knows Sybil and, after insisting Dr. Clarkson be trusted, finally blames Robert for Sybil's death when Dr. Clarkson's advice goes unheeded because people want to blame someone when tragedy strikes.

The Dowager's words to Robert sum up the theme of this plotline. She becomes the truth-teller (a role she plays periodically throughout the series), and her words also reveal a part of *Downton*'s ideology, which is that everyone makes mistakes and all people are culpable but forgivable. Lady Cora's trusting Dr. Clarkson supports this value. He has made mistakes, but his relationship with the family is more valuable than a title. Following each character leads to the idea that everyone is culpable but forgivable, but it is notably presented in this episode.[9]

BLAME THE MIDDLE CLASSES: PROTAGONISTS AND ANTAGONISTS

As every character on *Downton Abbey* goes through his or her own bouts with tragedy and comedy, each in turn has the chance to help or hinder another. Therefore, each character in turn may become either a protagonist or an antagonist. Viewers are aligned with different characters at different times in different situations. Even Thomas, whose underhanded schemes are in direct confrontation with Bates's happiness (he is almost always Bates's antagonist), is given moments of audience sympathy. When the staff hears the news of Sybil's death, Thomas leaves the hall, as he becomes overcome with emotion. Anna, who has also been at the receiving end of Thomas's jealous schemes (mostly because she loves Bates and is aligned with him), notices this. She comes up behind him, and Thomas says he does not know why he is crying, since a lady of the house would not notice if he had died. "You don't mean that," Anna replies, and Thomas answers, "No, no. I don't. In my life I can tell you not many have been kind to me. She [Sybil] was one of the few." Thomas may play the antagonist, but he earns Anna's[10] and the audience's sympathy as well. He will have his time as a protagonist, too, as will all the regular characters. He cannot remain a villain when viewers, and Anna, see where his motivations come from. Thomas has been hurt and has a hard time trusting people. This does not excuse his behavior toward others, but it does explain it, and both Anna and the audience can see it. This supports the ideology that everyone is culpable but forgivable. Knowing a person means understanding his or her real motivations. Thomas's behavior is at times inexcusable, but knowing why he acts the way he does makes it easier for other characters, as well as the audience, to forgive him.

Season 3, episode 5, pulls audience sympathy between Lord Grantham, Sir Philip, and the traditional class values they represent and Lady Cora, Dr. Clarkson, and the progressive social values they represent. Robert's traditional values reflect his life as a titled gentleman. Lady Cora's may reflect her heritage as American-born "new money." For this episode, both characters are protagonists. However, what they represent in this episode can be seen as protagonist and antagonist values.

Robert trusts the nobleman and the nobleman is wrong. Throughout the series Robert will at times prove that he is a gentleman in every sense of the word, but he will also make the pointed mistake of trusting titles over working-class sensibilities on notable occasions such as this one. His overarching character development is about the division between classes. Robert trusts his valet, Bates, and confides in him, even though Bates is his social inferior. However, Robert also exerts his title and influence over Tom, Matthew, and a host of other people, insisting that traditional social lines are important. Robert's complicated, sometimes competing, approaches to social divisions mirror the show's major subject matter. Social classes are changing (hence the show's setting in the early part of the twentieth century), and Robert reflects how traditional noblemen must endure the social shifts. In this episode, he errs on the side of trusting nobility over familiarity, and the consequences are dire.

Lady Cora, too, has moments of being a heroine and an antagonist. At the end of this episode, she will turn antagonistic, blaming Robert and "punishing" him for Sybil's death. For most of the episode, however, she represents trust in familiarity over titles. She trusts Dr. Clarkson. The local physician is someone who has made previous mistakes but has a relationship with the family. Sir Philip represents someone whose worth is seen only in his title since he does not know Sybil. Dr. Clarkson, however, knows her well since she served as a nurse under his direction during the Great War. Sir Philip is an obstetrician who has a more traditional and "hands off" approach.[11] Sir Philip tells the family of his medical successes. He is a trustworthy physician. Deciding which doctor to choose is a valid discussion. However, their choices betray obvious representations: Sir Philip represents traditional class values, Dr. Clarkson progressive ones.

The program's ideological concerns with personal culpability and value are at play even here. What makes a person of value and what makes a person culpable? Being a gentleman means responsibility but does not necessarily mean moral virtue. This seems to indicate that *Downton's* ideology reflects value for all people regardless of title or position, and perhaps even regardless of personal mistakes. The ensuing plot between Robert and Lady Cora reflects the idea that title and position do not indicate personal value and that instead "knowing" a person should build trust.

UPSTAIRS/DOWNSTAIRS: IDEOLOGY AND REDEMPTIVE VALUE

Downton Abbey's social commentary is more personal than political, but the nature of the subject matter means that it is impossible to separate it from political class values. However, in doing so it both celebrates and subverts "old world values." Writing for *Forbes* magazine, contributor Jerry Bowyer argues that *Downton Abbey's* political ideology goes against the progressive revolt. It celebrates and trusts the upper classes. "Films and series about Edwardian upper caste manners which portray the genteels uncharitably are boring," Bowyer says. *"Downton Abbey* is what George Gilder would call the entropic disruption to the background noise of revolt against the old world. To portray Lord and Lady Grantham as anything other than drunks, fools, hypocrites or either sexpots or sexual glaciers (or best of all, alternately both) is itself an act of cultural rebellion."[12] By not portraying the nobles as villains, the show supports them. Bowyer insists that is why leftists "bash" the show.

However, *Downton Abbey's* ideology seems to also support social progressivism. After all, Dr. Clarkson was right, not Sir Philip. Lord Grantham's fatal flaw was trusting titles over middle-class knowledge. The program's complicated relationship with social classes is evidenced in the choices of the characters. There is no decidedly overt political ideology. Instead, there is a personal ideology that, as we have seen, is more about how forgiveness, honesty, and caring trump bitterness, deceitfulness, and coldness.

Those values do reflect fruits of the Spirit. *Downton* makes commentary on religion, some of which is overt. In this episode, Sybil talks to Mary about her baby's christening. Tom wants the baby to be Catholic. Sybil knows this means a great deal to him and asks Mary to help her win the staunchly Anglican family over to the idea. "I do believe in God," she tells Mary, "but all the rest of it—feast days, vicars, deadly sins—I don't care about all that. I don't know if the vicar knows any more about God than I do." Sybil's opinion reflects a dominant ideology of the show. There is a morality, but it is not necessarily dictated or represented by the church.

When Anna discovers that Bates's dead ex-wife has plotted her own suicide in order to frame him so he will hang for her murder, she tells her husband she hopes the woman "burns in Hell." Bates replies, "Don't go down that road. Once you're on it there's no way off it."[13] Bates later reflects on Sybil's death by saying, "If I had any beliefs that would shake them." The church is not ultimately the purveyor of truth. However, love and caring, forgiveness and honesty, kindness and openness are all highly valued. Hate and wrath are dangerous roads. Characters act as protagonists when they reflect these values and as antagonists when they reflect the opposite.

In some sense, the way in which these opposite values are seen as each character makes good and bad choices or reacts to both terrible and wonderful circumstances supports exactly what Robert and Lady Cora are experiencing. We fear, we fight, we blame, we endure tragedy, and, somehow, we reconcile through honesty and love. Those events are catalysts for our growth. Happiness and pain, the show's plotlines insist, are not mutually exclusive. Neither are sorrow and pleasure. As good and bad reside in each person, so good and bad circumstances reside in each event. As everyone in the room realizes Sybil has died, her baby (who will also be named Sybil) cries from another room. Mary, Edith, and Tom saying goodbye to Sybil is intercut with Anna telling the family lawyer her evidence that Bates is innocent. Perhaps that is exactly what *Downton Abbey* is really all about. The sociocultural changes are a setting for personal development, and both events and people contain elements of good and bad. People are culpable, but getting to know them means understanding them. Situations are dramatic, but enduring them means seeing both the positives and negatives they bring.

These values are played out on a grand, dramatic, almost expressionistic stage that insists each moment be fraught with emotional danger. The heightened reality focuses on personal drama, but it also revels in its excess of feelings. For some viewers, this may be cathartic, allowing them to process and feel. For others, it may be misleading, causing them to misplace emotional ties and invest more in the vulnerability of the show's characters than the people around them. And for some, doubtless, the show's dramatic emotional mood swings will prove too much sentiment to take, making it melodramatic, overly sentimental, and self-absorbed. The high emotional content divides fans from foes, but the sheer number of fans indicates there is some pull, some desire, to experience the emotional highs and lows the show displays. In and of itself this may not be redemptive. It is a good example, however, of the idea that those looking for redemptive content may find it.

LOOKING FOR SIGNIFICANCE: FORMAL ELEMENTS AND SYMBOLS

The first moment of drama in every episode of *Downton Abbey* is the opening titles. With the show's signature stirring piano and strings score, slow sliding shots in shallow focus follow Lord Grantham and his dog Isis across the lawns of Downton, then shutters are opened to reveal a blinding white window before a bell in the servants' hall rings, a maid goes up the stairs behind letters sitting in a box, a pot on the stove is picked up, a silver place setting is measured beside a plate, a flower falls from an arrangement in a vase, a lamp flickers to life and a chandelier is dusted. The names of the actors appear in alphabetic order (a very democratic choice) over these highly dramatized simple moments. Then the opening graphic appears. Emblematic of the show, the graphic is divided horizontally. The top half is a pale sky with rolling clouds, the bottom completely black. The show's title is split with the word "Downton" appearing in black just on the edge of the sky section, and "Abbey" in white, just on the edge of the black. Likewise, an outline of the house itself splits the words and appears mirrored; the top image of the Abbey reflected in the dark half underneath.

The duality of the image plays off the themes that drive the show: upstairs and downstairs, good and evil, and comedy and tragedy. The show is about servants and nobles, but it is just as much about good and bad, joy and sorrow, happiness and pain. There are "levels" in the house, there are nobles and servants, in each character there is potential for good and evil, and in each situation there is happiness and pain. They are held in balance. The image reflects this. There is darkness in the sky, and light in the darkness. The image of the house itself is both dark and light, containing in its own identity the duality of the show's themes.

The shots themselves also reflect an inherent democracy. There is no one central character, and few people are given real isolated close-ups. While highly stylized, the show also relies on naturalistic images, with close attention to detail in crafting costumes and props and the use of real locations when possible. *Downton Abbey* is a heightened reality, but an attempt to reflect very faithfully what the experience of reality is. *Downton Abbey*'s hefty budgets affirm the very intentional choice to create a specific look, and that look is committed to a faithful representation of real experience. If *Downton Abbey* values more the realistic portrayal of life in a landed estate, of people who have the capacity for both good and evil, and of the sorrow and joy latent in dramatic circumstances, it reflects them in a heightened funhouse mirror. The props and costumes are realistic, but they are also period. They call attention to themselves simply by being so meticulously true to life.

The acting itself is also a heightened celebration of the real. One stunning example of this is the moment that the Dowager returns to Downton after Sybil's death. Mr. Carson, the butler who has been in service to the family for years, greets her at the door. "We've seen some troubles, you and I," the Dowager tells him, but "nothing worse than this." The music underneath the scene expresses the somber mood. The front hall is dim, and the Dowager all in black. She moves from Mr. Carson straight toward the camera, which trucks back so we can see her face. Mr. Carson, and further in the background, Alfred, remain in the shot. As it continues both the Dowager and the camera stop as she becomes overcome with emotion (an extremely rare occurrence for her character). She moves one hand from her cane to steady herself on a pillar, gathering emotional and physical strength, then raises her head and continues on as the camera remains static. It is *Downton*'s replacement for a close-up: a shot that intimates insight into a character's real feelings. The following shot is from behind as the Dowager moves across the hall, slowly and heavily burdened. Maggie Smith's performance is heavily dramatic, but true to the circumstances. She displays her grief in a dramatic way, but not an unrealistic one. In fact, it is so realistic it is compelling.

That is the art of *Downton Abbey*: so realistic it seems implausible, so compelling because it is so planned and yet so real. Is *Downton* drama or melodrama? Or is it a mellow drama, full of high emotional stakes and heavy viewer investment? The produced, planned, and plotted elements of the show seem false, and yet, so much of the show rings true. It is a drama that for some is over the top, and, for others, full of mellow drama—a softer, more balanced way to deal with life's tragedies.

NOTES

1. "Weepies" is another term for the kind of melodramatic films and television programs often marketed to women. *Dark Victory, An Affair to Remember, Doctor Zhivago*, and *The Way We Were* are all iterations of the "weepie."

2. Chris Harnick, "*Downton Abbey* Ratings: More Than 8 Million Tuned in for Season 3 Finale," *The Huffington Post*, February 19, 2013, accessed November 20, 2013, http://www.huffingtonpost.com/2013/02/19/downton-abbey-ratings-season-3-finale_n_2719786.html.

3. The now iconic filming location and exterior used as Downton Abbey is really Highclere Castle in Hampshire, England.

4. For example, in series 1 episode 7, Mrs. Patmore retorts to Daisy's "I was only trying to help" with "And I supposed Judas was trying to help when he brought the soldiers into the garden."

5. This genre goes by many names, including "melodramas," "soap operas," "three-hanky pictures," and "chic flicks," as well as "weepies." For more information see Marlee MacLeod, "Weepies," GreenCine.com, 2005, accessed December 18, 2014, http://www.greencine.com/static/primers/weepies.jsp.

6. Mary McNamara, "Critic's Notebook: An American's Take on 'Downton Abbey,'" *The Los Angeles Times*, February 5, 2012, accessed November 23, 2013, http://articles .latimes.com/2012/feb/05/entertainment/la-ca-critics-notebook-downton-20120205.

7. *Downton Abbey*, season 3 episode 5, DVD, directed by Jeremy Webb (2013, PBS, 2013).

8. Bates, who may be as much a main protagonist as Lord Grantham, or at least his main foil in the upstairs/downstairs class shift, is one good example of a character whose nature is in question. Is he a good man or a murderer? Can he really be trusted? Should Anna trust him? If she cannot, can anyone? Series 4 and 5 highlight this character development.

9. This episode proves vital, too, since it contains the death of a major series character mid-season, a startling plot twist that has also become a hallmark of the program.

10. Anna's character is perhaps the most sympathetic on the program. She, like Sybil, is someone who sees past another's flaws to care about that person. This is how she develops a relationship with Bates (itself a long and complex plotline) and keeps her relationship with Lady Mary. Anna may be the exception to "everyone is culpable" since she seems to act altruistically most, if not all, of the time. Her character is never in question. Another example might be Mrs. Hughes. Both characters are always "trustworthy" and tend to help and love the people they encounter, regardless of circumstance.

11. Sir Philip tells Matthew, who inquires for advice since he and Lady Mary have yet to get pregnant, to be patient and relax instead of proscribing some treatment or running a test.

12. Jerry Bowyer, "Down on Downton: Why the Left Is Torching *Downton Abbey*," *Forbes*, February 14, 2013, accessed November 23, 2013, http://www.forbes.com/sites/jerrybowyer/2013/02/14/down-on-downton-why-the-left-is-torching-downton-abbey/.

13. Bates's words prove prescient, as his own revenge plot will play out in future seasons.

Conclusion

In the course of my writing and research for this book, I experienced both a curious phenomenon that proved to me why the subject and approach were both necessary and useful, and an experience with a moving-image narrative that seemed the embodiment of self-reference, personal ownership, and the use of totems within a moving image. Working on the last chapter, I began watching *Downton Abbey*, which held my personal fascination. As I continued to watch, I found myself inexplicably caught up in the show, so much so that I found myself more emotionally invested in characters than in my own life. I did not like that, and I wanted to be free of it. At the same time, I came across the 2014 crowdsourced production *Empire Uncut*, the sequel to the Emmy-winning 2010 film *Star Wars Uncut*, which celebrated cinematic form and personal storytelling by reclaiming a Hollywood product at the same time it praised it.

My response to being swept up by *Downton* was the only logical thing for a film/television critic to do: I analyzed it and reminded myself of the totems necessary to bring me back to my own reality. Like Cobb fighting to leave his wife's memory and return to his children in *Inception*, I wanted to leave the dream world and come back to my own life. I wanted my investment to be in the present, living reality, not in a fictional piece of entertainment. So I worked through the ideas outlined in this text. I assessed the characters and the story, thought through the show's ideology, and, quite important in this case, used totems to remind myself this was a program with actors, not real life, and especially not my life.

The mental work I did to talk myself through the events of the show and its inherent non-reality gave me perspective. They gave me back the remote control. Understanding *Downton Abbey* and the effect it had on me gave me insight into myself as well as into the way moving-image stories work. Reclaiming the ability to separate myself from the show's influence meant I could control my emotional investment in it. I could now do the work necessary to invest more in my own life than a program, because I saw the program for what it was. Fiction did not prove to be a better reality than the world around me. Fiction proved to be a false reality, and demystifying it meant I could enjoy both the show and my own life more, because I no longer relied on a fictional story to induce my own emotional satisfaction. To put it shortly, I no longer relied on *Downton Abbey* to make me happy.

As I watched *Empire Uncut*, I followed a story arc I was familiar with, but I watched it being "performed" by different actors and filmmakers, as the film retold *The Empire Strikes Back* shot for shot with 15-second fan-made films. The cinematic style changed every quarter of a minute, and characters changed shape, form, dress, species (some segments starred dogs and other animals as the characters, with human voiceover), and gender along with them. I knew "what was going to happen," and I knew my favorite segments of the original film. What I was now watching was something that in no way looked like reality (not that *The Empire Strikes Back* does anyway, although it strives to help audiences get lost in the "realness" of the story). Nor did the multiple fan-made film strive to sweep me up into an emotional experience. It celebrated the well-known story by retelling it, often in creative and dynamic ways. As a viewer, I was always fully aware I was watching a performance. And yet, the enjoyment of the story and the telling was in no way lost. It was the opposite of *Downton;* I was entertained without being swept up. I was invited to critically participate, just as the filmmakers were invited to participate in telling the story. Cinematic form was different, but in no way less interesting.

The values of each were different, as were the production intentions. Both were made for fans and were made to entertain, and succeeded in doing so. However, one required of the viewer an intentional drawing back and registering fiction from reality. The other made its presence as artifice part of its appeal. As a viewer, I enjoyed both narratives. One required me to be very intentional about separating it from reality. The other did not require nearly as much effort and seemed to ask for critical participation. I critically examined both, practicing visual literacy in order to understand what I was watching. However, one took a great deal more effort than the other. What I realized, however, was that visual literacy could help me understand and appreciate both.

It is my hope that this text empowers readers to do just that: to take back the remote control, whether or not it is easy or hard to critically participate with it, and put films and television programs in their proper place. I have always loved movies and television. I have never gotten tired of watching or talking about them. However, I should not and do not have to rely on them for my emotional or personal satisfaction. Movies can celebrate story and ask audiences to actively participate with them at the same time. That is possible. And all stories should be critically assessed.

All moving-image narratives are not real life; they are stories. The tools outlined here are a way to regain remote control. We will enjoy movies and programs more when we no longer rely on them as substitute realities. When we understand how moving images work, when we take the time to understand what it is they are really saying and how they are saying it, we will regain control over the effect they have on us. We will enjoy them for what they are and what they can bring us: entertainment, enjoyment, encouragement, and insight. We will no longer need movies and television to be our moral compasses or our preferred realities.

In time, viewers can develop virtuous habits that make it easier and easier to gain control over moving images, but, as my story indicates, we may always be vulnerable. Virtue is a discipline and will require both intention and practice. If we do not choose to develop it, the virtue of understanding and controlling the effect moving images have on us will remain remote and far away. However, if we intentionally develop virtuous practices in understanding and demystifying the moving images we see, we will regain control, using the options available to practice "remote" virtue.

INDEX

Academy of Motion Picture Arts and Sciences, 24
Active and passive viewership, 29–30
Adichie, Chimamanda Ngozi, 96
Advertisements, 13, 14, 128
Affair, The (television series), 69
African American church, 44
Afterlife, 168
Albee, Edward, xi, 102
All about Eve (film), 26
Allen, Woody, 32
Althusser, Louis, 30, 32
American Beauty (film), 76
American President, The (film), 4–5
American values, 155
Anderson, Wes, 114
Animation, 128
Annie (film), 95
Antagonists, 62, 68, 72–73, 121–22, 126; in *Modern Family*, 151–52; in *Top Chef*, 136–38
Antiheroes, 71
Arbuckle, Roscoe "Fatty," 37
Aristotle, 97

Arngrim, Allison, 15
Arnheim, Rudolf, 24, 38, 103
Arnold, Martin, 50
Aronofsky, Darren, 2, 103
Arrested Development (television series), 145
Art, film as, 24–25
"Art for art's sake," 38–39
Artifice, 102, 114–15
Award shows, 128

Babel (film), 45
Babes in Arms (film), 92
Bacall, Lauren, 32
"Bad guys," 5, 62, 68, 89, 122. *See also* Antagonists
Balázs, Béla, 68
Bandura, Albert, 16
Basinger, Jeanine, 5, 6, 13
Battleship Potemkin (film), 28
Baudry, Jean-Louis, 31–32
Bazin, André, 28–29, 30, 38, 103
Beauty, arbitrary ideals of, 90
Bellafante, Ginia, 145
Ben-Hur (film), 17

Beresford, Bruce, 95
Biases, of moving-image makers, 5
Bible, objectionable content in, 99n.14
Big Sleep, The (film), 32
Body language, 75
Bogdanovich, Peter, 15
Boggs, Joseph M., 1, 55
Boredom, 2
Bowyer, Jerry, 181
Brakhage, Stan, 50
Breaking Bad (television series), 18, 66, 86
"Breaking the fourth wall," 154, 156, 157n.12
Breen, Joseph, 37
"Bringing to life," 103
Bringing Up Baby (film), 26
Brutality, 167–68
Bugs Bunny, 108
Burnett, Carol, 15
Burns, Ken, 52, 107
Butch Cassidy and the Sundance Kid (film), 71

Cable and satellite "pay" television, 16, 17
Caldwell, John, 11
Camera angle, 75–76, 124
Camera movement, 123–24
Campbell, Joseph, 65, 93–94
Cannes Film Festival, 45
Capra, Frank, 26, 44
Carey, John, 15, 16
Carol Burnett Show, The (television series), 15
Carrie (*Sex in the City* protagonist), 69–70, 75
Casablanca (film), 77
Catered Affair, The (film), 12
Catharsis, 97–98, 127, 154
Cat People (film), 77
Cavell, Stanley, 26
Censorship, 40

CGI (computer graphic image) software, 43, 103, 128, 170
Characters, 67–68, 120; actions of, 125; development of, 175–76, 180; in ensemble show, 146–47; redemption of, 74–75; sympathy for, 71–72, 74, 122–23, 128, 178, 180
Cheers (television series), 114
"Chic flicks," 184n.5
Childs, Julia, 139
Choices, in viewing, 20–21
Christ figures, 77
Christian film criticism, 35–44
Christian media, 42, 49
"Christian" reading of a movie, 95
Christ-like qualities, in protagonist, 127
Cinéma vérité, 106–7
Citizen Kane (film), 12, 28, 53
Class conflict, 180
Clockwork Orange, A (film), 69
Close reading, 27, 56
Close-up shots, 68–69, 71, 73, 120, 162, 163, 176
Close watching, 27–28, 29, 30, 57, 63, 78
Cohen, Keith, 54
Colbert, Claudette, 6, 56, 69
Colicchio, Tom, 132
College film programs, 36
Collins, Suzanne, 20
Color, 14, 76
Commercial ads, in television, 13, 14
Communism, 160
Community (television series), 110–11
Comolli, Jean-Louis, 2
Conflict, 28, 67–68
Conservative vision, of *Modern Family*, 146, 150
Consumerism, 139–40, 142, 159–60, 170
Consumption of movies, from community to individual event, 16
Content vs. programming, 18

Contest reality shows, 131–32
Cooking shows, 131, 139
Coppola, Francis Ford, 44
Corrigan, Timothy, 25, 27
Cosby Show, The (television series),
    67, 145
Costumes, 71–72
"Counter-cinema," 109
Cove, The (film), 107
Crisis, 121
Criticism, as response, 25–26
Crosses, as symbols, 77, 125
Cuarón, Alfonso, 17
Culinary arts, 139–40, 142
cummings, e. e., 52
Cutaways, 77

Dallas (television series), 108–9, 111
Darkness and light, 183
Darth Vader, 72, 73, 75
Deconstruction, 82
de Mello, Anthony, 81
DeMille, Cecil B., 12
Democratic values, of *Downton
    Abbey*, 182–83
Demystification, 62, 128–29,
    188–89
Derrida, Jacques, 82
Deviance, 26, 32
Diary of a Mad Black Woman
    (film), 43
Diawara, Manthia, 32
Dickens, Charles, 53
Digital sound, 18
Direct cinema, 106
Discernment, 9, 20
Dobson, James, 38
Documentary filmmaking, 102,
    106, 154
Douglas, Michael, 4
Downing, Crystal, 91
Downton Abbey (television series),
    18, 76, 129, 173–84, 187–89
Dramatic narrative, xi
"Dream factories," 3

Dreams, moving images as, 55,
    111–12
Dreyer, Carl, 54
DVDs, 16–18

Eagleton, Terry, 52–53
Edgerton, Gary, 49
Egg and I, The (film), 6, 69
Eisenstein, Sergei, 15, 28–29, 30,
    38, 50, 59n.12
Elf: The Musical (film), 114
Emojis, 58
Emoticons, 55, 58
Emotional highs and lows, 182
Emotional investment, control
    of, 188
Empathy, for characters, 69–70
Empire Strikes Back, The (film), 188
Empire Uncut (film), 187–89
Entertainment, 86, 106
Evangelical Christians, 36, 38
Explicit messages, 2, 4, 29, 61
External antagonists, 73

Face in the Crowd, A (film), 74, 78
Facing the Giants (film), 3
Fairbanks, Douglas, 24
Faith and Culture Conference
    (Baylor University), 95
Family, as protagonist, 150–51
Family life, 86, 156
Family sitcoms, 145–46
Family values, 153–54, 156
Fantasy, 86
Fassbinder, R. W., 81
Fast Food Nation (book and film), 52
"Feel good" movies, 4
Feiler, Bruce, 103–4, 146, 150
Fellowes, Julian, 173, 175
Fiction, as false reality, 188
Fiennes, Sophie, 1, 3
Film: began as purely visual form,
    12; changes reality, 28; as
    faithful to reality, 28–29; as
    "serious" entertainment, 24–25

Film criticism, xii, 23–33; evangelical Christians on, 39
Film festivals, 25
"Filmic" writing, 5
Film industry, 12, 15
Film School Criticism, 36
Film semiotics, 30, 54
Film theory, 23
Flaherty, Robert, 107
Focus on the Family, 40
Food labels, xiii
Forgiveness, 153
Form: of film, 28, 30, 45; of musicals, 93; reluctance to study, 39–40; of story, 81
Formalism, 30
42nd Street (film), 92
Foster, Harold M., 2–3, 49, 57, 61
"Frankenbiting," 141, 143n.12
Freedom, 72, 78
Freleng, Friz, 108
French Surrealism, 15, 55
Fruit of the Spirit, 84, 127
Fundamentalism, 38
Funhouse mirror, 8, 102, 156

Gable, Clark, 15
Gag reels, 128
Game of Thrones (television series), 18
Gary Shandling Show, The (television series), 17
Gender theories, 32
German Expressionism, 15
Gilder, George, 181
Godfather, The (film), 44
"Golden age" of American cinema, 33
Gone with the Wind (film), 40
Good and bad, 126, 182
Good and evil, 7, 183
"Good guys," 5, 61–62, 122. *See also* Protagonists

Gore, 85, 167, 169
Gosford Park (film), 173, 177
Gospel Films, 38
Grace, 84
Graphic novels, 168–69
Gravity (film), 17
Grey Gardens (film), 106
Griffith, D. W., 12, 53

Ham, Ken, 41
Handheld camera, 154
Happiness and pain, 182, 183
Happy Days (television series), 117n.20
Harnick, Chris, 173
Harry Potter and the Philosopher's Stone (book), 8
Harry Potter books, as "filmic" writing, 50
Haskell, Molly, 32
Hawking, Tom, 21
Hawks, Howard, 32
Hays, Will. H., 37
Hayworth, Rita, 15
HBO, 16, 17, 19
Hearst, William Randolph, 53
Hell, 167
"Hero" shots, 162
Hero's Journey, 93–94, 127, 154
Hitchcock, Alfred, 44, 76, 86
Hollywood, 12, 33; commodification of, 27; emphasis on entertainment not art, 29; on image, 37; studio system of, 26
Hollywood Production Code, 40
Home movies, 16
Honesty, 152–54
hooks, bell, 32
House of Cards (Netflix series), 5
Howard's End (film), 177
Hughes, John, 96
Hulu, 19
Humanity, 164, 167

Humility, 90, 139
Humor, 152, 153–54
Hunger Games (books), as "filmic" writing, 50
Hunger Games (film series), 20–21
Huxley, Aldous, xi

Iconoclasts, 37
Ideological State Apparatus, film as, 31
Ideology, 7, 67, 72, 123; of *Downton Abbey*, 179, 180, 181; of *Modern Family*, 147, 156; of *Top Chef*, 138; of *The Walking Dead*, 166, 179
I Love Lucy (television series), 145
Image: evangelical Christian wariness of, 39; Hollywood on, 37
IMAX films, 17, 29
Imitation of Life (film), 101–2
Implausibility, 67: of *Downton Abbey*, 175, 184; of musicals, 92; as totem, 114, 128
Implicit messages, 2–4, 29, 61
Inception (film), 111–13, 115, 189
Independent films, 18
Insdorf, Annette, 101
International Catholic Association for Radio and Television, 45
International Catholic Organization for Cinema, 45
Internet, 19–20
Interviews, 128
Investigative journalism, 107
"Invisible" filmmaking, 29
It's a Wonderful Life (film), 12

Jackson, Mahalia, 101–2
Jacobson, Roman, 52, 59n.12
Jakes, T. D., 44
Jane Eyre (book and film), 52
Jazz Singer, The (film), 12
Jesus, as storyteller, 83

Jesus Film, 39
Johnston, Robert K., 36, 45
Jones, Chuck, 108
Journalism, 106–7
"Jumping the shark," 114, 117n.20, 128, 169

Kazan, Elia, 74
Kerr, Philip, 9
Kirkman, Robert, 159–60
Kuleshov, Lev, 73–74, 106

Lacan, Jacques, 31–32
Lack, Andrew, 11
Lane, Rose Wilder, 101
Last Temptation of Christ, The (film), 44
Lause, Kevin, 8
Law and Order (television series), 110
Lewis, C. S., 94
Life, as a contest, 141
Lindvall, Terry, 35, 36–37, 38, 45
Literacy, xii, 51, 56–58
Literary criticism, xii
Literary traditions, 50
Literature, 52–56; adaptations into film, 49–50; as "highly valued writing," 53
Little House on the Prairie (television series), 15, 66, 96
Little Miss Sunshine (film), 18, 88–91
Lord of the Rings (film trilogy), 17, 73, 96
Love, 153
Lovely, characteristics of, 82, 87
Lucas, George, 65, 93

MacMurray, Fred, 6
Magic tricks, film as, 113
Main character, 120

Major Dramatic Question, 64–65, 70, 120–21; of *Downton Abbey*, 178–79; in dramatic television series, 66–67; of *Modern Family*, 148–50; in television sitcoms, 67; in *Top Chef*, 133–35; of *The Walking Dead*, 164–65

Man Ray, 52

Married life, in film, 5–6

Maysles, Andrew and David, 106

McCarey, Leo, 44

McLuhan, Marshall, xi

McMillan, Graeme, 5

McNamara, Mary, 175

Media, effects of, 26

Meet the Robinsons (film), 95

Mellow drama, 184

Melodrama, 174–75, 182, 184

Merchandise, as totem, 170

Message, as focus of evangelical Christian films, 38–39, 41

Meta-narratives, 93–94, 127

Metaphors, 78, 125–26

Metz, Christian, 30, 50, 54

Mirrors, as symbols, 76, 77, 125

Mitry, Jean, 30

Mockumentary, 111, 146, 150, 155

Modern Family (television series), 129, 145–56

Monogamous relationships, 146

Moral compass, 8

Moral judgments, 7

Mori, Masahiro, 107–8

Mothlight (film), 50

Motion Picture Production Code (1930), 2, 6, 37

Motorcycle Diaries (film), 45

Moulin Rouge (film), 76, 85

"Movie palaces," theaters as, 24

Movies and television: as alternative reality, 1–2; as commercial ventures, 5; differences between, 12–15, 23; as pure enjoyment, 8

Movie stars, as distant and glamorous, 15

Moving image, xi–xii: complexity of, 54; as conveyor of ideas, 62; as dream, 55, 111–12; engaging on its own terms, 42; layers of meaning in, 55; as mirror, 8–9; power of, xiii, 2, 57; relationship to literature, 53–56; seeing what one is disposed to see, 83; as stories, 189; truth in, 103

Mozzhukhin, Ivan, 73–74

Mulvey, Laura, 32

Munsterberg, Hugo, 23–24, 38

Murder She Wrote (television series), 67

Murphy Brown (television series), 145

Murrow, Edward R., 106

Music, 73, 123

Musicals, 91–93

Myers, Ken, 41

"Myth of Total Cinema," 28–29, 103

Nachbar, Jack, 8, 102

Nanook of the North (film), 107

Napoleon Dynamite (film), 18

Narboni, Jean, 2

Narrative elements, values and beliefs of, 62

National Endowment for the Arts, 50–51

Netflix, 19

Newhart (television series), 111

New York, New York (film), 115

Noah (film), 2, 41, 103–4

Nolan, Christopher, 111–13

Nonfiction, 107

Nuclear war, 160

Objectionable content, 85–88, 89–90; in the Bible, 99n.14

O'Connor, Flannery, 46, 49, 81, 83–84, 85, 98n.9

October (film), 28

Office, The (television series), 154

Oliver, Mary Beth, 2

Once upon a Time (television
    series), 86
127 Hours (film), 68
On the Waterfront (film), 76
Opening and closing titles, 113,
    126, 127, 128; of *Downton Abbey*,
    182–83
Opera, on Live HD, 19
Oral traditions, 50
Orange Is the New Black (Netflix
    series), 19
Ordinary People (film), 95
Ortiz, Gaye Williams, 45
Oscars, 24–25
Outtakes, 128
Over-the-shoulder (OTS) shots,
    120

Parable of the sower, 83
Paris, Texas (film), 45
Parks and Recreation (television
    series), 96, 110, 111, 154
Passage à l'acte (film), 50
Passion of Joan of Arc, The
    (film), 54
Passion of the Christ, The (film), 2
Patton, Paul D., 57, 85
Percy, Walker, 46, 49
Performers outside of character, as
    totems, 114
Perry, Tyler, 43–44, 45
Personal ownership, 127, 187
Pervert's Guide to Ideology, The
    (film), 1, 3
Phillips, Phil, 41
Picasso, Pablo, 102
Plagues on Egypt, 104
Plato's "cave," 31
Point of view, 62
Politics, 4–5
Pomerantz, Dorothy, 43
Popular culture, 41; as funhouse
    mirror, 8, 102
Pornography, 85
Postman, Neil, xi–xii, 106

Potter, Harry, 8
POV (point of view) shots, 69, 71,
    73, 120, 162, 163, 169, 176
Prestige, The (film), 113, 116n.18
Production Code. *See* Motion
    Picture Production Code (1930)
Programming, 13
Project Runway (reality show),
    142n.1
"Proofreading" movies, 41
Propaganda, 31
Prophetic sensibility, 85–86
Protagonists, 62, 68, 70, 121–22,
    126; in *Modern Family*, 150–51;
    in *Top Chef*, 136–38; turned
    antagonists, 178, 179–80
Protestants: on media, 42; on
    spoken word, 37
Psycho (film), 72
Psychoanalytical critics, 32–33
Psychoanalytic theory, 82
Pulp Fiction (film), 82
Purple Rose of Cairo, The (film), 32

Quicke, Andrew, 38

Race, 3–4
Racial/ethnic theories, 32
Radio, 13
Raging Bull (film), 76, 91
Raiders of the Lost Ark (film), 69
Rappe, Virginia, 37
Rashomon (film), 69
Ratings, 16
Reaction shots, 73–74, 77,
    123, 162
Reading, vs. watching, 50
Realism, 30; in moving-picture
    stories, 102
Reality, and imagination, 113
Reality television, 17, 21, 29, 102,
    105–7, 154; over-dramatization
    of, 142
Real World, The (television series),
    131

Rear Window (film), 76, 86
Reconciliation, 153
Red (color), 76, 77, 124
Redemption, 119, 126; of
 characters, 74–75; cost of, 98n.9
Redemptive narrative, xii–xiii,
 81–84, 93–94
"Refined in the fire," 139
Reiner, Rob, 4
Remember the Titans (film), 3
Remote control, 16, 20, 120, 188
Response, to moving image, 25–26
Responsibility, 152
Resurrection, 167–68
Return of the Jedi (film), 75
Return to Reason, The (film), 52
Revival, 3–4
Rice, John R., 35–36, 37, 41
Roberts, Alastair, 39, 45
Roman Catholic tradition, in film,
 42, 44–45
Romancing the Stone (film), 4
Romanowski, William D., 45
Romantic comedies, 5
R2-D2, 108–9, 115
Running Man (film), 21
Rupel, David, 106
Russian Formalism, 52, 59n.12

Sarcasm, 56
Saussure, Ferdinand de, 30
Schindler's List (film), 76
Schultze, Quentin J., 81, 89
Scorcese, Martin, 42, 44, 91,
 101, 115
Screwball comedies, 26
"Secular" culture, 41, 42
"Secular" films, 36
See It Now (television series), 106
Selflessness, 990
Self-reference, 110, 112, 113, 187
Self-sacrifice, 75, 127, 154
Semiotics, 30

Sentence Outline, 63–65, 70, 121;
 of *Downton Abbey*, 178–79; of
 Modern Family, 148–50; in *Top
 Chef*, 133–36; of *The Walking
 Dead*, 164–65
Sequences, 77–78
Sex, 87–88
Sex and the City (television series),
 69–70
Shadow of Doubt (film), 86
Shot-reverse-shot editing, 154
Sibley, Bryce, 46, 49
SIGNIS, 44–45
Silence of the Lambs (film), 72
Sirk, Douglas, 101–2
Sister Act (film), 82
Sitcoms, 67, 145–46
Sixth Sense, The (film), 76
Skywalker, Luke, 63–65, 70, 71–72
Sleepless in Seattle (film), 95
Slow pans, 170
Soap operas, 174
Social commentary metaphors, 160
Social media, 58
Social progressivism, 181
Sociocultural critics, 32–33
Sopranos, The (television series),
 17, 86
Sorkin, Alan, 4
Sorrow and pleasure, 182
Spectatorship theory, 82
SpongeBob SquarePants, 108
Sponsors, for television, 13
Star Wars: A New Hope (film),
 63–65, 68, 70, 71–72, 93, 108
Star Wars Uncut (film), 187
Steel Magnolias (film), 95
Stitt, Milan, 63
Stories, storytelling, 51–53;
 characters and conflict in,
 67–68; form of, 81; power of, xii,
 81; redemptive value of, 119
Studio system, of Hollywood, 26

Stuever, Hank, 159
Sunrise (film), 77
Supersize Me (film), 107
Survival, 168
Survivor (television series), 131
Suspending disbelief, 29, 114, 175
Suspense/horror genre, 169
Suture, 69, 77
Symbols, 76–78, 123–25
Sympathy, for characters, 71–72, 74, 122–23

Technology, 32; of moving images, 11–12, 26; of television, 16
Television: differences from film, 12–15, 23; on DVD, 17; emergence after World War II, 13; as medium of American home, 14–15; technological improvements on, 16
Television industry, 12
Television stars, as familiar, 15
"Television theory," 23
Tender Mercies (film), 95
Textual analysis, 26–27, 32
Thelma and Louise (film), 71, 72, 87, 88, 97
Theme, of story, 121, 123
They Live (film), 1
Thompson, Clive, 107–8
Thomson, David, 11, 67, 101
3D films, 17, 29
To Have and Have Not (film), 32
Top Chef, 129, 131–42
Top Hat (film), 92
Totems, 9, 112, 113–15, 128–29, 187; in *Modern Family*, 155–56; in reality shows, 140–42; of *The Walking Dead*, 169–70
Tourneur, Jacques, 77
Tragedy, 84
Truffaut, François, 15
Truman Show, The (film), 21

Truth: in fiction, 102, 175; in moving images, 103; in reality television, 105–7
Turner, Guinevere, 87
Twain, Mark, 175
24 (television series), 66
Twister (film), 68

"Untrustworthy narrator," 69
Upstairs/Downstairs (television series), 173

Vampires, 160, 167
VCRs, 16–17
VeggieTales videos, 42–43
Violence, 3, 16, 21, 26, 87–88, 167–68, 170
Virtual reality, 29
Virtue, 189
Vischer, Phil, 42–43, 44, 45
Visual literacy, xii–xiv, 57–58, 188; definition of, 61; practice of, 119–20; skills of, 61–62
Vogler, Christopher, 93
Voytilla, Stuart, 93–94

Walker, Alice, 96
Walking Dead, The (graphic novel), 50
Walking Dead, The (television series), 18, 129, 159–70
Walking the Bible (documentary), 103–4
Wall Street (film), 4
War Tapes, The (film), 107
Water, as symbol, 77, 125
Waugh, Evelyn, 46, 49
We Bought a Zoo (film), 95
"Weepies," 184n1, 184n.5
Wendt, George, 114
West Wing, The (television series), 4–5
What Dreams May Come (film), 111

White, Diane, 97
Who's the Boss (television series),
    110
Wilkinson, Alissa, 35, 41, 45
Williams, Joseph M., 23, 51
Wollen, Peter, 109
Women, in film, 32
Woods, Robert H., Jr., 57, 85
World Wide Pictures, 38
Writings on film, 27

X-Files (television series), 66, 67

Yang, Hyeseung, 2
Yehuda, Simone, 63
Yo, Gypsee, 108–9
YouTube, 19, 53

Zizek, Slavoj, 1–2, 3
Zombie narratives, 159–60,
    167–68, 170

ABOUT THE AUTHOR

JEN LETHERER, MFA, believes in the power of story and in the power of the moving image. With degrees in theater, creative writing, and film production, Letherer has been writing, directing, performing, and public speaking for most of her adult life. She teaches theater and media studies at Spring Arbor University. Letherer is the author of *The New Female Archetypes: Rethinking Women's Roles in Groups through Television* and keeps a film blog at AptMetaphor.wordpress.com.